VOCATIONAL EVALUATION
IN SPECIAL EDUCATION

VOCATIONAL EVALUATION IN SPECIAL EDUCATION

NORMAN C. HURSH, Sc.D.

Department of Rehabilitation Counseling
Boston University
Boston, Massachusetts

ALLEN F. KERNS, Ed.D.

Director of Human Resources Program
Department of Adult and Vocational Education
College of Education
University of South Florida
Tampa, Florida

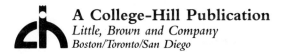

A College-Hill Publication
Little, Brown and Company
Boston/Toronto/San Diego

College-Hill Press
A Division of
Little, Brown and Company (Inc.)
34 Beacon Street
Boston, Massachusetts 02108

Library of Congress Cataloging in Publication Data

Main entry under title:

Hursh, Norman C., 1946-
      Vocational evaluation in special education / Norman C. Hursh,
Allen F. Kerns.
        p. cm.
        Bibliography
        Includes index.
        ISBN 0-316-38331-7
        1. Exceptional children--Vocational education--United States.
2. Special education--United States. 3. Vocational qualifications--
United States--Evaluation. I. Kerns, Allen F. II. Title.
LC3976.H87 1987   87-23716
371.9'044'0973--dc 19   CIP

ISBN 0-316-38331-7

Printed in the United States of America

CONTENTS

PREFACE

Over the past twenty years, education and vocational rehabilitation have realized tremendous growth in providing services to physically and mentally handicapped persons. The past decade has seen a series of legislative and consumer initiatives regarding both education and rehabilitation to provide more comprehensive services to individuals who are more severely disabled. At the same time, career education has become a dominant force in public education, directed toward providing students with knowledge and skills necessary to function in a variety of roles and positions necessary for vocational, personal, social, and community independence.

By 1977, the Rehabilitation Services Administration (vocational rehabilitation) and the U.S. Department of Education developed a position paper recognizing the many parallel roles and interrelatedness of function between the two agencies in providing services for disabled individuals. Education is concerned with "the overall life adjustment" of disabled students, including vocational adjustment, while vocational rehabilitation is involved in preparation, employment, and vocational adjustment of disabled adults. A need for cooperative efforts, open communication, and sharing of knowledge and information was recognized.

While it has been important to acknowledge that many similarities exist between education and rehabilitation, it is also important to note critical differences. Educators function within what may be identified as an educational model and are knowledgeable about curriculum design, teaching strategies, and characteristics of special-needs learners. To a great degree, special educators lack knowledge and skills related to vocational assessment, vocational adjustment, job placement, post-employment services, industrial analysis, and vocational functioning of disabled people in general. At the same time, vocational rehabilitation professionals, while knowledgeable about vocational factors related to disability, job placement, and job success, lack knowledge about the educational needs, characteristics, and practices with handicapped students and special education.

Several factors have influenced the thought and development of this text. Primary among these has been the need to reflect the resources and potential of vocational evaluation for vocational rehabilitation counselors and special educators who work with special needs learners. Through the mandates of the Carl D. Perkins Act of 1984, vocational evaluation for special education students involved in vocational education programs has become a priority for special education administrators. Although the form and content of these services are not specifically detailed in the legislation, guidelines indicate that this evaluation should at least consist of:

- Evaluation of vocational interest through structured interview, more formal interest surveys, and by observations of students by special educators using rating forms
- Identification of abilities, aptitudes, skills, dexterity, and coordination by using tests and simulated work activities
- Identification of learning style through classroom observation and additional formal evaluation.

The purpose of this book is to detail how vocational evaluation may be used effectively by both educators and vocational rehabilitation professionals in working with disabled students to identify relevant skills, develop career oriented educational activity, promote effective transition from school to work, and maximize vocational potential needed to link the special-needs student with the world of work. The text is divided into three sections. The first section provides a historical understanding of the growth, direction, and present emphasis of education and vocational rehabilitation of disabled individuals. The chapter detailing the more recent growth of the vocational evaluation profession also describes how vocational evaluation provides a unique contribution within the education system and throughout the career education process. The second section identifies the vocational evaluation process with special-needs students and assists the reader in understanding how to use the varied vocational evaluation tools, tests, techniques, and activities. The third section includes chapters identifying vocational evaluation emphasis with specific disabilities in order to demonstrate differences in evaluation emphasis and application.

CHAPTER 1

The Historical Development of Educational Services for Disabled Students

The growth and development of public education has been fueled by several significant forces, including federal and state legislation, vested advocacy groups, human service agencies, as well as philosophical and technological advances. Philosophically, education has always been accepted as a responsibility of the government and community and a right of all citizens. In practice, this responsibility has at times been quite narrowly defined and at other times quite broadly defined.

The objective of this chapter is to trace the historical roots of education and special education as we know it today and to identify the major influences on the current state of special education practice and philosophy.

OVERVIEW

The term *human services* has varied interpretations. Speaking generally, it encompasses various aspects of services that help people to reach the highest goals suitable to their interests and capabilities. Such services enable them to function more independently in school, home, community, and work environments. The service components that have had the greatest impact in develeoping the potential of individuals with handicaps are public education and vocational rehabilitation.

There is no definitive boundary, in the ultimate sense, between education and habilitation/rehabilitation. The verb *educate* stems from the Latin *educare*, meaning "to bring up, to rear," or "to train." Closely allied to this meaning is the word *habilitate*, which has as its Latin derivative the word *habilis*, which means "to make one physically vigorous," or "mentally skillful." To complete this triad, the word *rehabilitate* is derived from the Latin *rehabilitatus*, which means "to restore."

Therefore, these three terms are both relative and dependent, and they overlap in their meanings. A person who is free of mental or physical disability may be brought up, reared, or trained through the medium of education. But is any child in his or her preschool years, whether or not classified as disabled, really free of disability in the uitimate sense? If we withhold from a child for a few years the education of mind and body, that child will become disabled when compared with general societal norms (nebulous though these may be) relative to a mentally and physically educated person. When such a child reaches adulthood, the neglect of mental and physical education will result in that person being handicapped (a physical or mental disability necessitating assistance in training and/or work) in coping with both the social and vocational aspects of our contemporary society. Thus, the intent of education on behalf of a child who has no apparent disabling condition would be to habilitate the child by way of bringing about mental skillfulness and physical vigor.

Not only is education allied closely with habilitation, it bears a strong resemblance to rehabilitation. In viewing the eligibility requirements for a person who applies for the services of a public vocational rehabilitation agency, we note similarities in application to an educational institution. For an applicant to be eligible for vocational rehabilitation services he or she must satisfy three eligibility criteria. First, there must be a *specific* disability. That is, the person must have a diagnosable physical or mental disability. Second, the disability condition alone does not make that person eligible for services. The person may be incapacitated in some ways, but it must be demonstrated that the disability is a *handicap to employment*.

For example, a professional pianist, who through an accident sustains the loss of one or more fingers, may not be able to return to the same profession because of this incapacity. However, a truck driver who sustains a similar injury may be able to return to the same occupation after healing of the injured hand and fingers. Thus, the pianist has a handicap to employment, while the truck driver does not.

A third facet of the vocational rehabilitation eligibility requirement states that there must be a *reasonable expectation that services of the agency will render the person capable of engaging in remunerative employment*. Although it is vaguely possible that an orthotic device could be provided to enable the pianist to return to the same career, it is highly improbable. It is more likely that the pianist would have to be reeducated or retrained before entering another profession or occupation.

In education, whether it be a vocational technical center or a college or university, the same three requirements for eligibility could be applied to students in order to promote more realistic consideration of the meaning and future application of the course of study. The vocational technical center or the community junior college certainly should ask "Can the student benefit from this course of study?" and "Will the student be employable after training?" Currently, it is becoming more appropriate for colleges and universities to ask these questions, even though the degree may be in liberal arts or fine arts.

The educational institution should face the question of whether or not there is a reasonable expectation that the services it offers will render the person capable of entering into remunerative employment consistent with the training and with the person's interests and capabilities. Granted, there are other interpretations of the purpose of a general public education, but the question of vocational outcome should be considered far more than usually is the case.

Thus, the pervading philosophy of human services, including the role of education, entails both the concepts and practice of habilitation and rehabilitation.

The interrelation of education, habilitation, and rehabilitation may also be viewed from the aspect of socialization/resocialization (Kennedy & Kerber, 1973). If socialization is the process by which an individual develops capably within the ordinary institutions of society, education, family, religion, and employment, then resocialization entails the application of extra measures offered by these institutions, and probably the addition of other institutions. Kennedy and Kerber (1973) describe the process in this manner:

> Resocialization is that process wherein an individual, defined as inadequate according to the norms of a dominant institution(s), is subjected to a dynamic program of behavior intervention aimed at distilling and/or rejuvenating those values, attitudes, and abilities which would allow him to function according to the norms of said dominant institution(s). (p. 39).

The application of the more routine educational and habilitation services may involve the ordinary socialization process and may be adequate for much of the population. However, for the mentally and physically handicapped, and for the educationally, socially, culturally, and economically disadvantaged, a more dynamic process—or at least a higher degree of services in the form of rehabilitation or resocialization—may be necessary.

In any event, a major thrust of this book is to convey the idea of the interdependence between, and interaction of, the various educational, habilitation, and rehabilitation institutions and systems in human services. In our complex society, there is no one institution capable of fulfilling all of the educational needs for individuals that will enable them to become whole people in the sense of attaining their vocational, social, and economic aspirations. Cooperative effort and teamwork are essential if a human service delivery system is to be effective in developing a well-rounded and productive citizenry.

EARLY EDUCATION: DIRECTION AND EMPHASIS

The historical development of educational efforts within human services has its beginnings in the early development of our country, influenced heavily by the national British origins of the colonial settlers. The New England Puritans, following the English system, tutored their children at home, supplemented with Latin grammar schools for boys who would be going to college for ministerial training.

Compulsory education was initiated with the enactment of the Massachusetts Law of 1642, which required that all children be taught "to read and understand the principles of religion and the capitol laws of the country" and to be trained in learning and labor "profitable to the Commonwealth" (Cubberley, 1947, p. 17). The Puritan church leaders saw in a few years, however, that families could not be depended upon to adequately educate their children. Consequently, public education in America had its origins in the Massachusetts Law of 1647, which required every town of 50 households to appoint a teacher for reading and writing in an elementary school, and every town of 100 households to support a grammar school to prepare boys for entering the university.

THE POST-REVOLUTIONARY PERIOD

It was about 50 years after the adoption of the constitution before the creation of public, tax-supported state school systems became fairly commonplace. In New England (except for Rhode Island) and in New York, public education grew rapidly. Public land grants for educational purposes enhanced public education in the Old Northwest. Public and private schools became dominant in Maryland, Delaware, Pennsylvania, New Jersey, Virginia, and Georgia. In these states, children whose parents had declared themselves as paupers were educated in "pauper schools," while "rate schools" were provided for children of parents who were able to pay fees for supplementing school funds.

During this time, proponents of public education, among them Thomas Jefferson, saw education as a necessity for the advancement of popular government. This early perspective emphasizes how government saw itself as closely allied with education and how government and society could be strengthened only by a well-educated population.

THE CIVIL WAR THROUGH 1900

The first high school education program for boys was founded in 1821 in Boston. By 1860, however, the United States could boast only 321 high schools and about 85 percent of these were in New England, neighboring states, and states of the Old Northwest. This rapid growth in the New England area was a direct result of the rapidly developing industrial technology and a commercial society requiring educated and trained youth who would directly enter the work force.

1900 TO THE PRESENT

After 1900, public education increased rapidly. By 1960, about one-fourth of the population was enrolled in schools and colleges, making education a multibillion dollar business. Because of this growth, attendant problems arose such as teacher shortages, classroom overcrowding, financial burdens, and discipline problems. Following World War II, elementary and secondary curriculum evolved from a subject-centered to a more pupil-centered orientation, and the term *progressive education* was used in the arguments for and against the freedom of the student. The high school curriculum moved from emphasizing strictly college preparatory courses to offering courses in practical subjects such as bookkeeping, typing, cosmetology, automotive mechanics, and metal working.

VOCATIONAL EDUCATION
AND SPECIAL EDUCATION DEVELOPMENT

Vocational education had its beginnings in higher education in 1862 with the Morrill Act, and was enhanced financially by the second Morrill Act in 1890, when the federal government appropriated funds to each state to help maintain the agricultural and mechanical colleges. By 1910, 29 states had established vocational programs as a part of public education (Barlow, 1976). The Smith-Hughes Act of 1917 established and appropriated funds for a system of vocational education in the states, which matched state funds on a dollar for dollar basis.

The George-Barden Act of 1946 enhanced further the growth of vocational education by appropriating specific funds for vocational agriculture, home economics, trade, industrial, and distributive occupations. Most importantly, this act provided not only for administration and supervision but for teacher training and counseling and guidance. In 1958, the National Defense Education Act, Title VIII, known also as the Area Vocational School Act, extended the benefits of the Smith-Hughes and George-Barden Act by providing vocational education to areas that were served inadequately and by offering scientific and technological training for national defense purposes.

Continuing this growth, the Vocational Education Act of 1963 stipulated that funds be granted to persons of all ages and levels of achievement for training in any occupational area that does not require a baccalaureate degree. Thus, high school dropouts and the disadvantaged were being recognized as a previously unserved student group. Moreover, when matched by state monies, funds could be used for the construction of area vocational education facilities, and to support residential schools and work-study programs.

This act was one of the forerunners of cooperative agreements between education and other human service agencies. It stipulated that a state must have an approved state plan in order to receive federal funds, and a cooperative agreement between vocational education institutions and state employment agencies for counseling students and determining training areas, while information is transmitted from the schools to the employment agencies for use in counseling and placement of the graduates.

Secondary and higher education in general and vocational education in particular gained from this legislation by way of funding for construction purposes. Not only were area vocational schools, community and junior colleges, and universities offering terminal programs given construction aid, but vocational facilities of comprehensive high schools and specialized vocational high schools shared in these funds as well. Again, the law specifically recognized the disadvantaged, stipulating that junior colleges and universities receiving construction funds must admit to vocational courses persons who were not high school graduates.

As the country moved into the 1960s with increased affluence through economic and technological advancement, the commitment to education for all people continued. However, relative affluence and technological advances were also accompanied by social fragmentation caused by urban and rural poverty, racial inequalities, educationally disadvantaged populations and school dropouts, as well as manpower shortages during unemployment, and underemployment of large portions of the urban population.

RECENT VOCATIONAL AND SPECIAL EDUCATION LEGISLATION

While industry was relocating and market demands were shifting throughout the 1970s, traditional jobs disappeared or were altered as new jobs emerged. Vocational education offered a solution to these problems by helping to provide and maintain a flexible work force which was adequately skilled and educated.

Against this background, Congress passed the 1968 Vocational Education Act, which provided a legal basis and funding for expanding vocational education to a still greater variety of people. The act amended the 1963 Vocational Education Act to include special provisions to educate the handicapped and disadvantaged. Currently, 10 percent of the vocational education funds are set aside for services for the handicapped and 20 percent for the disadvantaged. National and state advisory councils and a formal state plan (with representatives from vocational education, exceptional education, and vocational rehabilitation) were required as a prerequisite to receiving the grants. Funds were appropriated specifically to help the school dropouts and to promote cooperation between public education and manpower agencies. Residential schools were funded, as well as work-study programs especially for unemployed youth enrolled in vocational educational programs. The Higher Education Act of 1965 was amended to provide stipends for training vocational education personnel.

Other vocational education legislation has been significant in the continuing process of making vocational programs available for an expanded segment of the population. Burkett (1973) described the impact of the 1972 legislation:

The Act called for integration of vocational education into the world of work as a continuing service for all segments of the community. Throughout their lives, people could enter and exit the system in order to develop new skills, adapt to change, and even change careers and develop new modes of recreation. (p. 68)

The Vocational Education Amendments of 1975 gave new impetus to certain features of the 1963 Vocational Education Act. Title I emphasized comprehensive statewide planning; Title II emphasized vocational guidance and exploration. Vocational education program support and funding was expanded through Title III for vocational education facilities of private, nonprofit, and proprietary institutions. Title IV paved the way for service functions; Title V accounted for applied research, curriculum development, exemplary demonstration and implementation programs, leadership development workshops, symposia, and special projects.

The federal government, then, has become increasingly influential in supporting and, consequently, in molding the tone and services of both general and vocational public education. The government's involvement in educational expenses, facility construction, pre-service and in-service training, vocational education, educational research, as well as tuition for veterans based on Public Law 346 (1944) and Public Law 550 (1952) has been significant.

EDUCATION FOR ALL HANDICAPPED CHILDREN ACT OF 1975

Undoubtedly, the most far-reaching educational legislation for special needs students has been the Education for All Handicapped Children Act of 1975 (Public Law 94-142). The act legislates that each state must provide a free and appropriate education, including vocational education, for all special needs students. In essence, the 1975 legislation has been heralded as a civil rights legislation for the handicapped student, as it guarantees several important educational rights, including:

- Provision of services for handicapped students between the ages of 3 and 22.
- Identification and establishment of goals that will provide "full educational opportunity" to all handicapped students, a detailing of the services and personnel needed, and a time table identifying when goals should be accomplished.
- Provision of a "least restrictive environment" for handicapped students between the ages of 3 and 22. Where applicable, students are to be mainstreamed into regular school programs.
- Development of procedures to evaluate handicapped students to determine the appropriale educational program.
- Annual evaluation of the student's progress and the effectiveness of various educational programs for meeting the student's identified needs.
- Provision by the states to inform parents or guardians of the programs being developed and the services to be provided.

The law also provides several safeguards for parents or guardians who question the individualized educational plan (IEP) developed for the student. These safeguards include access to educational records that describe the student's status, diagnosis, and/or program; the opportunity to obtain independent evaluations (including vocational evaluation) of the student that may be used in developing educational plans; written notice of the program or program changes that alter the educational status of the student; and the right to due process hearings and appeals if disagreements about an educational plan develop.

CARL D. PERKINS ACT OF 1984

The Carl D. Perkins Act of 1984 (Public Law 98-524) represents a major advancement and legislative mandate for vocational education services for special needs students, with specific reference for vocational evaluation of all special needs students enrolled in vocational school programs. In actuality, the law is an extension of the rights of special needs students provided under Public Law 94-142 promoting equal access to all programs in the least restrictive environment.

Under the law, schools are mandated to provide vocational evaluation services to all students accessing vocational education opportunities, and that includes:

1. Full range of programs and program supports
2. All occupationally specific programs
3. Cooperative education programs
4. Apprenticeship programs.

Department of Education guidelines suggest that the following vocational evaluation activities be utilized to develop accurate vocational plans for the student:

1. Identification of vocational interests, developed through a formal interest instrument, through a structured interview, or through formal observations of the student
2. Identification of aptitudes, abilities, skills and dexterity through use of hands on evaluation techniques
3. Identification of learning style through observation and formal evaluation

CAREER EDUCATION

Where has this historical evolution of the educational milieu of human services brought us relative to contemporary education? Since we have seen the change of emphasis move from a classical, "learning for the elite" type of education to a melding of the humanities with the practical and vocational means of learning and preparation, it would be well to view the current situation within the framework of career education.

Career education as a concept can be traced back, generally, to prehistoric days with reference to children learning the minimum vocations needed for survival—hunting, fishing, cooking, bodily care, and later, the planting and harvesting of food. Career education took on increasing significance as the vocational aspects of civilization became more formal and specialized.

EARLY ADVANCES IN THE UNITED STATES

In the twentieth century, Alfred North Whitehead (1929) was one of the first to give verbal expression to the concept of career education when he said, "There can be no adequate technical education which is not liberal, and no liberal education which is not technical: that is, no education which does not impart both technique and intellectual vision. Education should turn out the learner with something he knows well and something he can do well" (p. 74).

As evidence that we did not impart a reasonable combination of technology and intellectual vision, we need but look at our history of unemployment and social fragmentation. When asked in 1970 by the Secretary of Health, Education, and Welfare to become Commissioner of Education, S. P. Marland, Jr. (1974) recognized career education as an answer to this social fragmentation when he remarked:

> I cited my concern about disenchanted college and university students, unemployed youth, academic discrimination between things of the mind and the world of work, the aimlessness of high school and college students whose motivations, if any, were circular (to be in school or college because that was what was expected of them). I told him of my notions about the comprehensive high school and the need for greatly increasing the post-high school opportunities for young people in mid-career. I alluded to my still very fluid concept of a design for introducing awareness of work and the motivation intrinsic to the work idea, from early childhood education through the self-evident, work focused functions of the graduate professional school" (p. 7)

So when we speak of career education from kindergarten through professional schooling, we are speaking of a merging of the basic academic and humanities subject areas with exploration and training in the work world. When the concept of career education is followed, then the academic and the humanities are bolstered as the students learn more about, and participate in, the vocational world of which they are to be a part.

This merging of the academic and work world is given substance by Mangum, Becker, Coombs, and Marshall (1975) when they said, "To be effective, career education must link home, school, and institutions of the working world into a mutually reinforcing network that forms a comprehensive learning environment" (p. 10).

A more comprehensive definition is given for career education by the same authors as:

> The total effort of public education and the community to help all individuals become familiar with the values of a work-oriented society, to integrate these values into their personal value systems, and to implement these values into their lives in such a way that work becomes possible, meaningful, and satisfying to each individual" (p. 8).

Other writers have broadened the work/vocational aspect in defining career education in order to recognize the importance of community, social, daily living, and vocational roles necessary for more complete participation in society. A representative and widely accepted definition of career education is presented by Brolin and Kokaska (1979):

> Career education is the process of systematically coordinating all school, family, and community components together to facilitate each individual's potential for economic, social, and personal fulfillment" (p. 102).

IMPLEMENTATION

Generally, career education in the various states has followed a model similar to that of Oregon (Marland, 1974). The model is extensive in that it begins with a *career awareness* emphasis from kindergarten through the sixth grade and carries on to the post-high school level through occupational specialization and *career placement*. In the years between, *career exploration* is emphasized in grades 7 through 10, and *occupational preparation* in grades 11 and 12. Table 1–1 identifies the development nature of both the career education process and the career education objective, which are important at each stage. Two points are important to the success of career education with severely handicapped students. First, teachers from kindergarten through high school levels (K–12) must understand the developmental nature of functional career objectives to be able to build on past information, experiences, and skills, and to prepare the student for the next developmental stage. Second, career education training and program efforts must be infused with functional academic, vocational, and community experiences. For the more severley disabled, the education experience must be both community referenced and community based.

Georgia instituted a career education emphasis in the early 1960s when the career guidance function was added to the vocational education division and a network of comprehensive high schools was begun. The Skyline Career Development Center in Dallas, Texas, was opened to students in 1972. This impressive $21.5 million technological age high school had a curriculum composed of 27 clusters encompassing several families of careers.

In 1972 the Los Angeles City Schools together with five other school districts formed working models of career education as a national pilot project of the United States Office of Education. The contractor of this project was the Center for Vocational and Technical Education at the Ohio State University. The intent was to enable all school

TABLE 1-1.
Career Education Process Model.

Career Objectives	Process	Academic Level
Learn about roles in family, work, and society; Develop self-awareness of potentials; Develop work values and positive attitudes.	Career Awareness	Elementary Grades
Engage in hands-on activities to explore how skills, interests, abilities shape participation and choice in work and society.	Career Exploration	Middle School
Develop competencies in skills needed to function in home, work, and society.	Career Preparation	High School
Responsible participation in work and competitive employment; Develop support systems to maintain independent functioning.	Career Placement	High School & Post-Graduation

dropouts and graduates to have preparation and saleable skills for the world of work, and to provide opportunities for adults to become appropriately employable.

In 1973 and 1974, Florida instituted pilot programs in various school districts, including the Manatee Junior College Career Education Project (directed by Dr. Jim Selman), which worked with kindergarten through university levels in the development of career education curriculum and teacher training programs. In the 1970s career education set the tone throughout the country as the pervading educational philosophy.

LEGISLATIVE EMPHASIS

The first congressional endorsement of career education as an educational concept was expressed in the Educational Amendments of 1974 with the provisions of Section 406. In September of that year, the Secretary of Health, Education, and Welfare (HEW) approved, as HEW policy, a paper entitled "Career Education: Toward a Third

Environment," which described the Office of Education's interpretation of HEW's policy on career education.

The Educational Amendments of 1974 and 1976 provided major stimulus for research, training, demonstration, and programming projects. These amendments contributed in a major way to promoting career education at both state and federal levels. The Career Education Implementation Incentives Act of 1977 continued the major federal endorsement of career education and committed long term financial support to state programs.

It was projected that career education should continue and increase its influence on both the social and economic scene in our country. Bolino (1973) found that career education, as one of 23 economic factors, was improving the economic aspects of our society. He considered in his study only the more formalized aspects of career education such as adult and vocational education, apprenticeships, correspondence school, federal training, on-the-job training, private business schools, and special schools. It would be a tremendous task today to determine the effect of the career education emphasis in our elementary, secondary, and higher educational institutions on the social and economic milieu of our society. Bolino's earlier projection, without considering career education as a pervading educational philosophy in all of our educational institutions, would indicate that the impact is increasing tremendously.

THE CURRENT EDUCATIONAL SCENE

Elementary education curriculum and programs have sustained a wide variety of changes, even within the past 20 years. These changes, as noted by Collier, Houston, Schmatz, and Walsh (1976), entail primarily three different areas: "First, the content is organized in relation to the structure of the discipline itself. . . . Second, an increasing emphasis is placed on problem solving procedures. . . .Third, an emphasis is placed on the objectives the student is to obtain" (pp. 11–12).

In discussing the pressures of an increasingly complex technological society on secondary education, Tanner (1972) noted that:

Many educators, instead of seeking relevance through a new reconstruction and synthesis of the curriculum in general education, appear to be seeking relevance by injecting new offerings and options into the existing curriculum. In some cases efforts are made to provide for synthesis and relevance in the curriculum in general education, while also providing students with a wide selection of elective offerings" (p. 360).

From this historical review of the educational aspects we learn that the current services offered by education are vast, complex, and diversified. Also, historically, it has been evident that the federal government's interest in education has entailed the concept of national needs. Currently, interest in education at all levels of government appears to be a broader concern for providing needed manpower, as noted by Folger, Astin, and Bayer (1970) when they reported that:

> One primary concern of manpower specialists is whether the supply will be adequate to meet future demands in a number of specialized fields: Are people making vocational choices and receiving training for fields that are appropriate for society's needs? If not, can choices be influenced to insure that the necessary supply of trained talent will be available? These concerns about adequate manpower supplies should be tempered, however, with a recognition that there are a variety of mechanisms for adjusting to an ever-changing world of work; the interrelationships of occupations, the overlapping interests and abilities of people in different occupations, the adaptability of individuals to changing environmental demands and so forth. (p. 216)

It is this conceptualization that will maintain career education as a functional force within public education through the next decade. At the same time, there must be a recognition that society and technology continue to develop, diversify, adjust, and grow. Career education, as a responsive educational process, must be aware of changing demands and continuously evaluate how innovative education and training technology may respond to a changing society and work world.

TRANSITION PLANNING: A NATIONAL PRIORITY

Unfortunately, increased legislative mandates for expanded services to more severely handicapped students has not resulted in actual employment gains, increased independent functioning, or fuller participation in all areas of the community. Many handicapped students continue to be neglected with respect to occupational, vocational, and technical education programs (Brolin & Kokaska, 1979). Moreover, confusion among special education personnel still surrounds such issues as (1) the role and function of special education teachers in employment training and job placements, (2) the most appropriate curriculum and programmatic approaches for developing community-based vocational programs, and (3) the means by which school systems and service providers evaluate the process and outcome of programs for severely disabled students (Hursh, Shrey, Lasky, & D'Amico, 1982).

EMPLOYMENT OUTCOMES

Despite the hundreds of millions of dollars spent each year on special education by the state and federal governments, employment studies consistently document the significantly high levels of unemployment among handicapped individuals (Will, 1984). Several state-wide studies have highlighted the employment status of handicapped students recently completing special education programs. In Vermont, Hasazi, Gordon & Roe, Hall, Finck, & Salembier (1982) found that 50 percent of special education graduates were unemployed, with higher unemployment figures among individuals labeled severely handicapped. When full-time employment status was reported alone, only 37 percent of special education graduates could be considered employed (Hasazi, Gordon, & Roe, 1985). In Colorado, Mithaug, Horiuchi, & Fanning (1985) found that 69 percent of recent special education graduates were employed at the time of the study. When part-time jobs were excluded, however, the employment rate fell to 37 percent. Edgar, Levine, & Maddox (1985), reporting on a follow-up study in Washington, included sheltered workshop placement in their definition of employment and noted a 58 percent employment rate. The unemployment rates in a Virginia study (Wehman, Kregel, & Seyfarth, 1985), were found to be 60 percent and over 70 percent if controlled for part-time and sheltered employment status.

Special education graduates also receive lower wages than nonhandicapped graduates. Wolfe (1980) confirmed that disabled people earn significantly less than nondisabled people and, as in the study by Wehman and colleagues (1985), 75 percent of individuals earned less than $500 per month.

Along with poor income levels, high unemployment, and restricted occupational choices, handicapped workers receive few, if any, raises and negligible benefits. Wehman and colleagues (1985) reported that 70 percent of their subjects received no benefits, 66 percent received no vacation benefits, and 70 percent received no insurance benefits.

Finally, a majority of studies on employment of special education graduates (Harnisch, 1986) noted that handicapped workers are most likely to be employed in service, unskilled, or semi-skilled occupations. It appears that as the severity of the handicap increases, occupational options decrease and the individuals with multiple and severely handicapping conditions are in sheltered or service occupations (Edgar, Levine, & Maddox, 1985). If present special education methods remain unchanged, it appears that of the over 90,000 handicapped students leaving school each year, 80 percent will be either unemployed or underemployed and living below the poverty level within one year of graduation (Karan & Knight, 1986).

The studies previously cited are consistent with U.S. Commission on Civil Rights (1983) and Department of Labor (1979) statistics that report 50 to 75 percent of all disabled persons are unemployed. The employment studies of Wehman and Mithaug and colleagues are more disconcerting when one considers that the subjects were recent graduates of special education programs. It is discouraging and defeating to these individuals if they are not able to find employment quickly, with the usual consequence being to access a subsidy program or sheltered employment, with few future attempts to gain more competitive employment.

FEDERAL MANDATE: A TRANSITION INITIATIVE

As more attention and increased funding have been allocated to teaching special needs students, it is readily acknowledged that, given the advanced special education teaching technology, even the most severely and multiply handicapped student can learn. Although dramatic advances have been made in special education teaching technology, it is also apparent that traditional education approaches are not sufficient to overcome barriers that more severely handicapped persons find as they leave school and attempt integration into mainstream society. Severely handicapped students require a program that is characterized by long-term planning for community integration; coordinated services to respond to the individual's multiple and complex needs; exposure to and training in normalized environments; and supported training in the vocational environments in which they can be hired if skills are to be learned and generalized to community settings and if productive and independent behaviors are to be sustained.

The transition initiative developed by the Office of Special Education and Rehabilitation Services (Will, 1984) directs education to focus on developing the program and continuum of services that are necessary to provide an effective bridge between school and work (Figure 1-1). The transition initiative recognizes that:

- All handicapped individuals are capable of moving from school to employment
- Employment is the outcome of successful transition efforts
- All handicapped individuals must be served by the educational system
- Transition planning is long term, encompassing adolescence and adulthood, middle and high school years, and the years immediately following graduation
- Effective transition requires coordination among multiple services

Figure 1-1 conceptualizes the continuum of employment services that may be needed to ensure successful transition from school to work and

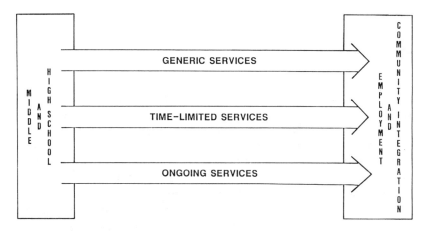

Figure 1-1.   Major components of the transition process.

community integration. Generic services include the range of employment services that most nonhandicapped individuals use, including local employment agencies and school guidance resources. Time limited services consist of specialized rehabilitation and adult service agencies that traditionally work with disabled individuals, such as the Office of Vocational Rehabilitation, Projects With Industry, or the Jobs Training Partnership Act resources. Ongoing services are those needed by severely handicapped individuals to support and maintain successful integration and performance in a job and in the community. These services may consist of supportive supervision, mobility aids, or continued involvement of adult service agencies.

The transition from school to the work place is not a one-step process and cannot be successfully performed in a vacuum. Wehman & Hill (1985) noted that it requires three stages, including (1) school instruction, (2) transition planning, and (3) placement into meaningful employment. Through effective planning and instruction, supported employment in a competitive work setting is a realistic goal. Special education is the foundation of effective transition and "preparing students to be independent in their living skills and employable in the marketplace should be the major goals for the educational system" (Wehman & Hill, 1985, p. 175).

SUMMARY

This first chapter offers a glimpse of the vast, moving panorama of the place of educational institutions in the historical development of human services. It is evident that the struggle to provide equal opportunities for persons in education generally, and for involvement in vocational education specifically, has been intense. Career education, as a viable focus since 1971, has had a relatively shorter, but equally active, history and shall continue to dominate educational efforts for the next decade.

At the national level, career education for handicapped students is also accepted and promoted as a national priority and as one critical to the students' full participation in the community (Martin, 1974). However, at the local education agency level, many educators, administrators, and guidance personnel continue to be uncertain and uneasy about how to assess handicapped students, develop career-oriented curriculum, and evaluation the process and outcome of career education activity (Hursh et al. 1982). Whereas the education goal, conceptually, is to provide the specific knowledge and range of skills for participating in work, community, social, and recreational activities, many students are not receiving the needed skills training or career-oriented programs (Brolin & Kokaska, 1979). Although specific and concrete career and vocational programs are provided, many students do not make the transition from school to productive jobs and relevant employment (Levitan & Taggart, 1977).

The process of evaluation, education, job placement, and follow-through is not a singular process or the sole responsibility of the educational system. Many handicapped students fail because the linkages between the service agencies within the human service delivery system are not fully developed and functional.

One objective of this book is to provide education personnel with a basic understanding of similar concepts and practices between education and vocational rehabilitation. With greater understanding of the vocational rehabilitation process as a component of the human services delivery system, linkages between career education efforts and vocational rehabilitation job placement efforts will be more viable.

As this text develops, we shall see the vastly expanding role of vocational evaluation in education, rehabilitation, business, and industry. It is hoped that we may see the integral part played by work in all of these areas of human processes. We shall view vocational evaluation as an intermittent and continuing process of vocational assessment which provides a key and a touchstone to the areas of education, rehabilitation, as well as to business and industry.

CHAPTER QUESTIONS

1. What historical factors play a significant role in developing today's present emphasis on career education, vocational functioning, and community adjustment of special needs students?

What are the most influential barriers (educational, societal, legislative, etc.) preventing stronger linkages between agencies/systems such as educational, vocational education, vocational rehabilitation, or industry and business that would promote education of special needs students?

2. If you were to be involved in drafting legislation needed to promote fuller integration of special needs students into the community, what would be the cornerstone of your arguments and what would you view as critical elements of your legislation?

3. Considering the limited budget of funding agencies, where should special education place major emphasis over the next 10 years?

    Advocacy   Technological development
    Legislation   Program development
    Research   Personnel development

    Perhaps other areas are equally important and should be discussed.

4. How can special education and vocational programming in particular be more relevant to available employment opportunities and to future employment trends?

CHAPTER 2

Vocational Rehabilitation: Links to Education

Work historically has played a significant role in American life. In our earlier agricultural society, it was felt to be expedient that all members of the family contribute their share of the work in some capacity to assure that the family farm provided a livelihood. In the early industrial society even children were often forced to work in order to provide sufficient income for the family welfare. Today it is not uncommon for both spouses to be employed outside of the home, and older children often work part-time after school.

Most people seem to feel that they experience a more satisfying life if they are able to work and be productive. People who are disabled, congenitally or traumatically, generally report a desire to work in order to develop their own ego strength and to make a worthwhile contribution to family and society. When, because of a disability, work activity is denied, a sense of restlessness and dissatisfaction often develops. If this state of existence is prolonged, the person is apt to move from despondency to a more passive acceptance.

Probably no other approach has accomplished more for disabled persons, by way of either habilitating those who never were able to work, or rehabilitating those who were denied work due to illness or injury, than has the field of human services known as vocational rehabilitation. In the philosophy of vocational rehabilitation, a disabled person is considered to be handicapped with respect to employment until services are provided which will make employment possible. The person still may be considered as disabled, but not as handicapped in securing employment.

Wright (1980) described the rehabilitation process as a planned, orderly sequence of services related to the total needs of the handicapped individual. It is a process built around the problems of a handicapped individual and the attempts of the vocational rehabilitation counselor to help solve these problems and thus to bring about the *vocational* adjustment of the handicapped person. When the vocational adjustment of the handicapped person is accomplished, the person still may be considered disabled, although able to enter into the world of productive employment.

Vocational rehabilitation practice, as we know it today, developed as a result of numerous individual and group efforts in both public and private sectors. The purpose of this chapter is to chronicle the growth of vocational rehabilitation within the human services field and to recognize the private and public influences that have contributed to its growth.

EARLY PRIVATE/PUBLIC SCHOOLS
AND AGENCIES FOR THE DISABLED

Recognition is given to education for providing the earliest formal efforts to train disabled persons in functional skills. A school established for deaf children in Baltimore in 1812 was the first educational institution for disabled children in America. Five years later in Hartford, Connecticut, the first public school for the deaf began admitting students. This school was established by Thomas Hopkins Gallaudet and Laurent Clere through a grant from Congress.

Samuel Gridley Howe (1801–1855) is identified as the foremost proponent of facilities for the blind in America. He founded the Perkins Institute, named after a wealthy Bostonian who donated his large mansion for the blind. In 1837 the Perkins Institute began to provide sheltered employment for blind students. The training and rehabilitation of the blind demonstrated early signs of more formal organization when the American Association of Instructors of the Blind was formed in 1853. The Perkins School for the Blind continues today as the leader of education and rehabilitation services for the blind and deaf-blind.

The Industrial School for Crippled and Deformed Children, established in Boston in 1893, was the first school for crippled children in America. Obermann (1985) noted that "by the year 1866 only seven states were caring for about 1,000 pupils in special schools" (p. 83). The first state legislature to provide support for the care, treatment, and education of crippled children was the Minnesota legislature in 1897, through the persuasion of a youthful orthopedic surgeon, Dr. Arthur J. Gillette.

SHELTERED WORKSHOPS

The sheltered workshop movement in America had its beginning as a result of the efforts of Henry Morgan (1825–1884), a deeply humanitarian minister who founded a chapel in 1868 in Boston's South

Side. He used this chapel, later to be known as Morgan Memorial, as a base of operations for his work among the disadvantaged of the area.

It was another minister, a Methodist, who built on Morgan's work and expanded it into the sheltered workshop movement with day care services, food and lodging, medical and social services, as well as the evaluation, training, adjustment, and placement services we know today. Plumb (1965) portrayed in vivid terms the exciting, but often frustrating, adventure of this man, Dr. Edgar James Helms (1863–1942), as he and a dedicated staff pushed ahead in their rehabilitation work at Morgan Memorial. In 1918, the Methodist church recognized Goodwill Industries as one of its responsibilities and began supporting it with funding and personnel. Thus, the Morgan Memorial Chapel was the foundation for the vast array of humanitarian services of Goodwill Industries. The unemployed were hired to collect used clothing and renovate furniture so that it could be sold at a price to provide a minimum wage. Today, Goodwill Industries is established in approximately 200 cities with collections and sales outlets reaching over 3,500 communities.

The Salvation Army, Volunteers of America, and the Society of St. Vincent de Paul also have programs and rehabilitation philosophies similar to that of Goodwill Industries (Nelson, 1971) and represent the expansion of both national and individual private and public sheltered workshops.

Workshop and rehabilitation centers have played an integral role in the rehabilitation of the disabled. Through both salvage, renovation, and subcontracts from industry, sheltered workshops have provided terminal employment, on-the-job evaluation, occupational training, adjustment skills training, and adjustment services (personal, social, work, and other counseling and medical services). Salvage and subcontracts are not able to provide all of the necessary funding to support a workshop, and consequently, government grants and cooperative interagency efforts have played an important role in the workshop movement.

REHABILITATION CENTERS

The International Center for the Disabled (known previously as the Institute for the Crippled and Disabled) was founded in New York City in 1917 to serve veterans of World War I. The Institute was founded by Jeremiah Milbank, a director of the Metropolitan Insurance Company, and grew with additional support from the Red Cross. Other important early workshops and centers were the Curative Workshop of Milwaukee (1919), sponsored by the Junior League, and the Cleveland Rehabilitation Center (1901), funded through local contributions.

At the 1947 National Conference of Social Work in Buffalo, Mr. Glenn Leighbody, Director of the Buffalo Goodwill Industries, called directors of workshops and homebound industries programs together for an informal meeting. Out of this meeting came the National Committee on Sheltered Workshops and Homebound Programs. In 1952 the Association of Rehabilitation Centers was established. Today there are over 4,000 facilities throughout the country which are classified as rehabilitation centers.

In 1955 the Joint Commission on Mental Illness and Health was authorized to evaluate the status, needs, and resources of mentally ill persons in the United States. As a result of this report, the Community Mental Health Center Act of 1964 was passed, establishing local community mental health centers nationwide. Today these centers provide a range of services for mentally ill persons and receive federal and state funds.

THE ROLE OF VOLUNTARY ORGANIZATIONS IN REHABILITATION

Jane Addams (1860–1935) was one of the foremost proponents of humanitarian programs for the disadvantaged and disabled during the last quarter of the nineteenth century and for more than a quarter of the twentieth century. After visiting Toynbee Hall in London, she founded Hull House in Chicago. This settlement house served as a focus for her crusade for social justice in housing, better factory conditions, and equal rights for women and children, immigrants, and Negroes.

The Red Cross made a great contribution to the rehabilitation effort through eleemosynary means. But another organization that was involved in rehabilitation efforts had its beginnings in 1904 in Philadelphia, when about 100 state leaders of societies for the prevention of tuberculosis formed the National Association for the Study and Prevention of Tuberculosis. In 1907 the Christmas Seals method of raising money was initiated, and by 1930 the association's national office authorized a Rehabilitation Service.

The National Society for Crippled Children and Adults came into existence as a result of a streetcar accident in Elyria, Ohio in 1907. When the 18 year old son of Edgar F. Allen died in this accident, which also resulted in injury to several others, Allen felt that his son's life may have been saved and proper care given to the others had there been a hospital in Elyria. As a consequence of Allen's intense interest in adequate medical care, a hospital was opened in Elyria in 1908, and an international organization was formed in the interest of the treatment and rehabilitation of crippled children. Interest in the care and treatment of children grew and subsequently resulted in the first state society in 1919, the Ohio Society for Crippled Children. A federation of state societies was formed in 1921, and was named the National Society for Crippled Children and Adults. The currently familiar Easter Seal method of raising funds for these societies was begun in 1934.

There are in existence around the country today many private and public diagnostic and rehabilitation centers, workshops, homebound programs, and multiple services for the orthopedically, neuromuscularly, and other disabled persons.

THE STATE-FEDERAL VOCATIONAL REHABILITATION PROGRAM

There may never have been a state-federal program of vocational rehabilitation had not private schools, facilities, and voluntary organizations helped to pave the way and work as teammates along the rehabilitation road. Nor would there have been a comprehensive vocational rehabilitation program had not the federal government backed public programs with forceful legislation and substance in the form of funding.

EARLY LEGISLATION

The forerunners of early vocational rehabilitation programs were the various benefit programs provided to veterans and those injured during war. The first veterans' benefits were approved by Congress on August 26, 1776, following the Revolutionary War, in the form of the first national pension law. In 1862, following the Civil War, Congress enacted the General Law (12 State. L., 566), which was to apply to veterans of future wars, and did apply in the Spanish-American War and still was in force during World War I. This law provided compensation for servicemen of the Regular Army and Navy for disability due to injury or disease related directly to incidents occurring in the military service. Since those who fought in the Spanish-American War were volunteers, they were not recognized with a disability pension until 1920.

The vocational education acts also were paving the way for, and subsequently helping to sustain, the vocational rehabilitation program. The Smith-Hughes Act (Public Law 347, 64th Congress), passed in 1917, established a federal-state program in vocational education and appropriated money for the training of vocational education teachers. This legislation, along with the National Defense Act of 1916, promoted vocational adjustment programs for servicemen. Congress, in creating a Federal Board for Vocational Education as authorized by the Vocational Education Act of 1917, established "a precedent for future legislation that would create programs to assist disabled workers to develop new skills for new jobs" (Switzer, 1969, p. 39). The first vocational rehabilitation program authorized by state law was instituted in Minneapolis as the result of a Minnesota rehabilitation act in 1919.

The Soldier Rehabilitation Act (Public Law 178, 65th Congress) was passed in 1918, authorizing the Federal Board of Vocational Education to organize and provide vocational rehabilitation programs for disabled veterans. Eligibility requirements dictated that disabled veterans were unable to participate in gainful employment. Two laws passed by Congress in 1919 enhanced rehabilitation services for veterans. Public Law 279 permitted the Federal Board for Vocational Education to use both public and private gifts and donations to reimburse veterans during training eligibility determination. Public Law 11 authorized the Board to provide funds for maintenance and support allowances while veterans were engaged in vocational rehabilitation programs.

FORMAL LEGISLATIVE COMMITMENT

The National Rehabilitation Act (Public Law 236, 66th Congress) passed in 1920, also known as the Smith-Fess Act, is recognized as the first formal beginning of a public rehabilitation program, and established the present federal state program relationship. The goal of the program was to facilitate gainful employment for physically disabled persons through the provision of limited areas of service. Allocation of the funds to state programs was authorized on a 50–50 matching basis according to population, and provided vocational guidance, training, occupational adjustment, prosthetics, and placement services. The legislation stipulated that services were for the physically disabled and were to be vocationally oriented. McGowan and Porter (1967) described the act as follows:

> This act was inaugurated under a special act of Congress to provide a program of rehabilitation for disabled civilians. It was stimulated by the success of the Soldier Rehabilitation Act. The primary purpose of the act was to encourage States to undertake similar legislation and provide similar services for disabled civilians. (p. 24)

Also of significance is that the legislation placed primary responsibility for vocational rehabilitation on the states rather than at the federal level (Obermann, 1965). Within 18 months, over 30 states passed legislation organizing vocational rehabilitation programs eligible for the federal matching funds.

In 1920, by the time the National Rehabilitation Act had been passed, many of the state Commissions for the Blind already were providing a wide variety of vocational services for blind clients. In 1931 the Pratt-Smoot Act was passed by Congress to provide for production of embossed books for blind adults, as well as for recorded "talking books." In 1952, the act was amended to provide the same services for children.

The Randolph-Sheppard Act was passed by Congress in 1936, giving the blind the primary rights for the establishment and operation of vending stands in public buildings. Switzer (1969) spoke of this act as "one of the most successful specialized approaches to the rehabilitation of a single category of disabled that we have ever had" (p. 42). In 1938 Congress passed the Wagner-O'Day Act, which Obermann (1965) described as having "given great stimulation to workshops for the blind by requiring the Federal Government Departments to buy products of those workshops under certain prescribed conditions" (p. 339).

EXPANSION LEGISLATION

The Social Security Act Amendments of 1939 gave a boost to the Vocational Rehabilitation programs by providing $3,500,000 in annual grants for the states. The Bardon-LaFollette Act, or the Vocational Act Amendments of 1943 (Public Law 78–113, 78th Congress), provided federal aid for the first time for the rehabilitation of the blind and mentally disabled. In addition, the act greatly expanded service provisions to include any services deemed necessary to facilitate return to work for the disabled person. These services included physical restoration, corrective surgery, and paid hospitalization up to 90 days (based on economic need); provision of transportation, tools, occupational licenses, and prosthetic devices; maintenance during training; and medical examinations. Separate state agencies were established for general vocational rehabilitation services and for rehabilitation services for the blind, both to operate within the federal-state framework and both to be eligible for federal funds.

In 1945, Public Law 176 (79th Congress) provided an opportunity for more public involvement in rehabilitation by a presidential proclamation designating the second week in October as National Employ the Physically Handicapped Week. In order to stimulate the interest of the youth in the disability and employment problems of disabled workers, the Committee in 1949 established an essay contest based on reasons for hiring the handicapped. In the same year, through Public Law 162, Congress appropriated $75,000 for operation of the Committee's activities. In 1962, the name was changed to the President's Committee on the Employment of the Handicapped. By 1962, there was a governor's committee in each state and over 1,000 cities had mayor's committees—all interconnected through the Washington Committee.

Today, the national, state, and local committees are active with study groups and conferences that deal with affirmative action legislation and activities.

The Vocational Rehabilitation Act Amendments of 1954 (Public Law 565, 83rd Congress) represented yet greater expansion and growth to the developing rehabilitation movement. The amendments changed the financing formula to one based on per capita income, so that the poorer states would receive a larger share of the appropriations, up to 66.66 percent matching funds. Critical to the development of a profession and a technology, research and demonstration projects were funded to support innovation in improving services and demonstrating application methods. Grants were provided on a state-matching basis to alter or expand rehabilitation facilities and workshops. Training grants for rehabilitation counselors, physicians, physical therapists, occupational therapists, and other specialists were established for long-term degree programs at universities and colleges and for short-term degree programs and in-service training. The annual appropriations provided through the act for all states was $30,000,000 in the first year, and was increased annually until it reached $65,000,000 in 1958.

In 1965 federal participation in vocational rehabilitation was broadened considerably through passage of the Vocational Rehabilitation Act Amendments of 1965 (Public Law 333, 89th Congress). Financially, the federal government agreed to pay 75 percent for the state-matching for rehabilitation services and vocational workshops. Disabled persons were provided extended services from 6 to 18 months for the purpose of evaluating vocational potential, employability, and determining eligibility. The act also expanded the base for service provision to include social handicapping conditions.

Statewide planning was made possible through Public Law 333, for projecting services for the disabled according to need and improved services. Economic need as a prerequisite for services was eliminated, but each state was given the right to use this criterion for services other than diagnostic, counseling, and placement services. A national commission on architectural barriers was created, and professional training in rehabilitation was extended from two to four years.

The Vocational Rehabilitation Amendments of 1967 (Public Law 90–99), further expanded the public vocational rehabilitation program. Highlights of this legislation were (1) disabled migrant workers were entitled to rehabilitation programs through project grants to the states; (2) development and operation of a national center for the deaf-blind; (3) continued funding for statewide planning; and (4) elimination of the residence requirement as a condition for receiving rehabilitation services.

The Vocational Rehabilitation Amendments of 1968 (Public Law 90–391) provided for broader and more specific evaluation and adjustment services for the disabled and disadvantaged. The law defined "disadvantaged individuals" as "individuals disadvantaged by reason of their youth or advanced age, low educational attainments, ethnic or cultural factors, prison or delinquency records, or other conditions which constitute a barrier to employment." Services were expanded to include follow-up of individuals after job placement, as well as aid to families, when aid advanced the rehabilitation potential of the individual.

Not only did Public Law 90–391 provide for the usual medical and psychological evaluation, it also provided for work evaluation and work adjustment services, which were defined specifically as:

> Services to appraise the individual's patterns of work behavior and ability to acquire occupational skills, and to develop work attitudes, work habits, work tolerance, and social and behavior patterns suitable for successful job performance, including the utilization of work, simulated or real, to assess and develop the individual's capacities to perform adequately in a work environment. (Sec. 15)

REHABILITATION ACT OF 1973

Although there were other intervening legislative initiatives, more significant changes in emphasis were made in the 1973 Rehabilitation Act (Public Law 93–112), known generally as the Rehabilitation of the Severely Disabled Act. The act placed emphasis not only on serving those whose severe handicaps made it difficult for them to be employed, but also provided for research and demonstration projects to determine the feasibility of methods to provide services for those who "cannot reasonably be expected to be rehabilitated for employment but for whom a program of rehabilitation could improve their ability to live independently or function normally within their family and community" (Sec. 130).

The act emphasized that services should be prioritized in order to service the more severely disabled first. Each state was directed io identify how this order of selection would be accomplished in the state plan.

In an effort to attain more client awareness and involvement, Public Law 93–112 mandated an Individualized Written Rehabilitation Plan (IWRP). In general, this plan was to be composed of a statement of the rehabilitation goals and the services to be utilized as objectives for attaining these goals—a contract between the counselor and the client.

The cooperation of business and industry was elicited in the special projects and demonstration section which is known, in part, as Projects With Industry (PWI). Under this provision, contracts may be made with employers and organizations for:

The establishment of projects designed to prepare handicapped
individuals for gainful and suitable employment in the competitive
labor market under which handicapped individuals are provided
training and employment in a realistic work setting and such other
services...as may be necessary for such individuals to continue
to engage in such employment. (Sec. 304)

Public Law 93–112 contained strong provisions for affirmative
action as contained in Title V of the act.

- Section 501 prohibits discrimination in federal employment against
  persons according to sex or race.
- Section 502 calls for barrier-free construction in federal and
  federally funded buildings.
- Section 503 requires an affirmative action hiring policy of those
  businesses and industries which have federal contracts.
- Section 504 mandates a nondiscrimination clause regarding
  employment and services for recipients of federal assistance—
  primarily federal grantees.

The Social Security Amendments of 1974 (Public Law 93–674, Title
XX) provide rehabilitation services to include not only training and
employment services, but combinations of services to meet the special
needs of children, the aged, the mentally retarded, the blind, the
physically handicapped, the emotionally disturbed, alcoholics, and drug
addicts. One major goal entailed self-support to prevent, reduce or elim-
inate dependency. This included counseling and other services related
to preparation for employment, as well as special services to youth who
are drop outs or who have been in trouble with the law. Another goal
was to prevent institutional care by providing community-based or
home-based care.

The Rehabilitation Amendment of 1974 (Public Law 93–516) mandated the removal of the Rehabilitation Services Administration from
the Social and Rehabilitation Service to the Office of Human Development headed by a Deputy Secretary of Health, Education, and Welfare.
In addition, the amendments authorized a White House Conference
on Handicapped Individuals to make recommendations to the Presi-
dent about solutions to problems experienced by handicapped persons.

In describing the four years of effort entailed in making possible
the passage of the 1973 legislation and the 1974 amendments, Mills (1976)
delineated the results:

The extensive hearings before both houses of the Congress afforded an opportunity for nearly every segment of the rehabilitation movement to participate
in the development of the legislation. The voice of consumers and

organizations of the handicapped were heard. The Congress was impressed by this testimony and reflected this in the committee reports and in the legislation.... *The widespread public support for the legislation resulted in the greatest grassroots involvement in support of rehabilitation programs and facilities* in the history of the movement. As a result, there was a substantial increase of public awareness of the program and of the needs of handicapped people. This public exposure may have opened a new era of concern for the rights and needs of physically handicapped and mentally handicapped people with severe vocational handicaps. (p. 20)

The Rehabilitation Act Amendments of 1978 increased the minimum state appropriation to $3,000,000. The legislation continued the emphasis on independent functioning of severely disabled persons by authorizing a program of comprehensive independent living services. Two other important provisions of this legislation included creation of a National Institute of Handicapped Research and a change in the definition of developmental disabilities to emphasize functional abilities.

PROMOTION OF COOPERATIVE EFFORTS

Teamwork, community involvement, and cooperation have been components of vocational rehabilitation legislation and philosophy since the beginning. Funding for the 1920 Smith-Fess legislation was very limited in scope. Legislation, therefore, encouraged the state programs to cooperate with state and local agencies to obtain the range of services a person might need to return to independent fuctioning, including medical treatment, prosthetics, and maintenance funds. In addition, the act required that states develop cooperative agreements with worker's compensation agencies to coordinate service provision for injured workers.

The Social Security Act of 1935 provided for cooperation at the state level between vocational programs and crippled children programs. The 1954 Vocational Rehabilitation Amendment recognized the tremendous growth of social welfare programs being developed through the 1950s and specified cooperation with public assistance and public unemployment agencies as well as the developing social welfare program.

The 1968 Amendments authorized state vocational rehabilitation agencies to develop agreements and programs with private industry and business. To further support and encourage cooperative efforts between both private and public agencies as well as business, the legislation allowed local vocational rehabilitation agencies to develop joint programs with more than one federal agency.

The Rehabilitation Act of 1973 confirmed the general legislative provisions promoting linkages between vocational rehabilitation and state and local agencies. The legislation was very specific in directing the Rehabilitation Services Administration to participate in interagency planning for coordinated services to disabled individuals. This directive filtered down to the state level, where states were required to develop written plans for interagency coordination and cooperation.

Thus, we see a panorama of contributing people, and influencing agencies, which has resulted in each state developing state-federal vocational rehabilitation programs to provide comprehensive services to disabled individuals. Congressional acts, fueled by the efforts of voluntary organizations, education and rehabilitation organizations, and representative bodies of disabled people, formulated concepts of service delivery. These concepts culminated periodically in the formation, expansion, and improvement of the state federal vocational rehabilitation programs. Today, many disabled persons are afforded the special services needed to become contributing members of our work force, and thus, live more independent and satisfying lives.

INTEREST GROUPS AND PROFESSIONAL ORGANIZATIONS

NATIONAL REHABILITATION ASSOCIATION

Nearly all facets of business and industry and education and rehabilitation have had professional organizations and unions which have played a prominent part in formulating and developing their professional roles, as well as projecting a certain image to society. Such organizations as the American Medical Association, the American Federation of Labor, Congress of Industrial Organization, the American Vocational Association, and the American Psychological Association, among hundreds of other varied organizations, have promoted the welfare of their professions.

The National Rehabilitation Association (NRA) has played a major role in the development of human service programs for the handicapped and disadvantaged. In 1923, W. F. Faulkes, Administrator of the Wisconsin Vocational Rehabilitation Division, spoke at a luncheon meeting proposing the formation of a separate and permanent national organization of state rehabilitation practitioners. At the same conference, D. M. Blankenship, Supervisor of the Virginia Vocational Rehabilitation Division, was elected Chairman of the group, which decided to call the new organization the National Civilian Rehabilitation Conference. The purposes of the new organization were to provide a forum, to conduct an educational campaign, to further agreement on principles and practices, and to set up a medium to give expression to views of the membership on pending legislation and public policies. All of this was in the interest of the vocational rehabilitation of disabled civilians and their consequent problems.

The organization was given its present name, the National Rehabilitation Association (NRA), at the conference held in Memphis in March, 1927. In 1945, the *Journal of Rehabilitation* was designated as the official organ of the association. It was not until 1931 that the Executive Committee took legislative action to separate vocational rehabilitation from vocational education. The establishment of an NRA office in Washington, D.C., served to promulgate this and other future legislative actions.

The NRA has grown from the early days of limiting membership to those working with the civilian disabled to professionals in all categories of rehabilitation efforts. Currently, the association comprises seven divisions. The National Rehabilitation Counseling Association, founded in 1958, has among its members not only rehabilitation counselors but counselor educators, researchers, students in training, and counselor aides. This division publishes a newsletter and the *Journal of Applied Rehabilitation Counseling*.

The second largest division of NRA is the Vocational Evaluation and Work Adjustment Association which achieved status as a professional division in 1967. Its membership consists of vocational evaluators, adjustment services specialists, and related personnel. It publishes a quarterly journal, the *Vocational Evaluation and Work Adjustment Bulletin*.

In 1964, two new divisions were admitted. One was the National Association of Disability Examiners, composed of those who evaluate Social Security applications for disability benefits. The other was the Job Placement Division, consisting of those whose work entails job development and placement of the handicapped.

Other divisions include the National Association of Rehabilitation Secretaries, the National Congress on the Rehabilitation of Homebound and Institutionalized Persons, and the last division to be recognized, the National Rehabilitation Administration Association.

A new division is forming, designated as the National Association of Workshop Instructors. These persons are employed in sheltered workshops and rehabilitation centers as instructors of the disabled, teaching trade and basic academic skills.

Today, the NRA has a membership of approximately 40,000 persons. Over the past decade, the NRA has come to recognize the obligation to give disabled individuals, who are the recipient of services, a louder voice in its operations and conferences. Thus, the consumer increasingly plays a more active role in both NRA activities on the national and local levels, as well as in actual rehabilitation agency activities and services.

THE CURRENT STATUS OF VOCATIONAL REHABILITATION

Obviously, there continues to be a dire need for services to rehabilitate disabled people. In 1929, according to the *Social Security Bulletin* (Skolnik & Dales, 1976), vocational rehabilitation services were budgeted $1,600,000 out of a total social welfare expenditure of $3,921,100,000, or only .0004 percent of the total budget. By 1975, vocational rehabilitation services were allotted only $950,000,000 out of a total social welfare expenditure of $286,674,000,000 or .0033 percent of the total budget.

If we were to compare the budget for vocational rehabilitation services against the total national budget, the amount would be infinitesimal in comparison. And yet, if we were to project the gains in person-years and wages through the services of vocational rehabilitation, we would find that such agencies not only pay for themselves, but repay the taxpayer many times over.

Teamwork, community involvement and cooperation, and state-federal coordination always have been the modus operandi of the vocational rehabilitation movement. Not only has vocational rehabilitation been generally involved in the concept of the therapeutic community, it also has been one of the foremost proponents of formalized agreements with other agencies and organizations. These have been in the form of contractual agreements, such as with the Social Security Offices of Disability Determination and with the Social Security Trust Fund.

As legislation has increased funding for vocational education, special education, manpower programs, mental retardation, and other human service organizations, vocational rehabilitation similarly continues to reach out in a larger cooperative effort on behalf of the disabled and disadvantaged clientele.

SUMMARY

The brief history in this chapter describes the expanding services offered by the field of vocational rehabilitation. As vocational rehabilitation has grown, so has the knowledge base and range of skills and involvement of the rehabilitation counselor. As noted in the previous chapter, changes in education emphasis toward a more career/vocational focus have functioned to bridge the gap between vocational rehabilitation and education. Through Public Law 94–142, public schools have assumed more responsibility for providing comprehensive career and vocational education services to special needs students. As a result, rehabilitation counselors are being called upon to work cooperatively with special educators in evaluation, vocational curriculum design,

career development counseling, and in linking students with the world
of work after graduation.

CHAPTER QUESTIONS

1. What do you view as the major influence(s) in the development
   of formal services to disabled adults and how have this/these
   influence(s) contributed to today's vocational rehabilitation delivery
   system?

2. How is the vocational rehabilitation system the same/different from
   education and special education in providing services to handicapped individuals? What core services are present in each system
   and what skills and competencies are characteristic of professionals
   in each system?

3. Place yourself in the position of a legislative aide who has been asked
   to develop a brief or short report on special education and vocational rehabilitation. Your charge is to develop arguments pro and
   con for the plan to subsume the Office of Special Education and
   the Rehabilitation Services Administration under one federal/state
   department to facilitate more effective and efficient delivery of
   services.

CHAPTER 3

Vocational Evaluation Development

Although vocational evaluation is often viewed as a relatively new profession, the practice of vocational evaluation dates to biblical times when Gideon used a "situational assessment" technique to identify skilled warriors (Pruitt, 1986). However, over the past two decades, vocational evaluation as a profession has experienced rapid and dynamic growth in terms of a theoretical body of knowledge, research, professional standards, and level of technology.

Definitions of vocational evaluation are numerous (Dahl, Appleby, & Lipe, 1978; Kulman, 1975; Nadolsky, 1976; Neff, 1985) and are indicative of a growing and expanding profession that is responding to an increasing range of individuals that may be served. Despite rapid professional growth, the basic goals of vocational evaluation practice have remained constant:

- to provide an understanding of the individual's vocational potential;
- to assist in decision making regarding career direction;
- and to predict performance in a work setting.

Vocational evaluation remains a *functional* process rather than the more static descriptive process that is common in psychometric diagnostic evaluations or testing procedures.

The purpose of the present chapter is to briefly detail the growth and development of vocational evaluation, leading to its present role and function within special education.

WHAT IS VOCATIONAL EVALUATION?

Work personality has long played a central role in the development of vocational evaluation theory and practice. Although work personality is basically an abstract concept, Gellman (1968) gave substance to work personality when he stated:

The work personality consists of the characteristic pattern of work activity displayed by a person in a work situation. The work personality incorporates work attitudes, behavioral work patterns, attitudes, value systems, incentive and abilities—the behavioral configuration regarded as necessary to function effectively in a work setting. It is a constellation distinguishing work roles from other societal roles. (p. 99)

Vocational evaluation, then, must be viewed as an assessment of these work attitudes, behavioral work patterns, value systems, incentives, and abilities. Gellman again maintained the centrality of the work personality when he stated:

Vocational evaluation assesses a client's work personality to determine (a) developmental level, (b) characteristic performance patterns, and (c) appropriateness of behavior in a work situation. Other aspects of vocational evaluation deal with the person's relationships to the labor market. (p. 99)

Instrumentally, when we speak of the role of work personality in the evaluation process, we are placing the person (client, student, evaluee) at the center of the process. Vocational evaluation, in the final instance, is culminated only when the person makes his or her own individual assessment of personal work behaviors and performances. A major principle of vocational evaluation states that the individual must be an active participant in the evaluation process—the process cannot be imposed upon the person.

So, in this context, what do we mean by vocational evaluation? Common usage indicates that the terms *vocational evaluation* and *work evaluation* have been used synonymously. The Tenth Institute on Rehabilitation Services (Mills, 1972) designated both terms in its definition:

Vocational (work) evaluation is a comprehensive process that systematically utilizes work, real or simulated, as the focal point for assessment and vocational exploration, the purpose of which is to assist individuals in vocational development. Vocational (work) evaluation incorporates medical, psychological, social, vocational, educational, cultural and economic data in the attainment of the goals of the evaluation process. (p. 2)

The study group report of the Tenth Institute commented on the fact that the two terms were used interchangeably, but noted, "The fact that the word 'vocational' is used first and outside the parentheses indicates that it is the preferable term" (p. 2).

A more recent study group, as a part of the Vocational Evaluation Project Final Report, provided another detailed definition of vocational evaluation in which the term *work evaluation* was not included (Ehrle, 1975). Vocational evaluation is:

(1) The process of observing behaviors and interpreting them against some criterion;

(2) The process of assessing what an individual does and how well he does it, i.e., his "calling" (grounded in interests, abilities, needs and opportunities) against some criterion;

(3) One function of a personalized delivery system that obtains and synthesizes information pertinent to persons with vocational problems to assist them in identifying and planning (an) appropriate vocation(s);

(4) [The Tenth Institute's definition];

(5) A specialized form of clinical assessment requiring a specialized technology and environment, requiring a period of several days or even weeks of close observation and judgement, characterized by the use of real or simulated work tasks and activities in a situation which simulates some of the demands of work environments. (p. 86)

The previous definition is quite comprehensive and provides a broader picture of the scope of the vocational evaluation *process*. Roberts (1970) differentiated between vocational evaluation and work evaluation by denoting the former as the broader categorization and the latter as an assessment process within vocational evaluation, which emphasizes work as the focal point of the evaluation.

As vocational evaluation has developed a professional identity, the literature has further refined the definition of vocational evaluation. Nadolsky (1971) delineated both the objective and the somewhat subjective aspects of vocational evaluation when he stated that it "may be defined as a process that attempts to *assess* and *predict* work behavior and vocational potential through the application of a variety of techniques and procedures" (p. 226). As he continued his definition, he pointed out some of the arguments related to the subject, but concluded that all vocational procedures do share a common goal:

Some of the techniques and procedures are directly related to work, while others are unrelated; some are standardized, while others are not. However, what is *common to all* vocational evaluation procedures is the *goal of assessment*. They all attempt to assess and predict work behavior and vocational potential. (p. 227)

In summary then, vocational evaluation is a comprehensive, systematic process that utilizes various techniques in the assessment and prediction of vocational interest and potential aptitude. In essence, this entails an assessment of the total work personality, incorporating medical, psychosocial, educational, cultural, and economic data, in addition to vocational data. Some of the techniques at which we will be looking are psychological testing, work samples, situational assessment, and on-the-job evaluation.

Work evaluation, per se, is a process of vocational assessment in which real or simulated work situations such as work samples, situational assessment, and on-the-job evaluation are the primary components. In general, vocational evaluation may be considered as the overall process of *assessment*—a descriptive term—whereas work evaluation is geared more specifically to work-oriented *assessment procedures*. However, the terms are used interchangeably and often the term *evaluation* is used to describe one or both procedures.

We find that vocational evaluation procedures have application in various milieus in education and rehabilitation, as well as in business and industry. Vocational evaluation offers a prescription for vocational guidance for various types of individuals in educational and rehabilitation institutions, as well as offering a prediction, or prognosis, of the probability of success in a particular vocational area.

The next section of this chapter will look at a short history of vocational evaluation with reference to vocational evaluation growth in special education.

HISTORY OF VOCATIONAL EVALUATION

EARLY INFLUENCES

Although vocational evaluation is a profession in its own right, it has drawn from and been influenced by several related sources.

If we accept a general definition of vocational evaluation to be a method of matching the right person with a particular job, many incidents in history could be considered the forerunners of contemporary vocational evaluation. Various cultures have used different methods for determining which persons would have the responsibilities of the different duties necessary to carry on tribal customs and tasks.

However, vocational evaluation as a science or formalized methodology of assessment was not a reality until the twentieth century. One of the first known pioneers in work sample development was an industrial psychologist, Hugo Munsterberg, who developed a simulated streetcar operator's control panel for the Boston Railway Company for the purpose of selecting qualified streetcar operators (Bregman, 1969).

Early vocational evaluation by rehabilitation workers involved questioning clients about their vocational interests and abilities, administering psychological tests, and trying the clients in various vocational courses. This hit-and-miss method was in vogue in the 1930s when the Minneapolis Veterans Administration Hospital demonstrated several new vocational counseling procedures and the Institute for the Crippled and Disabled (ICD) in New York instituted simulated work evaluation techniques and procedures, which later in the 1950s would become a vocational evaluation system known as the Testing, Orientation, and Work Evaluation in Rehabilitation (TOWER) System (Institute for the Crippled and Disabled, 1967).

The views of Whitehouse (1953) were representative of some of the early literature on vocational evaluation when he pointed out the advantages of the work sample process to the rehabilitation team at the ICD in New York. Soon after that, Bailey (1958) emphasized the work trial method of vocational evaluation for the attainment of the mutual goals of the disabled client and evaluator.

PSYCHOLOGY AND PSYCHOMETRIC TESTING

Psychometric testing must be recognized as both a forerunner and a present-day component of vocational evaluation. As late as 1850, psychology still was, to a great extent, a part of philosophy. By 1900 psychology was struggling to be accepted as a science in its own right as it began to ally itself more with the physical and biological sciences, and it became more conscious of measurement through adoption of the experimental method. Although the early psychologists of the nineteenth century were concerned more with the formulation of generalized descriptions of human behavior than they were with measurement of individual differences, it was left to Wilhelm Wundt to pave the way for developing and standardizing psychological measurement. In 1879, Wundt developed strict measurement procedures to evaluate speed of response in a laboratory setting.

However, it was Sir Francis Galton, an English biologist, who was more solely responsible for the contemporary testing movement. He and other English scientists, under the direction of Karl Pearson, improved the techniques for the analysis and description of patterns of individual differences. Soon after the turn of the century, Alfred Binet, who later teamed up with Theodore Simon, designed the first formal intelligence test.

It was an American psychologist, James McKenn Cattell, who, before the turn of the century and under the influence of Galton, first used the term *mental test* in the psychological literature. In an article concerning a series of tests administered annually for the purpose of determining the intellectual level of college students, we find a kinship to our contemporary vocational evaluation efforts. Anastasi (1976) provided this description:

The tests, which had to be administered individually, included measures of muscular strength, speed of movement, sensitivity to pain, keenness of vision and of hearing, weight discrimination, reaction time, memory and the like. (p. 9)

Vocational evaluation continues to rely on and adhere to the contributions psychology has made in the test development principles involved in standardizing testing procedures, developing representative norm groups, establishing reliability measures, and validating tests.

INFLUENCES OF INDUSTRY

Industry has had a long-standing interest in evaluating potential workers and employees for selection and promotion as well as for improving productivity. As noted earlier, the first formal work sample was developed by Munsterberg in an attempt to identify causes of industrial accidents in electric railway positions. The work sample was a simulated trolley car control apparatus. It entailed simulated operator's equipment, including the levers that moved cars, with figures representing people, animals, and cars that might move in front of the trolley car.

The experiments in Munsterberg's Harvard laboratory resulted in the railway company being able to screen potential accident-prone operators when the findings showed a rather high correlation between efficiency in the experiment and efficiency in actual service.

Industry has been interested in production, motivation, job satisfaction, as well as in selection and screening of workers. As vocational evaluation has a similar interest, it has drawn from the advances industry has made in job analysis, job evaluation, situational assessment, performance appraisal, production and personnel data gathering, behavioral rating scales, and observational principles (Landy & Trumbo, 1976).

EVALUATION IN MEDICAL INSTITUTIONS

One of the earlier references to vocational evaluation in general medical institutions was a description of the team approach utilized in a prevocational evaluation and rehabilitation setting at Massachusetts General Hospital (Watkins, 1959). A situational assessment approach was used as the evaluation methodology by placing the patients at job stations in various departments of the hospital.

Another general medical hospital that pioneered in vocational evaluation was the Highland View Hospital in Cleveland, Ohio (Garrett,

1959). This was a long-term hospital that made sheltered workshop evaluation available to the patients in an effort to place the patients in outside employment appropriate to their interests and talents.

The Institute of Physical Medicine and Rehabilitation in New York City was one of the earliest users of vocational evaluation (Garrett, 1959). The Institute utilized standardized tests and prevocational evaluation and therapy for the disabled. Comparative results of the psychometric test and vocational evaluation approaches were also researched.

EVALUATION IN THE UNITED STATES EMPLOYMENT SERVICE

The United States Employment Service (USES) offers a broad range of services to the person seeking work. Almost all services of the USES relate to vocational evaluation and vocational planning. Evaluation is essential if the person is to be matched with the appropriate job. The USES utilizes various aptitude and interest tests, foremost of which is the General Aptitude Test Battery (GATB) and its counterpart for the nonreader, the Non-verbal Aptitude Test Battery (NATB).

In job matching, the *Dictionary of Occupational Titles*, the *Occupational Outlook Handbook*, the *Standard Occupational Classification Manual*, and other pertinent occupational literature and tools are utilized. The job bank in microfiche form makes job matching current, and job search and relocation services offer job matching on a geographical basis. More recently, the interviewers in some of the larger cities have been able to use a computerized job matching system.

Employment counseling is a service that utilizes the previously mentioned placement service, but is geared to those who have special needs, such as the disadvantaged, the handicapped, the older worker, the displaced homemaker, and others.

The labor market information and occupational analysis services offered by the USES are actually tools of vocational evaluation in that the evaluator and the counselor are made aware of labor market trends, thus having a more adequate knowledge of the job market. The *Standard Industrial Classification Manual* is utilized as the format in making these projections. Other industrial services are provided by employer service representatives who help employers and unions with employment and apprenticeship problems. Usually these services entail job/person matching, as when an employer wants a worker with some unique skill, or needs many workers on short notice.

Vocational evaluation has been involved in the training and retraining activities of the employment services in such programs as WIN and

CETA and, more recently, the Job Training Partnership Act (JTPA), in order to match the person with the most feasible training and/or employment slot.

Historically, the USES has been heavily involved in vocational evaluation to fulfill its mission. Usually this has not entailed work samples per se, and consequently, the USES has sent some of their applicants and counselors to a rehabilitation facility or school vocational evaluation facility for a more formalized vocational assessment.

ADDITIONAL INFLUENCES AND CONTRIBUTIONS TO VOCATIONAL EVALUATION GROWTH

In addition to the influences cited, there have been and continue to be significant factors contributing to the dramatic growth of vocational evaluation practice and technology.

REHABILITATION FACILITIES

Historically, Goodwill Industries has engaged in primary use of the situational approach to vocational evaluation because of the opportunities afforded by their production workshops. However, Goodwill Industries recognized the benefit of all forms of simulated work evaluations and developed many standardized work sample approaches. The Goodwill Industries of Chicago and Cook County developed the Multidimensional Objective Vocational Evaluation (MOVE) system, which entails both work tasks and paper and pencil tests, and correlates with the *Dictionary of Occupational Titles* worker trait group.

The Jewish Vocational Service (JVS) surely ranks with Goodwill Industries as one of the earlier pioneers in vocational assessment. The JVS in Philadelphia gained prominence not only because of its contributions in evaluation and adjustment services (Leshner & Snyderman, 1965), but also because of the development and dissemination of the JEVS Work Sample Battery (Jewish Employment and Vocational Service, 1968). This work sample battery was developed under a Manpower Administration Contract in cooperation with the Pennsylvania State Employment Service.

There are other JVS agencies that are representative, historically, of the evaluation programs offered by this institution. The St. Louis JVS (Bitter, 1967) provides services for the mentally retarded, including work samples, standardized tests, and on-the-job evaluations. Examples of the provision of vocational evaluation services for the mentally ill and behaviorally disturbed are seen in the joint program between the

Camarillo State Hospital and the JVS in Los Angeles (Goertzel et al., 1967), and the Newark, New Jersey JVS (Coun, 1969).

One of the earlier devotees of formalized vocational evaluation and the initiator of the first systematized vocational evaluation system is the Institute for the Crippled and Disabled (ICD) in New York City. Jeremiah Milbank, founder and a perpetuator of the ICD, established a multiservice rehabilitation center, whose services emphasized programs for the severely handicapped when the term *severely* was not in popular usage as it is today. The Guidance Testing Class was the predecessor of the Testing, Orientation, and Work Evaluation in Rehabilitation (TOWER) Work Sample Battery which was developed by the ICD staff. TOWER, as practiced at the ICD, is correlated not only with the *Dictionary of Occupational Titles* (especially with the occupational group arrangements), but also with specific jobs in local industry.

LEGISLATION

As noted in the previous two chapters, legislation and subsequent federal funding have played a significant role in the growth of vocational rehabilitation, vocational education, and special education. Vocational rehabilitation legislation has emphasized expansion of services to severely disabled individuals, and this focus has resulted in development of vocational evaluation technology to identify the vocational potential of individuals with more severe and multiple handicaps.

Similarly, special education legislation has made comprehensive services more available to special needs students, and the service focus has been on competencies that students will need at home, on the job, and in the community. Recent legislation (the Carl Perkins Act of 1984) has made vocational evaluation available to all special needs students involved in a vocational education program. In addition, transition from school to work, as a national priority, has made vocational evaluation an integral component of individualized education planning, and necessitates evaluation of vocational skills needed to perform in different work settings.

TECHNOLOGICAL ADVANCES

Technological advances in the computer field allow individuals to manage an ever-increasing amount of information. Computer technology has been developed in vocational evaluation that assists the evaluator in several ways. Several paper and pencil tests (Strong Vocational Interest Blank, Career Assessment Inventory, Work Values Inventory) as well as selected work evaluation systems (Sage, TAP,

McCarron-Dial, MESA, Apticom) have computer scoring systems to evaluate and interpret the results and to profile the individual's interest and aptitude against vocational factors. Through this process, the evaluator can compare the individual's interests, aptitudes, and abilities and physical limitations to the requirements of worker trait demands and different occupational clusters.

Job matching software programs will compare the individual's characteristics, identified through test and work samples, and will cross-walk the resulting individual profile through the various occupational classification systems, including the DOT, GOE, SIC and available local employment resources to identify suitable vocational areas for the student. Other software programs will have local employer data bases so that the individual's vocational profile may be matched with local employers.

Computer technology enables the individual to manage increasing information about the person and the world of work to

- Develop effective evaluation information
- Organize available occupational information
- Compare information about the individual with information in different occupational resource systems.

VOCATIONAL EVALUATION IN SPECIAL EDUCATION

Testing in education and special education has had a long history, dating to the early 1900s when Alfred Binet was commissioned to develop a testing devise to differentiate between normal and mentally retarded students. Testing activity continues to be developed and used primarily to screen students who may have difficulty in educational activities and/or to establish an accurate diagnosis that would identify students as eligible for special education services.

Traditional educational testing methods use interview, observation, and psychometric testing procedures to evaluate the student and make decisions about program needs. Unfortunately, there are several limitations to these procedures when they are used to gather information for vocational planning. Traditional testing procedures were not developed to identify vocational skills, abilities or behaviors, and are not capable of providing information about vocational program development. In addition, educational testing results have little relationship to vocational outcome or little ability to predict future vocational success. Educational testing models useful for academic planning are far too restrictive and not well suited for identifying the range of skills and abilities that special needs students will need as they transition to community and vocational environments.

Vocational and transition planning requires an evaluation model that is community-referenced and that seeks to identify the range of skills, supports, reinforcers, and specific environmental characteristics that promote effective and productive levels of independent functioning.

For the purposes of this text, vocational evaluation that is responsive to the needs of the student and to the special education system is defined as follows: an ongoing and systematic process that utilizes information from a multidisciplinary team as well as from work or simulated work activity to identify individual strengths and weaknesses in addition to curriculum, program, and placement needs in order to develop vocational potential.

PRINCIPLES AND CHARACTERISTICS OF VOCATIONAL EVALUATION IN SPECIAL EDUCATION

1. Vocational evaluation is an "ongoing and systematic process" within special education. As such, it functions throughout the education process (K–12) from elementary levels, through middle and high school, to job placement (Peterson, 1985; Sitlington, 1979; Sitlington, Brolin, Clark, & Vacanti, 1985). Rather than a peripheral and independent educational service, it is an integrated component of career education, vocational programming, and transition planning (Stodden & Ianacone, 1981).

2. Vocational evaluation is a developmental process. Early in the education process, vocational evaluation contributes to the student's awareness of his or her abilities and interests as well as a developing understanding of why people work. As the student develops an understanding of his or her potential as a worker, he or she begins to explore how individual skills and abilities apply to and interact with different work situations and demands. As the individual becomes more familiar with occupations, vocational evaluation helps to crystallize choices and to develop tentative vocational objectives.

3. Vocational evaluation is not a static process that measures isolated traits, but a dynamic process that exposes the individual to varied tasks and situational demands. The process recognizes that successful work performance is an interactive process between the student and his or her skills and limitations, and the demands and supports of the work environment

4. Vocational evaluation is experientially based. Whereas much of education is verbally oriented, special needs students learn best through "hands-on" performance activities. Vocational evaluation uses multiple tasks and settings, including curriculum, simulated work, and on-the-job evaluation settings to provide exposure to and exploration of different work demands.

5. Vocational evaluation provides a varied and flexible assessment approach. As vocational evaluation has many tools, tasks, and tests as well as levels of simulated work experiences, the evaluator is able to examine student strengths and limitations from different perspectives and situations. In addition, the evaluator may systematically vary the supports and demands of a task to evaluate performance potential in several work situations.

6. Vocational evaluation is a learning process. Through involvement in a range of hands-on practical work tasks in a supportive and noncompetitive environment, the individual learns about himself or herself in relation to the world of work. Evaluation is an instrumental process promoting self awareness and self understanding, as well as personal and vocational growth.

7. Vocational evaluation is a decision-making process. The individual is able to organize the vocational, medical, social, cultural, psychological, and functional academic information to evaluate vocational alternatives, identify needed program efforts, and develop realistic vocational plans.

8. Vocational evaluation is a student-centered and individualized evaluation process. Evaluation activities are based on the student's vocational development rather than on a standardized evaluation battery administered to all students. The student has a responsibility to participate in evaluation planning and to make decisions about vocational programming.

9. Vocational evaluation is an outcome-oriented process. It is important for both the evaluator and the special education practitioner to be aware that, by definition, vocational evaluation is both student-centered and program-centered, as the process functions to enhance vocational growth for the student and to provide concrete information to program planners about the unique characteristics of the student.

10. Vocational evaluation recommendations are directed toward training and program activities that facilitate independent functioning in work and community settings.

VOCATIONAL EVALUATION COMPONENTS

Vocational evaluation consists of three primary evaluation components: psychometric tests, work samples, and situational assessment.

PSYCHOMETRIC TESTS

Psychometric tests, or paper and pencil tests, have been widely used in education and special education but have restricted use in vocational evaluation with students having severe handicaps. Major limitations of psychometric tests are inadequate norm groups, restrictive standardized administration procedures, inappropriate test content, and limited ability to modify testing procedures. In addition, paper and pencil tests are familiar experiences for special needs students and have historically represented failure.

Although many psychometric tests reflect the criticisms cited, many still may be used in support of simulated work evaluation. Testing may be useful if it identifies a specific behavior or skill level and if the results are in a format that is understandable to the student. Psychometric tests that measure aptitude, interest, functional academic ability, and dexterity are particularly useful.

Interest inventories such as the Wide Range Interest-Opinion Test (WRIOT) and the Gordon Occupational Check-List provide the opportunity for exploration of vocational alternatives at an early age. Achievement tests are a relatively quick method of gaining insight into functional academic ability or monitoring progress in career education training. Vocationally related aptitude tests such as the Bennett Mechanical Comprehension Test or Minnesota Clerical Test can be compared with the student's practical work on a simulated work task.

Chapter 7 will review how psychometric tests may be modified and used in a flexible way as an integral part of comprehensive vocational evaluation planning.

WORK SAMPLES

Work samples are standardized, well-defined work activities that use tools, materials, equipment, and supplies found in an actual job. Vocational evaluators use commercial work sample systems such as the SINGER, JEVS, Valpar, VIEWS, SAGE, and/or McCarron-Dial Work Evaluation System. By involving students in work sample activity, the student is exposed to a wide range of occupational activities in a relatively short period of time. The student may work on a mannequin in a cosmetology sample, connect pipes in a plumbing sample, use a soldering iron to perform electrical tasks, or sort screws, nuts, washers, or bolts to examine basic discrimination skills. Because work samples use norm groups to evaluate performance, the student may be compared to peers, industrial applicants, or employees.

In addition to commercial work samples, many school systems and rehabilitation agencies develop in-house work samples that more directly meet the needs of the student as well as the employment market of the community. In-house work samples allow the student to explore the work tools and equipment as well as the simulated work activities of local industries and businesses. The benefit of a work sample is its reality orientation.

Modifications of work sample evaluation will be discussed in a subsequent chapter.

SITUATIONAL ASSESSMENT

Vocational evaluators are able to use job stations within the school setting or industry-based job setting to evaluate vocational potential. The student is placed in a realistic setting, rather than the controlled and standardized format of a work sample, and is evaluated not only on technical ability to perform on the job but also on his or her ability to interact with co-workers, supervisors, and the public. Usually, the student is in one job for a day or longer and has the opportunity to adjust to expectations over time. In addition, the evaluator has the opportunity to vary characteristics of the setting, for example, work demands, supervision style, quality demands, or working alone or with others, to assess how the individual adjusts to work demands and environmental supports. Systematic observation skills and behavior analysis are assessment tools used to evaluate adjustment behavior, interpersonal skills, and readiness for more direct placement. Situational assessment is also a useful tool to identify the accommodations that a student may need in a transition or supported work setting.

FUNCTION OF VOCATIONAL EVALUATION

Rather than primarily a descriptive, diagnostic, eligibility, or placement determination service, vocational evaluation serves multiple functions:

1. Vocational evaluation *assists the student* in developing an understanding of how his or her unique skills, abilities, limitations, interests, and work values interact with the demands and opportunities of the world of work.

2. Vocational evaluation functions to provide information about career education and vocational transition *program development* needs. For example, identifying present and needed job skills; identifying the most appropriate program activity (supported work, work-study, job shadowing, job station, job club); developing training objectives and identifying how transition priorities should be established; identifying the accommodations, modifications, or aids that will promote more independent work.

3. Vocational evaluation functions to provide the planning team with information that facilitates decision making. For example, Is the student ready for a work site placement? In what kind of job should the student be placed? Should the student be placed in a particular residence? What kind of additional evaluation is needed?

4. Vocational evaluation functions to monitor the transition skill development process. Vocational evaluation should provide information

that is useful to both program and process evaluation. For example, Are training objectives being met in a timely way in a particular training site? Is the transition program as efficient as it can be?

5. Vocational evaluation functions to evaluate vocational and transition program efforts. Vocational evaluation can provide information about the program effectiveness of the vocational transition program efforts. For example, Are the transition programs resulting in increased jobs for students, increased quality of placements, and increased independent community functioning?

SUMMARY

Over the past two decades, vocational evaluation has experienced rapid professional and technological growth and development. Legislation, consumer advocacy, and an elightened community have resulted in a greater emphasis on quality services to more severely disabled individuals. This emphasis has resulted in the development of an evaluation technology to assess and identify vocational potential for these individuals. Growth in technology has been matched by development of professional standards in the vocational evaluation field. Professional standards have been developed and a certification process has been in place since 1981. At present, the professional organization, the Vocational Evaluation and Work Adjustment Association, is the second largest division of ihe National Rehabilitiation Association. Although vocational evaluation has always been closely aligned to vocational rehabilitation, there has also been recent expansion to provide service in manpower development programs, occupational medicine, private rehabilitation, and school systems. Legislation has mandated vocational evaluation services for all special needs students involved in vocational education programs. Schools are increasingly taking responsibility for vocational evaluation, vocational programming, and improved vocational outcomes for special needs students.

CHAPTER EXERCISE

1. Members of the evaluation team view the function of vocational evaluation in different ways. Assume the position of a
   Teacher
   Parent
   Guidance Counselor
   Program Administrator
   Student

What would you see as important primary functions of vocational evaluation? Develop a rationale for why each individual views the function of vocational evaluation as important/different.

2. You have been asked by your administrator to develop an organization and service delivery plan to comply with state special education directives on vocational evaluation. State the advantages and disadvantages of vocational evaluation service provided:

■ In-house
■ Through regional education centers
■ By purchasing service through a local vendor
■ By other means.

Decide whether vocational evaluation should be a function of the local education agency or should be performed outside of the school, and how special educators should be involved in the process.

CHAPTER 4

Implementing Vocational Evaluation in Special Education

$\mathbf{R}$ather than primarily a descriptive or diagnostic process, vocational evaluation provides information related to:

- functional strengths and limitations
- curricula, services, and program needs
- optimal career/vocational/transition outcome activities

The impact of vocational evaluation on the special education student is broader than traditional vocational evaluation activities performed in rehabilitation agencies. In the first place, vocational evaluation has students for far longer periods of time and is able to monitor, assess, and adjust evaluation and program recommendations over time. In addition, in special education, the evaluator is dealing with youth rather than adults and must consider developmental stages of the student that are not always present in adults. The vocational evaluator is also working with far more individuals and agencies, from parents and teachers to adult service agencies and multiple advocacy groups. Also, special education organizational systems are far different than vocational rehabilitation systems in terms of regulations, responsibilities, and entitlements.

The purpose of this chapter is to describe the planning, procedures, and outcomes of vocational evaluation activity within special education.

VOCATIONAL OUTCOMES

The goal of vocational evaluation in special education is to provide information that contributes to an educational process that maximizes the vocational potential of the student. Vocational evaluation activity is organized to provide information about (1) student outcomes, (2) vocational program outcomes, and (3) transition planning outcomes.

Vocational evaluation does not function solely to identify the optimal vocational program activity for the student. The evaluation process is also capable of promoting career awareness, self understanding, and personal and vocational growth; contributing to programmatic and training development; and promoting linkages with adult service agencies and industry. Typical outcomes resulting from systematic vocational evaluation activity include the following:

STUDENT OUTCOMES

- Orientation to the world of work
- Development of worker role identification
- Identification of strengths, skills, abilities in areas of:
    functional academic abilities
    work adjustment behavior
    work attitudes
    interpersonal and social skills
    specific job-related skills
    job-seeking skills (interview techniques, application completion)
    community resources utilization
- Exposure to a range of vocational alternatives and opportunities available in the world of work
- Recommendations for short-term training objectives and long-term transition goals
- Awareness of how interests, skills, abilities, and limitations match job demands and work environments
- Determination of employability and job readiness status
- Increased motivation to be involved in training and transition programs

VOCATIONAL TRAINING OUTCOMES

- Information and recommendations for development of vocational and transition IEP objectives
- Recommendations to meet IEP objectives through specific program content and curriculum activities
- Recommendations to incorporate learning style and instructional techniques into vocational training or curriculum activity
- Recommendations for placement option that consider vocational development, e.g., job shadow activity, supported work, school work site, work study, community placement
- Identification and recommendations for use of accommodations and work aids that result in productive functioning in the least restrictive environment

- Recommendations for vocational program development that utilize information from job analysis of community or industry setting; training objectives will match task analysis and worker trait characteristics
- Evaluation of process and outcomes of special education efforts

TRANSITION ACTIVITY OUTCOMES

- Identification of the services that students will need as they transition from school to work
- Involvement of industry and community agencies in vocational and transition planning early in the students' training, at least during middle school
- Involvement of adult service agencies (Division of Vocational Rehabilitation, Commission for the Blind, Department of Mental Health) to identify and provide services as the students transition from school to work

Because of the range of tests, tasks, procedures, and resources available to the evaluator, multiple outcomes are possible. Vocational evaluation is capable of providing outcomes as shown in Figure 4-1 and as described here.

Figure 4-1. Vocational assessment capability.

ORIENT THE STUDENT TO THE WORLD OF WORK

Through exposure to vocational alternatives, opportunities, and work demands, the individual begins to develop a realistic understanding of his or her "role as a worker." This is an important outcome in vocational evaluation, as in the past, many students would leave school with little understanding that they could participate in the work world and with a poorly developed worker identity.

Vocational evaluation should serve to organize and present a wide range of information about occupational clusters, work settings, job duties and requirements, activities, salary levels, and employment outlook of the local job market. The process should also provide the individual with a means of understanding the information and making decisions about vocational options.

Many special education students have a limited understanding of the different occupational opportunities available. Vocational choice is often based on what parents feel the student *should* do, or on the vocational areas that have been successful for special education students in the past. Because of specific handicaps, a student may have difficulty organizing and utilizing information in a meaningful way. The student may subsequently choose a vocational area based on his or her most recent experience or upon the most available opportunity.

IDENTIFY THE SPECIFIC SKILLS, STRENGTHS,
AND LIMITATIONS OF THE STUDENT

Whereas many diagnostic procedures concentrate on the individual alone, vocational evaluation stresses the importance of understanding the student in relation to the vocational and community situations in which the student is or will be functioning. In this respect, vocational evaluation is industry- and community-referenced and identifies the present and needed level of functional academics, interpersonal and social skills, mobility, independent living skills, specific job skills, as well as job-seeking skills.

Successful work performance results from the interaction between the individual and his or her environment. Vocational evaluation seeks to identify how this interaction helps or hinders acquisition and utilization of vocational skill.

Initial emphasis in evaluation is on identifying the strengths or skills (rather than deficits) that the individual may display across several environments. The evaluator then seeks to understand the supports and reinforcers that may be present in the environment that promote productive activity. Supports may take many forms, including people, type of production demand, type of reward, and/or other characteristics of the environment that may be present or needed.

Elaboration of relevant skills provides a framework for ongoing interest exploration and continuing evaluation direction.

IDENTIFY THE VOCATIONAL PROGRAMMING NEEDS

Based on an understanding of the student's strengths, skills, and interests, vocational evaluation is able to develop short-term training objectives and long-term transition goals. These objectives and goals result in recommendations for program placement as well as new program development.

Program information is *student-centered*. Recommendations state how short-term objectives should be implemented through different training options such as classroom training, job shadowing, supported work, or on-the-job training. Outcome objectives to result from program activities should be clearly defined and related to vocational or community expectations.

Vocational evaluation program information is also *program-centered*. Vocational evaluation uses job analysis to identify requirements and characteristics of a job and work environment. This information is then used to develop industry-referenced vocational training curricula and programs. Ongoing job analysis information keeps programs current with local job expectations.

IDENTIFY SOCIAL AND INTERPERSONAL SKILLS

Job-related social skills are often classified as work adjustment behaviors such as personality, neatness, attention to task, or ability to follow directions. For many special needs students, social and interpersonal skills are often the behaviors that "make or break" a student on the job. For this reason, it is recommended that evaluators look at the student's social skills apart from other adjustment (or prevocational) behavior. For our purposes, vocational evaluation examines how the individual responds and interacts with co-workers, supervisors, and the public. The evaluator looks at the individual's interviewing behavior, whether or how the student is able to assume the "worker role" in dealing with the public, how the student may respond differentially to co-workers and supervisors, and how he or she is able to monitor emotional responses in work situations.

One of the benefits of ongoing evaluation activity is that the evaluator is able to assess how one particular training activity (summer employment) may be effective over time in developing a particular job-related social skill (adapting to worker/customer role demands).

IDENTIFY INDEPENDENT LIVING AND COMMUNITY INTEGRATION SKILLS

If the student is to integrate (not just interact) with the community, he or she must be able to demonstrate a range of community-based competencies. The responsibility of vocational evaluation is to assess all factors that may impact the vocational success of the student.

Although the vocational evaluator may not perform a comprehensive evaluation of all independent living or community living skills, sufficient informaiion about how different functional areas may or may not support work activity must be gathered, with requests for more formal information to be made as necessary.

IDENTIFY LEARNING STYLES AND EFFECTIVE INSTRUCTIONAL TECHNIQUES

A function of vocational evaluation is to evaluate effective instructional approaches and optimal learning styles of the student within different work environments (McCray, 1979). By involving the student in diverse work tasks under different working conditions, the evaluator identifies how auditory, visual, and/or kinesthetic cues complement different instruction techniques. In addition, one student may learn effectively through a step-by-step, structured, and highly organized instructional process. Another may learn best from hands-on tasks with instructional support that allows for more experiential exploration and that is far less structured. Information on how to most effectively teach or train the student is useful to both vocational instructors and employers.

While observing the student's performance on concrete work simulations, the evaluator also may identify or develop compensatory strategies that are effective for the student and that may be useful in training situations as well as actual work situations. (At the same time, the evaluator may identify certain "learning" situations that could result in poor performance or failure in a future job and that should be avoided on a job.)

IDENTIFY COMPENSATION STRATEGY AND REMEDIAL NEEDS

As the individual develops from adolescence to adulthood, he or she may have unique and highly individualized ways to compensate for skill or processing deficits. Evaluation experiences should be organized to allow the individual to experiment with different ways of performing a particular work task. The evaluator may note how the student compensates for a performance deficit in one area (academics) and implement assessment strategies to examine how a similar strategy may be used in another area (vocational). Recommendations for implementing these strategies in training or employment situations can be very specific.

IDENTIFY ACCOMMODATIONS NEEDED TO PERFORM
IN A PARTICULAR WORK ENVIRONMENT

Evaluation is a particularly useful time to determine the accommodations that will allow the individual to perform productively or to adapt and adjust to a particular environment. The effectiveness of transition and supported work activity often depends on the vocational trainer having an understanding of the accommodations that support work production and that the individual requires to work in a competitive work environment.

PLAN FOR COMMUNITY SUPPORT/IDENTIFY AND
INVOLVE ADULT SERVICE AGENCIES

A cornerstone of transition planning is the involvement of adult service providers in both planning and programming. Planning for future community involvement should begin early in the student's educational experience, no later than middle school. Evaluation can facilitate this process by projecting whether the student will be capable of independent competitive employment upon graduation and by identifying the range of transition supports (adult services, transportation, supported employment) that will be necessary as the student moves from school to work.

IDENTIFY JOB PLACEMENT STRATEGIES

Job placement is a critical concern for the evaluator and job placement coordinator. The evaluator will have information about the individual's vocational objective; a detailed description of vocational skills, production levels, and work adjustment behaviors; the type of work environments in which the individual best functions; the student's job-seeking skills; the range of supports that will facilitate optimal performance in a work setting; any compensatory work aids that assist the student, such as jigs, tape recorders, measuring aids; as well as a current knowledge of the work expectations, and duties and requirements of community work environments. This information can be used to develop a coordinated job development and placement plan for the student.

INCREASE MOTIVATION

By identifying specific skills, understanding the range of occupational areas available, exploring how skills may transfer from one work setting to another, and by developing a step-by-step plan to reach specific goals, the confusion surrounding job choice and the uncertainty about the role and value as a worker is replaced by a realistic appraisal of what the student can and cannot do. As the individual directly experiences and receives feedback on his or her vocational strengths, interest in participating in goal-oriented vocational transition activity develops.

These multiple outcomes demonstrate the range of vocational evaluation capabilities that respond to special education needs. Vocational evaluation in special education settings must do more than compare the individual to specific norm groups and determine that the student does or does not have the ability to perform as well as others. The information needs of the student and the special education practitioner are varied. At one time, the evaluator may work with the student to promote vocational exploration. At another time, the evaluator may work with the teacher to develop curriculum that is based on the skill demands of community-based evaluation criteria. Later, the evaluator may work with the job placement specialist to anticipate problems or to develop solutions to a particular placement problem.

The vocational evaluator fails if he or she does not move beyond norm group comparisons to draw upon the full potential of varied vocational evaluation activities and to provide special educators with program information for career education, transition planning, and job placement.

VOCATIONAL EVALUATION PLANNING PROCESS

To realize the multiple outcomes described in the previous sections, vocational evaluation must function as an integrated component of career education, vocational education, and transition planning (Stodden & Ianacone, 1981). Isolated referrals to outside evaluation resources do not result in evaluation results that recognize the school's resources, the range of available occupational programs, or the student's vocational and developmental history. Integrated evaluation recognizes the interaction between the student, available program alternatives, and the capability of special education to respond to the student's unique vocational characteristics.

Should the evaluation activity be the ongoing responsibility of the school system? Without question.

Vocational evaluation planning also recognizes that career education is a developmental process that occurs from kindergarten to grade 12 and is available to the student post-graduation. Vocational evaluation complements the developmental education process with age-appropriate and curriculum-appropriate evaluation information and activities.

As a developmental process, vocational evaluation will provide information relevant to the student's career/vocational developmental stage and to the program's developmental activity. Vocational evaluation planning is highly interactive with special education curriculum, vocational program activity, teachers and guidance personnel, and innovative technological development.

The following sections discuss in detail how vocational evaluation is implemented within the special education system to realize student and system outcomes outlined in the previous section. The vocational evaluation planning model is depicted in Table 4-1.

ELEMENTARY SCHOOL LEVEL

At the elementary school level, the career education and vocational development stage focuses on career awareness (Brolin & Kokaska, 1979). The career awareness stage teaches the student about the different responsibilities he or she will have in community, vocational, and learning environments. Teaching objectives include money management, homemaking skills, using local community resources, and developing problem-solving strategies. Vocationally, students learn about the range of occupations in the world of work and develop self-awareness and understanding of their potential role as productive workers. Specific skill development centers on work habits, adjustment behaviors, attitudes, and interpersonal skills.

VOCATIONAL EVALUATION FOCUS

The focus of vocational evaluators at this stage is on developing the student's work personality (Brolin, 1985; Gellman, 1968) and orienting the student to the work world.

VOCATIONAL EVALUATION ACTIVITY

At this stage in vocational evaluation, Curriculum-Based Vocational Assessment (CBVA) is implemented (Peterson, 1985; Sitlington, Brolin, Clark, & Vacanti, 1986). Peterson (1985) defined CBVA as an

"informal, less intensive process of vocational assessment in which development of student prevocational skills, career awareness and

TABLE 4–1.
Vocational Evaluation Integrated Process Model.

School Level	Elementary School	Middle School	High School	Post Graduation
	Occupational Orientation		Transition Planning	
Career/ Vocational Development Stage (Brolin & Kokaska)	Career Awareness	Career Exploration	Career Preparation	Career Placement
Vocational Evaluation Focus	Work Personality (Brolin, 1985; Gellman, 1968)	Occupational Match	Skill Development	Employment
Vocational Evaluation Activity	Curriculum Based Vocational Assessment (CBVA)	CBVA: Vocational Evaluation Level 1	CBVA: Vocational Evaluation Level 2	Vocational Evaluation Level 2
Student Outcomes	Functional academics, independent living, self awareness, work habits, worker role identification, work adjustment, work attitudes, motivation.	Learning style, occupational information, interest and skill awareness, skills assessment, match of student/ work characteristics.	Identify skill development, accommodations and aids, adult services involvement, job field match, job seeking skills.	Work adjustment, productivity, accommodations, adult service needs.
System Outcomes	IEP development, training goals, curriculum development.	Vocational program development, alternative training sites, community involvement, family involvement.	Supported work options (Enclave, industry based) vocational program development, industry/ community linkage.	Cooperative agreement with adult service agencies.

vocational skills are monitored from elementary school through adulthood. Curriculum-based vocational assessment uses existing data and records, informal techniques of vocational assessment such as teacher and counselor observations, parent and student interviews and basic vocational testing that may include vocational interest, aptitude and awareness testing" (p. 11).

CBVA is carried out by teachers and/or guidance personnel and relies on medical, psychological, social service, and instructional information.

STUDENT OUTCOMES

Vocational evaluation at this stage focuses on developing the individual's work personality and on orienting the student to the world of work. Evaluation outcomes promote the development of functional academic skills, independent living skills, as well as work habits, adjustment behaviors, and social skills. The student is exposed to different occupations and develops a worker role identification. In addition, the student becomes aware of what workers do, how productive work results in a service or product, that productive work is reimbursed with money, that different jobs require different training, that one may have different jobs throughout one's career and, most importantly, that he or she will become a part of the work world.

MIDDLE SCHOOL LEVEL

At the middle school level the career education and vocational development stage focuses on career exploration. Within this stage,the student begins more comprehensive self exploration related to how his or her specific skills and attitudes match community, vocational, avocational, leisure, and recreational activities. Transition planning occurs as community and adult services agencies become involved in direct training activities. Educational activities directly involve the student in community-based activities, for example, field trips, job shadowing, shopping simulations, and library, post office, and job site activities.

VOCATIONAL EVALUATION FOCUS

Vocational evaluation is a highly active and interactive activity during this stage. Activity involves exposing the individual to different occupational demands in order to compare the individual's skills, interests, work values, and aptitudes with opportunities and characteristics of different work environments.

VOCATIONAL EVALUATION ACTIVITY

Curriculum-Based Vocational Assessment continues to be a primary evaluation component during the career exploration stage. Teachers and vocational instructors involve the student in vocational training, and job shadowing experiences and observe and discuss interest, skill levels,and work values with the student. In addition, students are involved in *Level 1 Formal Vocational Evaluation* activity involving paper and pencil interest, aptitude and achievement tests, performance tests, and commercial and in-house work samples. At this stage, work sample evaluation does not use norm-based comparisons as much as criterion-referenced interpretations. The evaluator is more interested in observable behavior, skill level, tool usage, and achievement observations than comparisons to industrial norm groups. Behavior and skill level information guide formulation of vocational IEP objectives and subsequent curriculum planning.

STUDENT OUTCOMES

Results of CBVA and formal vocational evaluation are described in terms of identification of vocational interest; skill level identification; recommendations about teaching methodology; work behavior characteristics; observations of work skills, interests, and limitations in relation to varied work environments. Transition planning begins and the student becomes involved with community agencies and adult service agencies.

HIGH SCHOOL LEVEL

At the high school level, the student enters the stage of career preparation in his or her career development. Career preparation in a real sense takes place from elementary school through high school and continues long after graduation (Brolin & Kokaska, 1979). However, the specific focus at this time is on developing proficiencies in community, vocational, leisure, and recreational areas. While recognizing that job choice is still tentative, specific vocational skill development begins.

With severely and multiply disabled students, skill development occurs through community based experiential learning.

VOCATIONAL EVALUATION FOCUS

Throughout this stage, vocational evaluation functions to identify student and program characteristics that promote vocational skill development and productivity.

VOCATIONAL EVALUATION ACTIVITY

CBVA continues as an informal evaluation activity, but *Level 2 Formal Vocational Evaluation* activity is far more extensive. Work sample evaluation is used to evaluate skill behavior to criterion levels as well as to develop program planning objectives. For certain students, work sample norm group comparisons may be utilized, especially when job placement personnel need information on specific levels of performance. Situational assessment, including job simulations, work stations, and on-the-job placement alternatives provide the evaluator with information about social interactions with co-workers and supervisors, physical tolerances to perform for varied periods of time, as well as work adjustment behaviors and technical skill to perform. Situational assessments rely on behavioral observations over time and can provide information about how the individual adapts, adjusts to a job, and learns new tasks.

STUDENT OUTCOMES

During career preparation, vocational evaluation provides information on varied program recommendations based on identified behavior and skill development levels. The evaluator recommends accommodations that may be needed; for example, transportation, mobility aids, structured supervision, job modifications, and work aids, and evaluates their impact on performance. Based on productivity, work behaviors, need for ongoing support, and available community resources, the evaluator will recommend transition objectives to facilitate vocational transition from school to work. Adult service agencies will be directly involved in evaluation to identify service needs upon graduation.

POST-GRADUATION

The next stage in career development involves community placement activity. The focus of career preparation is not only community interaction, but community *integration*. Career placement activity dictates that the student be interactive with all facets of community life, including work, leisure, civic, recreational, and educational areas. Vocational placement involves alternatives ranging from supported work alternatives or on-the-job training to direct community placement. Education efforts are directed at involving family, community agencies, advocacy groups, adult service agencies, and industry in the transition efforts. This stage also recognizes that life-long learning opportunities are essential to severely disabled individuals and that career planning is a necessary and ongoing process. Follow-up, interagency interaction, and post-employment supports and services demonstrate that this stage is not the final stage of learning for the "student/worker."

VOCATIONAL EVALUATION FOCUS

The focus of vocational evaluation activity during career placement is to identify and organize information about work behaviors, productivity levels, needed work environment supports, as well as other information that will support job acquisition and promote sustained employment.

VOCATIONAL EVALUATION ACTIVITY

At this stage, primary vocational evaluation activity is systematic behavioral observation in a job setting, job analysis, and vocational interviewing. The role and function of the evaluator in the work site is very different from that in the school environment, as not as many environmental factors can be modified.

STUDENT OUTCOMES

Evaluation outcomes focus on identifying the behaviors, skills, and work demands and supports that function to maintain or improve productivity on the job. The evaluator will use job analysis information to identify aptitudes, functional academics needed, work environment characteristics, and naturally occurring reinforcers in the work environment. Information about instructional methods to train the student as well as use of work aids will be reviewed with the work supervisors. The vocational evaluator also identifies factors outside of the work environment that support or hinder work performance such as family support, SSI benefits, transportation, and lack of social or recreational activities.

SUMMARY

The previous description of career development stages and vocational evaluation development appears to depict a smooth progression throughout the student's educational life. In practice, this progression is not so smooth or so clearly defined. The stages that students go through in choosing career alternatives and defining a specific vocational objective are often characterized by spurts of progress and periods of confusion and uncertainty. At the same time, although we have depicted vocational planning as a linear process, students continually recycle the evaluation process—identifying new skills, becoming aware of new capabilities, experiencing new opportunities, making decisions about alternatives, and using these decisions to develop new awareness and to fuel further exploration. Figure 4-2 depicts the development and cyclical nature of this process.

Actually, this is a normal process, one that we all are involved in on a day-to-day basis. The difficulties that students with severe handicaps have are in organizing the information, problem solving, and making appropriate decisions. The structure of vocational evaluation assists in this process and supports the student in his or her ongoing exploration and career decision making. At the same time, discussions with program professionals develop new interventions to promote more independent functioning.

Like career education, vocational evaluation is a dynamic process that uses didactic tools such as tests, and dynamic processes such as simulated work and real work, to contribute to a developing vocational potential.

Figure 4-2. Career education developmental model.

CHAPTER EXERCISE

Below is a list of aptitudes and work skills. Along the horizontal axis are typical occupational curriculum areas common to many school programs, with several slots left blank. Fill in the blank slots with curriculum areas that you presently offer, that are occupational areas in which special needs students frequently find jobs, or for which you plan to develop curriculum offerings. Evaluate the level of aptitude or skill needed for successful performance in the curriculum (or job) using the following criteria:

E = Essential
I = Important
Blank = nonrelevant aptitudes

Curricula

Aptitudes	Clerical Occupations	Food Service Occupations	Health Aide	Stock Room	Horticulture	Building Maintenance	Data Entry	Grounds Maintenance			
G (General)											
V (Verbal)											
N (Numerical)											
S (Spatial)											
P (Form Perception)											
Q (Clerical)	E										
K (Motor Coordination)											
F (Finger Dexterity)	E										
M (Manual Dexterity)	I										
E (Eye-hand-foot)											
C (Color Discrimination)											

FA (Functional Academic)	E											
MA (Measuring Ability)	I											
SD (Size Discrimination)												
HT (Hand Tools)												
VI (Verbal Instruction)	I											
MI (Model Instruction)	I											
OA (Organizational Ability)	I											
RA (Routine Task)	E											
AT (Attention on Task)	E											
QS (Quality Standards)	E											
MT (Power Tools, Machines)	I											
PM (Physical Ability)												
QC (Check Work)	I											
Others Important To Your Curriculum												

CHAPTER 5

Occupational Information Resources in the World of Work

The purpose of this chapter is to introduce the occupational information resources available to the special educator and to demonstrate how each resource may be useful in providing information for vocational evaluation and transitional programming.

All too often, teachers and rehabilitation practitioners become confused about how to identify the abilities or characteristics of students that are important for a particular job. Similarly, they are uncertain about how to organize information about the world of work in a manner that is understandable for the student. Vocational evaluators must be familiar with the characteristics of jobs available in the local market, the work performed in these jobs, and the occupational requirements and particular skills needed to perform successfully.

Fortunately, there is a standardized format to describe specific jobs and to organize the information about the world of work that is both comprehensive and comprehensible. The occupational information resources described in this chapter assist the evaluator in providing:

1. A comprehensive and standardized format for describing jobs and organizing the world of work
2. A systematic process of organizing information about an individual's interests, work values, abilities, vocational aptitudes, and physical functioning capacities
3. A framework for organizing evaluation and career preparation that relates directly to vocational characteristics and job requirements in the world of work

UTILIZING OCCUPATIONAL INFORMATION RESOURCES

Occupational information systems and resources are necessary to ensure that a person chooses and prepares for an occupation most fitting his or her personality, interests, and abilities. In addition, both students and evaluators desire a job choice in a field where there are potential job openings and a competitive salary. By providing a source of knowledge outlining job requirements relating to the individual's specific abilities and traits, available occupational information sources assume a significant role. Securing and providing accurate and complete occupational information becomes a prime responsibility of vocational evaluators. The following sections highlight several reasons for the evaluators and students to have access to realistic occupational information about jobs and the world of work.

VOCATIONAL EXPLORATION AND CAREER DECISION MAKING

The importance of making an appropriate vocational choice has been stressed by Hoppock (1976), in pointing out that individual choice often affects how easily a person may be employed, whether the chosen occupation will be enjoyed or detested, whether success or failure will follow, or the degree to which the job will influence other aspects of the individual's life. Accurate information about characteristics of a job or career area form the basis for vocational exploration activity as well as subsequent success the individual has on the job.

The occupational resources that are discussed in this chapter provide a systematic description of jobs, their working environments, and detailed job requirements. The individual is able to compare one job with another and determine whether or how his or her vocational interests, work values, and individual abilities and aptitudes match a particular job or occupational field. Fry (1978) viewed occupational information as an adjunct to vocational evaluation, enabling the individual to "read about, look at and listen to occupational information so that additional learning about the active world of work may take place during the time that the client's abilities, skills, aptitudes and interests are being evaluated" (p. 2).

As additional questions are identified through vocational exploration about what jobs the individual may be interested in, or whether he or she has abilities for a particular job, specific vocational evaluation activity is developed. As additional information about interests and abilities is obtained, occupational resources aid in identifying particular jobs for which the individual may be well suited. To the degree that the evaluator and student are able to access and use occupational systems and resources, they are able to participate in exploration activity in a systematic manner and are able to make appropriate vocational choices. As the student sees that the information being gathered during evaluation relates directly to concrete jobs, he or she participates more actively and responsibly in vocational exploration. The evaluation and exploration process becomes a highly personal experience for the student and the validity of the vocational decision-making process is enhanced.

VOCATIONAL PREPARATION AND CAREER EDUCATION

The importance of occupational information in substantiating a career education curriculum cannot be emphasized enough, especially as teaching about jobs permeates the curriculum of middle and high school occupational skill development courses, as well as academic subject areas. Pucel (1972) expressed this succinctly, stating:

> The role of the school and the educator in the vocational development process. . . is to help individuals better understand themselves, occupations and the relationships between themselves and occupations in light of the many influences on the perceptions of the individual. In order to accomplish this role, opportunities must be incorporated into the curriculum for students to better understand themselves, occupations and the relationships between themselves and occupations. The incorporation should take the form of integrating such opportunities into the existing courses, since the vocational development process leading to an occupational choice is continual and not a point-in-time event. *Teachers can accomplish this integration by continually pointing out the relationships between what is being taught and its use in occupations.* They can also provide opportunities for students to take part in a variety of experiences that relate the subject matter being taught to occupations. Subject matter content need not be changed to assist students more effectively with their vocational development, but *teachers must emphasize the relevance of the content to occupations.* (p. 47)

Although infusing academic courses with related occupational information adds relevance to formal academic classes, available occupational information is critical in the development of all occupational skill preparation programs. To effectively prepare special needs students for the demands and expectations they will face in transitioning from school to work, the vocational program and curriculum must be based on an analysis of jobs and community environments in which the students will be functioning when they leave school. In other words, the curriculum must be community based and criterion referenced. Performance and curriculum objectives must reflect the work activities, work situations, skill requirements, and utilization of material, tasks, equipment, and supplies that are found in local jobs.

VOCATIONAL TRANSITION AND JOB PLACEMENT

An understanding of job and work environments is obviously important at the time of job placement. The evaluator must develop an accurate description of the individual's performance levels that will parallel the performance requirements for a particular job. An understanding of job requirements and work environment characteristics assists the evaluator in assessing whether the individual is employable in the competitive work environment.

For many severely disabled students, determination of employability is not a clear-cut decision. In the past, many teachers felt that the only resource for severely handicapped students was referral to a sheltered workshop. However, with an accurate understanding of work demands and work environments, the evaluator is able to develop vocational transition objectives and identify the accommodations and supports that will allow the individual to function in a competitive environment.

The following resources are available to assist the evaluator and special educator in organizing occupational information.

DICTIONARY OF OCCUPATIONAL TITLES

The *Dictionary of Occupational Titles* (commonly called the DOT) represents the primary resource for providing practitioners with information about jobs. The DOT provides a standardized format for defining the over 12,099 jobs in the national economy (a recent supplement has identified over 300 additional jobs that have been developed since the DOT was written in 1977), as well as a code number to classify each job. The DOT has become the lexicon of communication between the evaluator and the teacher in the classroom, vocational educator, guidance counselor, or rehabilitation counselor to identify and discuss jobs, job requirements, and characteristics of occupational groups.

Every teacher or educator who is remotely involved in developing the vocational potential of special needs students should have access to a copy of the DOT for reference. No matter what subject is being taught, from addition and subtraction to calculus, from biology to personal and medical health care, from English grammar to developing a business letter, the DOT is pertinent to the process of bringing reality to the school subject and adding relevance of the subject being studied to the world of real work.

Initially, the DOT may appear to be an imposing volume with very technical verbiage (and such small print!); however, with only a brief orientation to the DOT format, even the casual user will find that it can provide information for a variety of uses. For the individual who is involved directly with vocational guidance, instruction, or job placement, it is important to have a thorough working knowledge of the DOT's capabilities.

DEVELOPMENT OF THE FOURTH EDITION OF THE DOT

The fourth edition of the DOT appeared in 1977. This edition, based on over 75,000 on-site analyses conducted by public employment service staff from the 11 State Occupational Analysis Field Centers, added over

2,100 new occupational definitions, while deleting some 3,500 obsolete job definitions contained in the previous edition. Thus, there are approximately 20,000 jobs contained in the new edition.

Jobs are grouped into "occupations" based on their similarities, with definitions of the structure and content of all occupations listed. The occupational definition is divided into six components which present data about each job in a systematic manner. These components include:

1. Occupational Code Number
2. Occupational Title
3. Industry Designation
4. Alternate Titles (if any)
5. Body of the Definition
   a. Lead statement
   b. Task element statements
   c. "May" items
6. Undefined Related Titles (if any)

A typical DOT definition is shown in Figure 5-1, with each of the six parts labeled.

PARTS OF A DOT DEFINITION

In Figure 5-1, the parts are labeled for the DOT definition of Cloth Printer (652.382-010). The following is an abbreviated explanation of the DOT Occupational Code Number.

THE OCCUPATIONAL CODE NUMBER

The nine-digit occupational code (652.382-010) is the first item in an occupational definition. Each set of three digits in this code has a specific purpose or meaning. When taken as a whole, this identification code differentiates a particular occupation from all others.

The first three digits identify a particular *Occupation Category* according to one of the clusters of the nine broad *categories* (first digit), such as machine trades occupations (6), in Figure 5-1. These categories are divided into 82 occupationally specific *divisions* (first two digits). These divisions are separated into small, homogeneous *groups* (first three digits combined).

The nine primary occupational categories include:

0/1 Professional, technical, managerial occupations
2   Clerical and sales occupations
3   Service occupations
4   Agricultural, fishery, forestry, and related occupations

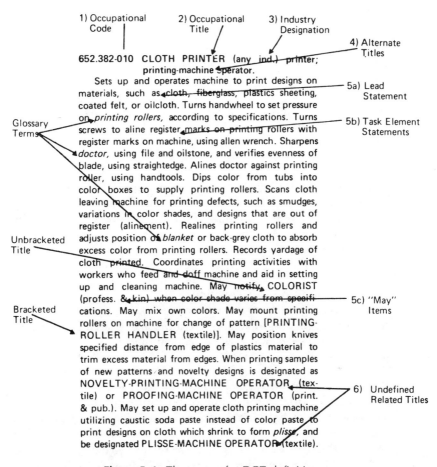

Figure 5-1. The parts of a DOT definition.

5   Processing occupations
6   Machine trades occupations
7   Bench work occupations
8   Structural work occupations
9   Miscellaneous occupations

In the example (Cloth Printer, 652.382–010), the first digit (6) indicates that this particular occupation is found in the Machine Trades Occupations.

The second digit, when combined with the first digit, refers to a division within the category. The divisions composing the Machines Trades Occupations category are:

60	Metal machine occupations
61	Metal working occupations, n.e.c.★
62/63	Mechanics and machinery repairs
64	Paper working occupations
65	*Printing occupations*
66	Wood machining occupations
67	Occupations in machining stone, clay, glass, and related materials
68	Textile occupations
69	Machine trades occupations, n.e.c.

In the example in Figure 5–1, the second digit (5) thus designates the occupation as a part of the printing occupations division.

The third digit, when combined with the first two digits, defines the *occupational group* within the division. The groups within the printing occupations division are:

650	Typesetters and composers
651	Printing press occupations
652	*Printing machines occupations*
653	Bookbinding machine operators and related occupations
654	Typecasters and related occupations
659	Printing occupations, n.e.c.

The third digit in the example given in Figure 5–1 then locates the occupation in the printing machine occupations group.

The middle three digits of the occupational code make up the *worker functions* ratings of the tasks performed in the occupation. Each job requires a worker function to some degree relative to data, people, and things. Each job must have three digits—one from each of the following three columns, in order to express the worker's relationship to each of these functions:

DATA (4th digit)	PEOPLE (5th digit)	THINGS (6th digit)
0 Synthesizing	0 Mentoring	0 Setting-up
1 Coordinating	1 Negotiating	1 Precision Working
2 Analyzing	2 Instructing	2 Operating-Controlling
3 Compiling	3 Supervising	3 Driving-Operating
4 Computing	4 Diverting	4 Manipulating
5 Copying	5 Persuading	5 Tending
6 Comparing	6 Speaking-Signaling	6 Feeding-Offbearing
	7 Serving	7 Handling
	8 Taking Instructions-Helping	

★Occupations not fitting logically into more precisely defined divisions or groups or that could fit into two or more equally well are designated "n.e.c." (not elsewhere classified).

Although a definition of each of these worker functions is given in the DOT, it is included in Appendix A of this text for easier reference.

Worker functions (data, people, things) that involve more complex responsibility and judgment are assigned lower numbers (nearer to zero), whereas functions less complex have higher numbers (nearer the bottom of the column). For example, "synthesizing" (0) and "coordinating" (1) data are more complex tasks than "copying" (5) data; "instructing" (2) people involves a broader responsibility than "taking instructions helping" (8) and "operating controlling" (2) things is a more complicated task than "handling" (7) things.

The Worker Functions code (382) relates to the middle three digits of the DOT occupational code and has a different meaning and no necessary connection with the group code 652 (first three digits).

The Worker Functions code (382) may relate to numerous occupational groups. It signifies that the worker is "compiling" (3) in relation to data; "taking instructions-helping" (8) in relation to people; and "operating-controlling" (2) in relation to things. The Worker Functions code indicates the broadest level of responsibility or judgment required in relation to data, people, or things. It is assumed that, if the job requires it, the worker generally can perform any higher numbered function (less complex, nearer the bottom of the column) listed in each of the three categories.

The last three digits of the occupational code number indicate the alphabetical order of titles within the six-digit code groups.

HOW TO FIND AN OCCUPATIONAL TITLE AND CODE

There are three different arrangements of occupational titles in the DOT: the Occupational Group Arrangement, the Alphabetical Index, and the Industry Designation. All of these can assist in identifying and classifying jobs.

THE OCCUPATIONAL GROUP ARRANGEMENT (PP. 15–946)

It is preferable to utilize this section first in identifying or classifying jobs. However, this can be done only if one has an adequate knowledge of the industry and the job to be able to pinpoint the job by the Occupational Group Arrangement. This section may be used as follows:

1. Obtain all of the relevant facts about the job.

2. Find the one-digit occupational category (p. xxxiv) which seems most likely to contain the job. Each category is explained at the beginning of each of the nine numbered sections of the Occupational Group Arrangements starting on page 16.

3. Find the most appropriate two-digit occupational division of the category.

4. Find the best three-digit group within the division

5. Examine the occupational definitions under the group you have selected. If the definition does not correspond closely to the job information you have collected, it may be necessary to repeat steps. When you are trying to find the most appropriate definition in the occupational group selected (step 5), remember that jobs requiring more responsibility and independent judgment have lower worker functions numerals (nearer zero on data, people, things in the middle three digits) and will be near the beginning of each group. Those requiring less responsibility and less independent judgment have higher numbers (nearer the bottom of each data, people, things column in the middle three digits) and will be found nearer the end of each occupational group.

THE ALPHABETICAL INDEX OF OCCUPATIONAL TITLES (PP. 965–1156)

If you know only the title of a job, you can search through this index for a lead to an appropriate classification. To use the Alphabetical Index:

1. Look through the index for the title of the job as you know it. If you find it, write down the nine digit code found at the right of the title. Using this code as a guide, look up the definition for the title numerically in the Occupational Group Arrangement. Read the entire definition before deciding whether it is the most appropriate classification.

2. If you cannot find the title, or if the definition appears inappropriate, look for another title. Some clues are:

■ Invert the title: maintenance carpenter—CARPENTER, MAINTENANCE
■ Contract the title: rubber belt repairer—BELT REPAIRER
■ Find a synonym: car mechanic—AUTOMOBILE MECHANIC

Consider such factors as:

■ Job location—PARKING LOT ATTENDANT; STOREROOM CLERK
■ Machines used—PUNCH-PRESS OPERATOR; MACHINE FEEDER
■ Materials used—LOG LOADER; PLASTIC-TILE LAYER
■ Subject matter—ACCOUNTING CLERK; CREDIT ANALYST
■ Services involved—CLEANER & PRESSER; BROKER
■ Activity performed—TEACHER; INSPECTOR
■ Job complexity—MACHINE SETTER; WELDING MACHINE TENDER

*OCCUPATION TITLES ARRANGED BY
INDUSTRY DESIGNATION (PP. 1157–1361)*

This index may be useful if you have limited information about a job. You may know the industry in which the job is located, but have little or no information about such things as products made, materials used, services rendered, and other essential data. The Industry Designations can be of assistance if a person wants to work in a particular industry, or if more information is needed about related jobs in the industry. To use this index:

1. Look through the industry titles and read their definitions. Select the one most likely to contain the job for which you are searching.

2. Survey the occupational titles listed under the selected industry and choose the title which seems appropriate to your job. Write down the nine digit code found at the right of the title. Using this code as a guide, find the definition in the Occupational Group Arrangement.

The basic purpose and use of each of the three arrangements of occupational titles is shown below in Table 5–1.

GUIDE FOR OCCUPATIONAL EXPLORATION

The Guide for Occupational Exploration (GOE) was designed and developed by the United States Employment Service under the direction of William B. Lewis, Administrator. The combined efforts of the various USES Occupational Analysis Field Centers, a number of state employment services, other divisions of the USES, and the contracted services of the Appalachia Educational Laboratory made possible the development of the GOE. A recent edition (1984) has been edited by Thomas Harrington and Arthur O'Shea and is distributed by the American Guidance Service.

The GOE groups occupations by interests, abilities, and traits required for successful work performance. Descriptive information is provided for each work group, thus enabling persons to identify and explore work areas in which they are highly interested and whose job requirements are more closely related to their skills and vocational potential. The GOE is a "readable" resource and may be used as an aid for the vocational evaluator or vocational counselor who works directly with individuals in career exploration and planning.

ORGANIZATION AND CONTENT OF THE GOE

INTEREST CLASSIFICATION

Information in the GOE is organized into 12 interest areas, 55 work groups, and 348 subgroups. The *interest areas* equate with the interest factors resulting from the research and development activities in interest

TABLE 5–1.
The Use of Arrangements of Occupational Titles.

Use...	If you...
THE OCCUPATIONAL GROUP ARRANGEMENT	Have sufficient information about the job tasks
(pp. 15–946)	Want to know about other closely related occupations Want to be sure you have chosen the most appropriate classification using the other arrangements
OCCUPATIONAL TITLES ARRANGED BY INDUSTRY DESIGNATION	Know only the industry in which the job is located
(pp. 1157–1361)	Want to know about other jobs in an industry. Have a client who wants to work in a specific industry

measurement conducted by the Division of Testing in the U.S. Employment Service. The interest factors represent not only the broad interest requirements of occupations, but also the vocational interests of individuals. A two-digit code identifies the interest area followed by a short definition, for example:

01—Artistic: Interest in creative expression of feelings or ideas.

WORK GROUP

There are 66 *work groups* within the 12 interest areas. Each work group is a group of jobs containing descripiive information in narrative form and listing of jobs. The jobs within each work group are homogeneous regarding the adaptabilities and capabilities required of the worker and the general type of work performed. A unique four digit code and title is designated for each group. The number of groups in an interest area varies from a range of two groups in interest area 12 (Physical Performing) to a dozen work groups in interest area 5 (Mechanical). An example of a work group in the Artistic interest area is:

01.01—Literary Arts

Jobs are arranged by *subgroups* within each worker trait group to provide even more homogeneous clusters, which facilitate the reader's distinguishing among jobs. Again, each subgroup has its own unique code and title, as exemplified by this subgroup under the literary arts work group:

01.01.02 Creative Writing

The jobs within the 348 subgroups are arranged alphabetically by industrial classification, for example, motion picture, professional & kindred, radio & TV broadcasting, printing & publishing. The industries, likewise, are listed alphabetically within each subgroup.

The following is an illustration of the components of the GOE structure by subgroup with jobs listed alphabetically by industry:

01	ARTISTIC	(Interest Area)
01.01	Literary Arts	(Work Group)
01.01.02	Creative Writing	(Subgroup)

Screen Writer (motion pic., radio & TV broad.) 131.087–018
Crossword-Puzzle Maker (print & pub.) 139.087–010
Editorial Writer (print. & pub.) 131.067–022
Biographer (profess. & kin.) 052.067–010
Copy Writer (profess. & kin.) 131.067–014
Humorist (profess. & kin.) 131.067–026
Librettist (profess. & kin.) 131.087–030
Lyricist (profess. & kin.) 131.067–034
Playwright (profess. & kin.) 131.067–038
Poet (profess. & kin.) 131.067–042
Writer, Prose, Fiction and Nonfiction (profess. & kin.) 131.067–046
Continuity Writer (radio & TV broad.) 131.087–010

Immediately following the description of each work group, and preceding the listing of subgroups within the work group, is a set of questions and occupational information regarding the jobs listed in the subgroups. These questions in the GOE format are worded as follows:

   1. Work performed: *What kind of work would you do?* Gives examples of types of work activities included in the work group.

   2. Worker requirements: *What skills and abilities do you need for this kind of work?* Indicates the worker requirements, or characteristics required of the worker to successfully perform jobs in this work group.

   3. Clues for relating worker to requirements: *How do you know if you would like to do or could learn to do this kind of work?* Indicates types of work experience, extracurricular activities, hobbies, and other types of experiences and activities, as well as types of skills, potentials, and interests relevant to occupations in this work group.

4. Training and methods of entry: *How can you prepare for and enter this kind of work?* Indicates the kind of training, work, and other experiences desired by employers and explains the means of entry into the field.

5. Other considerations: *What else should you consider about these jobs?* Indicates the employment opportunities, promotional possibilities, competition for jobs, any unusual or dangerous situations in the job, or other information that may be important in weighing advantages or disadvantages of the job. Special considerations are discussed, such as the need for licenses or certification and addresses of organizations and agencies that may be able to provide additional information.

The 1984 edition of the GOE also provides information on physical strength factors that are important for specific jobs and describes the level of competency needed in mathematics and language, as well as the vocational preparation time needed on the job.

ROLE OF THE GOE IN COUNSELING AND VOCATIONAL EVALUATION

The GOE provides clusters of occupations and fields of work within each major interest area—broad fields (four-digit work groups) and narrower fields (six-digit subgroups)—which evaluators and students can explore and to which they can relate occupationally significant information that has been developed about the student.

The 1984 edition of the GOE provides a step-by-step description of how to use the guide that is a useful format to follow when initiating vocational evaluation. The student first explores vocational interest, work values, leisure activities of interest, home activities of interest, school subjects, and any work experience. These interests are then matched against the work groups and interest areas on an Occupational Exploration Worksheet provided in the GOE. The student is assisted in identifying work groups that are considered most suitable to interest and ability and an initial action plan is developed to gather more information about the field.

OCCUPATIONAL OUTLOOK HANDBOOK

The Occupational Outlook Handbook (OOH) is a publication of the U.S. Department of Labor (1984–1985) that presents a wealth of information that is useful to the individual involved in vocational exploration, training, or placement. Unlike the DOT, the text is very readable and the format encourages the individual to explore jobs and occupational areas more deeply.

The OOH divides the world of work into 19 occupational groupings. Under each occupational grouping, representative jobs are identified and discussed in depth under the following topical areas:

NATURE OF THE WORK. The OOH discusses what workers typically perform on the job, what tools or equipment are used, the type of supervision that is typical and how the position relates to others in the workplace.

WORKING CONDITIONS. Discussion involves working conditions that some individuals may find satisfying while others find quite disagreeable. Information is given about overtime potential, evening or night shift requirements, characteristics of the worksite that might involve noise, heat, cold, danger, or change in the routine of performed tasks. In a general way, information is provided about the physical demands and activities required, such as standing, lifting, or climbing.

TRAINING REQUIREMENTS. The section provides information on training that is necessary for positions within the occupational field. It notes whether high school or vocational technical courses are necessary or whether college and graduate school is recommended. Some jobs can be obtained through on-the-job training or apprenticeship training.

For each occupation the OOH identifies the preferred training as well as alternative training available. It will note also if a particular job is not open to entry-level job applicants and will cite the prerequisite experience and training needed for the position.

As available, the OOH will identify opportunities for career advancement and discuss the steps individuals would take to advance in the field.

JOB OUTLOOK. The information is particularly important to individuals involved in vocational exploration: whether there is an employment market for the job in which they may be interested. The OOH identifies the expected growth for a particular job through the 1990's. For example, autobody repairers (DOT 807.381–010) are expected to increase about as fast as the average for all occupations with an expected growth of 20 to 29 percent in employment.

EARNINGS. Although no single statistic can adequately identify a specific salary for a particular job, the OOH will give entry level salaries, average salaries, and top salaries. Also, salaries will be projected for individuals with different experience, credentials, and education. If benefits are included, such as tips for food service workers, they will be noted.

RELATED OCCUPATIONS. If a particular occupation appeals to the individual, the OOH will also identify related jobs for future consideration. Usually these jobs are those that require similar aptitudes, interest, education, and training.

ADDITIONAL INFORMATION SOURCES. The OOH will also identify unions, associations, agencies, or other organizations that may provide information on careers. Names and addresses of resources are provided to aid in research and exploration.

The U.S. Department of Labor also publishes the *Occupational Outlook Quarterly*. This is issued four times a year and provides up-to-date information on emerging occupations, labor force trends, unusual jobs, and new technology. The magazine format is interesting to read, similar to the OOH, and useful to the evaluator and educator who is working with individuals involved in vocational exploration.

HANDBOOK FOR ANALYZING JOBS

The Handbook for Analyzing Jobs was published by the Department of Labor in 1972, but continues to be the standard used to systematically evaluate the characteristics of a specific job. The process of job analysis forms the foundation for all job information found in the DOT and other occupational resources, as well as the criteria for the development of many psychometric and criterion-referenced tests used in vocational evaluation.

The Handbook describes job analysis as a process of identifying and describing in a systematic and detailed manner:

■ What the worker does in terms of activities or functions.
■ How the work is done—the methods, techniques or processes involved and the work devices used.
■ Results of the work—the work produced, services rendered or materials used.
■ Worker characteristics—the skills, knowledge, abilities and adaptabilities needed to accomplish the tasks involved (worker trait characteristics).
■ Context of the work in terms of environmental and organizational factors and the nature of the worker's responsibility and accountability.

Worker trait characteristics are defined as the requirements made on the worker in terms of worker functions (complexity of the work in relation to data, people, and things), physical demands, environmental conditions, general educational development, specific vocational preparation, work aptitudes, work activities, and work situation.

The Worker Trait Factors are defined as follows:

WORKER FUNCTIONS

Worker functions are the ways in which a job requires the persons to function in relation to Data, People, and Things. A more detailed description of worker function has been described in an earlier section (DOT) and is detailed in Appendix A.

PHYSICAL DEMANDS

Physical demands identify the physical requirements of the job and the physical capacities the person must have to meet those requirements. These factors include:

strength (Sedentary, light, medium, heavy, very heavy)
lifting, carrying, pushing, pulling
standing, walking, sitting
climbing and/or balancing
stooping, kneeling, crouching, and/or crawling
reaching, handling, fingering, and/or feeling
talking and/or hearing
seeing

A detailed description of Physical Demand Characteristics is found in Appendix B.

ENVIRONMENTAL CONDITIONS

Environmental conditions represent the physical surroundings of the worker in a specific job, including:

Work Location, inside, outside, or both
Extremes of cold and temperature changes
Extremes of heat and temperature changes
Wetness and/or humidity
Noise and/or vibration
Hazards
Fumes, odors, toxic conditions, and dust

Appendix C defines each working condition.

GENERAL EDUCATION DEVELOPMENT

General educational development (GED) contributes to the acquisition of job skills and knowledge, including:

Reasoning development
Mathematical development
Language development

Appendix D describes the GED levels in detail.

SPECIFIC VOCATIONAL PREPARATION

Specific vocational preparation (SVP) is the amount of time needed to learn the work techniques, acquire job information, and develop the abilities needed for average performance on the job. Appendix E defines SVP levels.

SPECIFIC WORK APTITUDES

Eleven aptitudes have been identified as being relevant for average successful performance on jobs and have been identified and listed as follows:

(G) General learning ability
(V) Verbal
(N) Numerical

(S) Spatial
(P) Form perception
(Q) Clerical perception

(K) Motor coordination
(F) Finger dexterity

(M) Manual dexterity
(E) Eye-hand-foot coordination
(C) Color discrimination

The aptitudes are defined in Appendix F.

WORK INTERESTS

Work interests are a liking or a preference for a vocational activity. The Handbook lists interests in a format of opposites (bi-polar). Appendix G lists and defines these bi-polar interests. Twelve areas, defined and discussed earlier (GOE), have been identified which represent the potential interests of individuals and include:

01 Artistic
02 Business Detail
03 Scientific
04 Selling
05 Plants and Animals
06 Accommodating
07 Protective
08 Humanitarian
09 Mechanical
10 Leading-Influencing
11 Industrial
12 Physical Performing

JOB WORKER SITUATIONS (TEMPERAMENTS)

Work situations are the adaptabilty requirements made on an individual by specific types of jobs. These factors are defined in Appendix H and include:

D—Directing activities
R—Performing repetitive tasks
I—Influencing people
V—Performing a variety of tasks
F—Expressing personal feelings
S—Working under stress
T—Attaining tolerances
P—Dealing with people
J—Making judgements and decisions

THE DICTIONARY OF WORKER TRAITS

The *Dictionary of Worker Traits* (DWT) by Kerns and Neeley (1987) represents the only resource that provides complete worker trait data for all occupations in the Fourth Edition of the *Dictionary of Occupational Titles* (DOT) and the 1982 supplement.

Volume I contains 109 Worker Trait Groups (WTGs) composed of 12,379 DOT codes and job titles that are grouped by similar worker functions (Data, People, Things) and worker traits. Each job listed is rated on 19 different worker traits and cross referenced with other sources such as:

- The Guide for Occupational Exploration (GOE)
- Selected Characteristics of Occupations Defined in the DOT (SCOD)
- Standard Occupational Classification Manual (SOC)
- Classification of Instructional Programs (CIP)

The Qualification Profile lists the number and percentage of jobs at each level of functioning on the 19 worker traits. In addition, the number and percentage of jobs by each worker function (Data, People, Things) are listed, as are the GOE codes.

All too often, special needs students find themselves restricted to a food service-custodial-benchwork job syndrome. Through this resource, the evaluator, rehabilitation counselors and teacher are able to cross-reference the student's worker trait characteristics with a wider range of job listings that the student may be able to perform. The Appendicies demonstrate how Worker Function and Worker Trait characteristics, such as General Educational Development, Specific Vocational Preparation, Aptitudes, Interests, Temperaments, Physical Demands, and Environmental Conditions, can be cross-walked to different Worker Trait Groups.

Volume II of the DWT contains the DOT Job Indices and Data. The Alphabetical Index of Occupational Titles lists 12,379 job titles along with the DOT code, Worker Trait Group Code, Industry Designation Code, Materials, Products, Subject Matter, Services and Work Field Codes. The numeric index lists the same information, numerically, for each of the 12,379 jobs.

The Appendices of Cross Referenced Resource Data provide codes, levels, definitions and illustrations on many resources to support information in the Qualifications Profiles on each of the 109 Worker Trait Group Sections.

ADDITIONAL OCCUPATION INFORMATION RESOURCES

There are two additional resources that may provide the evaluator and special education practitioner with information useful to career exploration, program development, and job placement:

- *Selected Characteristics of Occupations Defined in the Dictionary of Occupational titles*. (1982). U.S. Department of Labor
- *the Classification of Jobs According to Worker Trait Factors*. (1984). VALPAR, Tucson, AZ

Although these resources may be considered secondary resources after those discussed previously, they each provide information in a form that is unique. For this reason, the evaluator should be familiar with each and understand when one may be useful in vocational planning.

The Selected Characteristics of Occupations Defined in the Dictionary of Occupation Titles (SCOD) actually is a supplement of the DOT and provides more detailed information on worker trait characteristics of jobs found in the DOT. In Part A of the SCOD, occupations are grouped according to the 66 Work Groups of the GOE. Of particular use to the evaluator is that occupational groupings are made according to similarity of physical demand requirements of jobs. All sedentary jobs are listed together, all light jobs are together, etc. Data is included on environmental conditions, GED (math and language) levels and specific vocational preparation (SVP).

The Classification of Jobs According to Worker Trait Factors (COJ) provides comprehensive worker trait data on occupations in the DOT. The COJ is divided by sections as follows:

- Section 1—Job Profiles: A complete worker trait factor profile on each job in the DOT. In addition, the GOE Code is provided for each occupation.
- Section 2—Jobs by GOE Code: A listing of occupations by GOE code with DOT code, DPT, occupational title, and physical exertion level. Only sedentary and light occupations are listed.
- Section 3—Jobs by Data/People/Things Number: A listing of sedentary and light jobs as clustered by DPT codes and cross referenced to DOT, GOE, occupational title, and exertion level. This provides the user with a reference to jobs of increasing complexity within a DPT framework.

CHAPTER EXERCISE

OCCUPATIONAL INFORMATION

Purpose: This exercise is designed to familiarize you with the basic occupational information available in the *Dictionary of Occupational Titles*, (D.O.T.), *Selected Characteristics of Occupations Defined in the Dictionary of Occupational titles, Occupational Outlook Handbook*, and the *Guide for Occupational Exploration*. The information available in these resources is critical to vocational evaluation planning data. The information presented in these resources makes the complex process of developing a realistic vocational objective, a more concrete, structured, and attainable activity for special needs students.

For the occupational title provided, identify the following information from the resource cited above:

1. Occupational Title

Laboratory Technician

2. Occupational Code Number (9 digit)

3a. Occupational Category

  b. Occupational Division

  c. Occupational Group

  d. Worker Function Rating Data (defined)

     People (defined)_____

     Things (defined)_____

4. Work Group Title and Code Number (6 digit number; GOE Code #)

5. Physical Demands (define)_____

6. Environment Conditions_____

7. General Education Development (define)_____

8. Vocational Preparation Needed_____

9. Related Jobs (Title and Dot #)
    a. _____
    b. _____
    c. _____
10. Employment Outlook_____

CHAPTER 6

Test Selection Issues in Special Education

Vocational evaluators are presented with a number of assessment questions from teachers, administrators, and parents.

- What abilities does the student have?
- How does the student's handicap limit employment opportunities?
- What are the student's vocational interests?
- What type of work will the student be capable of performing?
- Is the student employable?
- Will the student transfer skills from the classroom to the work environment?
- Does the student have appropriate personal and social behaviors?
- Can the student benefit from supported work?
- What training does the student need to reach vocational goals?
- What kind of accommodations will the student need in a work environment?

How the evaluation determines which test, tool, or activity to use to obtain the necessary information to respond to different questions depends on several factors. The evaluator must consider the abilities and limitations of the student, the information needs of the teacher, and the kinds of decisions that are being made by the education system.

At the same time, in considering test selection for individuals with disabilities, the evaluator often is faced with tests or evaluation tools that have inadequate norms, inappropriate test content, unknown predictive capability, and testing procedures that are not adapted to the individuals' abilities and disabilities. This is particularly true when evaluating students with severe disabilities. A testing activity measuring mechanical aptitude may have a time limit as well as writing requirements that are inappropriate for the student with a prosthetic arm and hand. For many students, modification in test administration is required because of the students' disabilities. However, procedural modifications often cloud interpretation of test performance and raise additional questions about confidence in interpreting test results.

The question becomes how to select an evaluation instrument and use it with confidence to acquire accurate information, to answer specific questions raised by teachers, parents, and students, and to generate realistic recommendations for the student. The following sections review issues in selecting tests for students with severe special needs.

CRITERION ISSUES

NORM-REFERENCED TESTS

The majority of tests used in education and vocational evaluation are classified as norm-referenced tests. These tests compare the performance of the individual being tested to the performance of a group of similar individuals on the same test (Bolton, 1976). In essence, the individual's performance is evaluated based on the performance characteristics of a standardized sample of a particular population.

A basic assumption in norm-referenced testing is that the individual or group being tested is similar to the sample or population on which the test was normed. The adequacy of the norm group for special needs students, and more severely disabled students in particular, becomes a question of particular concern to the evaluator. How do we begin to evaluate the adequacy of the norm group? The test manual will provide information about standardization procedures, including:

- the number of individuals in the group sample;
- the representatives of the sample population to the individual being tested;
- the relevance of the norm group to the questions being asked.

Among information about the norm group, the evaluator should look for the date of the sampling, the age range of the population (school age and/or adult norms), education and/or grade level, sex, geographic distribution, racial characteristics, employment or occupational levels, and handicapping conditions.

The relevancy of the norm group relates to the questions being asked about the individual being evaluated and the type of decisions to be made. Often, questions about diagnosis or level of perceptual or language ability dictate that the norm sample have a national representation. In other instances, a more circumscribed population may be desired. For example, questions about job placement or employment readiness may rely on achievement tests or simulated work samples that have been normal on trade groups, applicants for skilled trade positions, and employees in selected skilled trade occupations. At the time of placement, the evaluator is more interested in comparing the student to a specific population than to a broader group.

Critics of tests used with disabled students often point out that few tests are normed on samples having disabled-student-population characteristics and that such tests have limited usefulness in special education. However, in vocational evaluation, a more realistic understanding of the individual's performance or vocational potential is gained if the person is compared with industrial or business norms or general population norms rather than sheltered employment or handicapped norms (Botterbusch & Michael, 1985). When making decisions about employability or placement readiness, it is important to compare the individual's performance level against the performance expectations present in the competitive environment.

In determining the usefulness of a norm group, the evaluator should look for tests that use norm groups that are current, well-described, sufficient in size, and that relate to the questions being asked by the student and special education system.

CRITERION-REFERENCED TESTS

Norm-referenced tests are based on statistical procedures that allow the evaluator to compare the student's performance with that of individuals in a related sample. The purpose of evaluation with norm-based comparison tests is to rank order individuals and to determine the relative standing of the individual among the sample group. To the extent that the test discriminates performance, the evaluator is able to make an interpretation about the person's ability level or performance.

In contrast, criterion-referenced tests provide information about the individual's ability to perform specific behaviors, skills, or activities or to demonstrate mastery over a particular skill domain. The testing procedure "compare(s) the performance of the individual being tested against the content of the material to be acquired or learned" (Mauser, 1981). Rather than asking how Rebecca will perform compared to classmates (norm-referenced), the criterion-referenced test asks "Does Rebecca assemble the widget correctly?" or "How many safety rules is she able to identify?" or "Can Rebecca make change from $20?"

In criterion-referenced tests, interpretations are tied to performance criteria rather than to performance characteristics of a relative norm group. Norm-referenced tests tend to mask individual skill strengths and deficits within global test-derived scores. Criterion-referenced tests allow interpretation about the individual's present and needed levels of behavior. Norm-referenced tests result in statistically derived scores that are not always easily understood by students or their families. In contrast, descriptions of skill mastery levels are more readily understandable and provide a rationale for the development of program activity.

Because criterion-referenced tests provide information about behavior or skill level and content mastery, results are useful in developing learning objectives, individualized education program (IEP) goals, and curriculum or program development activity.

VALIDITY

The primary criteria for determining the usefulness of a test is its validity. The norming sample may be adequate and the test may demonstrate reliability over time, but unless it demonstrates acceptable validity, it is of little use to the evaluator. The validity of a test is defined in terms of the extent to which a test measures what it was designed to measure (Bolton, 1976). However, it is important to understand that the validity of a test should not be measured in a vacuum. Test validation is specific to the population sample as well as to the purpose(s) of the instrument (Power, 1984). A test may be useful (valid) in answering certain questions about one specific population but not others. Power (1984) highlighted the importance of this last point in noting that validation of tests on disabled individuals is a rare occurrence. The validity of a test is not absolute and must be evaluated for different individuals and for different assessment questions.

In the context of vocational and transition planning in special education, test validation refers to how the test activity measures the knowledge, skills, abilities, and worker trait characteristics needed for successful job performance and community integration.

TEST VALIDATION DESCRIPTION

There are four methods of describing test validity: content validity, construct validity, predictive validity, and face validity.

CONTENT VALIDITY

Content validity is determined by evaluating the representativeness of the test items to the content area or domain under question. Content validity asks the question, "How well does the content of the test sample the subject matter being evaluated?" Achievement tests measuring math ability should have test items (addition, multiplication) that reflect the scope and range of the math material (content domain). Similarly, a work sample has adequate content validity if it is representative of the job knowledge, skills, or abilities needed for successful job performance. To the degree that the work sample simulates the types of tasks, the range of tasks and the typical tasks of a worker, it is said to have adequate content validity.

CONSTRUCT VALIDITY

When evaluating a hypothetical construct or theoretical concept, a test is assessing a characteristic that is not always directly measurable or clearly evident. Construct validity measures the extent to which test results relate to the theoretical concept that the test is attempting to measure. Abstract concepts such as intelligence, anxiety, mechanical aptitude, or creativity are actually constructs developed to identify particular aspects or traits of the person. Determining whether a person has "good" learning ability, creativity, artistic ability, or spatial ability is not as easily quantifiable as is whether the person is able to add, subtract, or multiply, or to identify three continents in the Northern Hemisphere. Construct validity in vocational evaluation determines whether the test measures a trait and whether the trait relates to job performance.

As constructs are not easily observable, it is desirable to obtain validation data from as many different sources as possible to substantiate the presence, lack, or degree of skill or ability.

Construct validity is developed through several means. A test may be compared with an instrument that is accepted as a valid measure of the construct. In addition, experts in the field may assess items in the test item/activity pool. Also, the test may be used with individuals who test well or poorly in the area to determine whether accurate discrimination occurs. Vocational tests will use job analysis procedures to determine the job functions or tasks that relate to the construct and that are necessary for successful performance in a job. In this way, mechanical comprehension may be evaluated through demonstration of competency with pulleys, leverage, weights, motors, and gears.

PREDICTIVE VALIDITY

Predictive validity demonstrates the relationship between performance on a test (the predictor) and performance on a criterion measure in the future. Predictive validity is determined by administering the test and examining performance on a criterion in the future. Because of its practical utility, it is a desirable validity measure for special education, when questions are asked about the student's ability to perform adequately in a training site or on a job.

FACE VALIDITY

Face validity is the subjective appraisal about whether a test actually will measure what it is supposed to measure. As a subjective judgment, face validity adds very little statistical evidence to the understanding of the validity of an evaluation instrument. An instrument may have very high face validity (it looks like it measures clerical skills), but in fact, may have little ability to measure the individual's skills or to predict success in the area.

Face validity has value to the vocational evaluator to the extent that the person being evaluated accepts the process as realistic and important. Based on this belief, he or she may invest more energy and motivation in test performance.

VALIDATION CONSIDERATIONS IN WORK SAMPLE DEVELOPMENT

Validity entails studying the relations of the measuring device (the work sample or the predictor) to things other than itself (the criteria) and is concerned with the soundness and accuracy of the detailed interpretations of the test score (Bolton, 1976) or of the work sample ratings. The primary tools available to the vocational evaluator for establishing the validity of the various commercial and self-developed work samples are the *Handbook for Analyzing Jobs*, the *Dictionary of Occupational Titles* (DOT) and the *Dictionary of Worker Traits*.

A thorough job analysis should be accomplished on the job that the work sample is to simulate. The *Handbook for Analyzing Jobs* will delineate information on worker functions; machines, tools, equipment, and work aids (MTEWA); materials, products, subject matter, or services (MPSMS); and the worker traits involved in the job.

When information is identified, the evaluator may compare information with the job description in the DOT and with the appendices on worker traits listed in the *Dictionary of Worker Traits* or in the appendices in the back of this text.

With the work sample as the assessment tool and functioning as the predictor, the results and time and quality ratings of the individual evaluee's performance ratings will be correlated with the criterion based on the job analysis and delineated in a qualifications profile.

DEVELOPMENT OF WORK SAMPLE VALIDATION

There are three specific types of validity that the evaluator can utilize in developing a work sample.

CONTENT VALIDITY

Content validity entails a systematic examination of the work sample content, situations, and performances to determine whether they cover a representative sample of the job that they purport to simulate. If, as Anastasi (1976) noted, "content validity is built into a test from the outset through the choice of appropriate item" (p. 135), then it behooves the evaluator to make sure that the performance, equipment, and material components of the work sample are representative of the ultimate job criterion.

Some subjectivity is allowed in determining content analysis. Landy and Trumbo (1976) stated that "content validity is a qualitative evaluation based upon logical analysis and expert judgment, rather than on a statistical analysis" (p. 63). Goldman (1971), concurred when he said that a test has content validity when it "has been judged by competent persons to measure certain skills, knowledges and understandings, usually those specifically labeled achievement and proficiency" (p. 82). The problem for the vocational evaluator would be to select the most dependable judges and competent experts to be involved in identifying the validity of the predictor. These certainly would include vocational instructors, job development specialists and, of course, workers and supervisors. Correlating the predictor (work sample) components with the ultimate criteria of the job tasks can be accomplished by comparing the tasks of the job as detailed in the DOT with the tasks in the work sample. An example of this procedure on a carburetor mechanic (620.281–034) work sample is shown in Table 6–1.

Since the carburetor mechanic work sample consists only of the carburetor, apart from the engine and the automobile, the work sample cannot provide for the tasks that involve starting the engine and adjusting the carburetor. Nor does it provide for the two "may" items—the last two tasks listed. Thus, out of the six basic tasks described in the DOT, our work sample has five of them, which is an overlap of 83 percent. This would be acceptable-to-good content validity, even if the task of starting the engine and regulating the carburetor were weighted slightly heavier than the others. The evaluator could look forward to the time that a total automobile engine could be placed in the vocational evaluation center. Of course, to simulate the total job situation the engine would need to be in an automobile. Then, we would have a job sample, rather than a work sample.

CONSTRUCT VALIDITY

Construct validity is determined to the extent that the test or work sample measures a theoretical construct or trait. When there are many constructs to be measured, a requirement of construct validation is that

TABLE 6-1.
Content Validation for Carburetor Mechanic (620.281-034)

DOT Task Listing	Work Sample Tasks
Disassembles carburetor and gasoline filter units, using handtools	Disassembles carburetors and gasoline filter units, using handtools
Examines parts for defects and tests needle valves with wire gauges and flow meter	Examines parts for defects and tests needle valves with wire gauges
Cleans parts in solvent to remove dirt and gum deposits	Cleans parts in solvent to remove dirt and gum deposits
Repairs or replaces defective parts	Repairs or replaces defective parts
Reassembles carburetor and gasoline filter and installs them in vehicle	Reassembles carburetor and gasoline filter
Starts engine and turns adjustment screw to regulate flow of air and gasoline through carburetor, using testing equipment	
May operate drill press, lathe, and other power tools to retap jets, ream throttle bodies and chokes, and machine seating surfaces of carburetor housings	
May install and repair mechanical devices that convert conventional systems to use of other fuels	

information from a variety of sources be accumulated gradually over a period of time. Thus, construct validity, compared with other validity measures, tends to focus on a broader and more enduring type of behavioral description (Anastasi, 1976).

Factor analysis is a pertinent process in establishing construct validity, since every attempt should be made to refine the number of constructs to a few more common and essential traits pertinent to the job that the work sample simulates. This statistical procedure analyzes the relationships of this behavior data by using a correlation known as factorial validity (Anastasi, 1976), which with the work sample may correlate the factors entailed in the sample with those in the qualifications profile relating to the particular job or worker trait group.

Brolin (1976) noted that since the job sample so closely approximates the actual job, construct validity is built into the sample, even though "the psychosocial and financial conditions of the real job cannot be replicated" (p. 111). Andrew and Dickerson (1974) reiterated the use of DOT information and job analysis as built in aspects of construct validity in the work sample process and also recommended the use of the Minnesota Job Requirements Questionnaire (Desmond & Weiss, 1970; Hendel & Vessey, 1970).

FACE VALIDITY

Face validity, although not validity in the technical sense, should not be shunted aside as having no importance in the work sample validation process. Face validity entails the work sample "looking like" the job it simulates. If the sample is very similar to the job, student/client motivation tends to increase (Bolton, 1976; Brolin, 1976). Face validity can be a desirable feature of a work sample, making it look more related to job performance expectations, and actually entails good public relations. It pertains to how valid the work sample or test looks to "the subjects who take it, the administrative personnel who decide on its use and other technically untrained observers" (Anastasi, 1976, p. 139).

RELIABILITY

Reliability is the extent to which the results of an evaluation instrument are consistent and stable from one measurement to another. If the test is reliable and the skill, behavior, or trait is not effected by instruction, learning, or maturation, the person would receive the same or similar scores in repeated testing. Several ways of establishing reliability are available.

TEST-RETEST RELIABILITY

Test-retest reliability provides an index of stability and is determined by administering a test to a large sample of individuals and readministering the same test to the sample after a period of time. The scores are correlated and the resulting correlation is called the *stability coefficient.*

The time between initial testing and follow-up testing is important, as learning or familiarity with the test items or activity may affect true test reliability estimation. The form of error that may occur is labeled a time sampling error.

ALTERNATE FORM RELIABILITY

Alternate form reliability is obtained when a sample of individuals is tested and then retested with a different test covering the same content, skill, or behavior. Error variance in the reliability may be introduced in two ways. Time sampling errors may result, similar to test-retest methods, depending on the interval between testing. Also, *content sampling* errors may be introduced when the test items on one test are different from test items on the second form.

SPLIT-HALF RELIABILITY

Split-half reliability is determined when test items are divided into two item pools (odd-numbered and even-numbered items, for example) and the individual's performance on one test item pool is compared with performance on the second test item pool. The split-half reliability estimate provides a measure of internal consistency. Split-half reliability does not provide an estimate of stability or consistency over time and cannot be used with timed tests.

CORRELATION COEFFICIENT

Correlation coefficients are the numerical indices that quantify the relationship between variables. The correlation coefficient identifies the extent to which two variables "go together," how changes in one variable may be accompanied by changes in the second variable.

Correlation coefficients are used in estimating the reliability and validity of the instrument and can range in value from 0 to + 1.00 or − 1.00. A correlation coefficient of 0 indicates that there is no relationship between two variables, that changes in one variable are independent from changes in the other. A correlation coefficient of + 1.00 indicates a positive or direct (perfect) relationship; as one variable increases, the other variable increases. Similarly, − 1.00 is a perfect negative or indirect relationship, as in Figure 6-1.

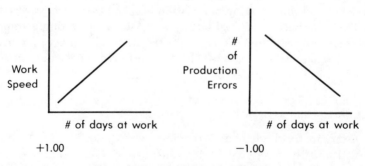

Figure 6-1. Correlation coefficients.

Power (1984) identified the strength of correlations as:

.80 – 1.00   Very high correlation
.60 – .79   Substantial correlation
.40 – .59   Moderate correlation
.20 – .39   Little correlation
.01 – .19   Practically no correlation

In reviewing the validity and reliability coefficients for a particular test, the evaluator is confronted with questions of how substantial (how reliable or valid) the correlation coefficient for a test should be. Unfortunately, there are no clear cut-off scores available to answer this question, but there are guidelines to assist the practitioner in evaluating the test.

The strength of reliability and validity coefficients is influenced by the following:

■ The method of estimating reliability/validity. For example, the method of estimating reliability should be examined. If the interval between testing is short in test-retest reliability, the reliability estimate may be higher than if alternate-form methods over time are used.

■ The type of test (intelligence, personality, work sample) used. Achievement tests have a higher reliability and validity than tests measuring constructs or more abstract concepts. In general, the evaluator would be satisfied with reliability coefficients ranging from .80 to .95. Validity coefficients range from .30 to a more acceptable .65.

■ The population sample. The test manual provides information on the characteristics of the population on which the test has been validated. Often, different validation studies have been performed, with different correlation coefficients resulting, and the evaluator can compare the usefulness of the test with different population samples.

■ The purpose of testing. Content validity is the most common validation measure cited in testing manuals. Although the evaluator uses tests to predict or estimate the individual's performance in a particular setting, predictive validity measures are rare, due to the cost in time and money to perform long-range follow-up testing. The question becomes, "How useful is a test in predicting behavior when the content validity is .68?"

The nature of the decisions being made also affect how valid a test must be. When decisions about job placement with a new employer are being made, there is need for more confidence in the predictors. However, if a test is being used to stimulate career exploration, recognizing that interests may change over time, the strength of the predictive validity may not be as important.

USEFULNESS OF TEST MEASURERS

Validity and reliability are psychometric standards used to evaluate the characteristics of a test. Understanding the validity and reliability allows the evaluator to use the instrument with confidence in subsequent test interpretations. Based on assessment of test validity, the evaluator can evaluate the importance of test performance against external criteria. Based on understanding of test reliability, the evaluator can be confident about the instrument demonstrating internal consistency.

Bolton (1976) has reminded us that reliability and validity concepts cannot be independent of the client when interpretations of performance are made. Reliability must be examined against the nature of the trait being measured (stable versus developmental) and how the test is to be used (measure of current behavior or a predictor of future performance). Based on these questions, the evaluator will more realistically examine the types of reliability estimated and how each may impact interpretation.

Similarly, the evaluator examines the method of validation used (content, predictive, construct), the characteristics of the norm group, and the characteristics of the student.

Aside from these considerations, the value of a test finally rests in its usefulness in assisting the evaluator to make decisions with the client. Bolton (1976) discussed the concept of "incremental validity" in pointing out that instruments or test activity may be reliable and valid but add little to the decision-making process. A testing procedure is useful if the test facilitates and promotes accurate decision making for the client.

SUMMARY

Vocational evaluation involves a process of identifying a series of tests appropriate to an individual student, administering the test in order to gain additive information about the student, and interpreting testing results in order to make decisions about programming and placement. The question for the evaluator becomes one of selecting the test that is best suited to the student, the information needs, and the decisions to be made. This chapter has discussed several issues related to the psychometric principles involved in test selection.

CHAPTER 7

Vocational Evaluation Tools: Psychometric Tests

Vocational evaluation has many tests, tools, techniques, and procedures to evaluate the vocational potential of special needs students. These evaluation tools include:

- Paper and pencil tests
- Observation activity
- Work samples
- Situational assessment
- Job site evaluation
- Computer-aided evaluation and job matching systems

Historically, the most widely used evaluation method in special education has been paper and pencil or psychometric tests, undoubtedly due to their excellent ability to screen for disability and establish a diagnosis. Vocational evaluators favor work samples or simulated work activity, often not accepting the contributions of psychometric tests in measuring specific aptitudes as well as psychomotor and cognitive abilities that are not so easily measured by work simulations.

Psychometric tests are particularly useful to supplement work simulations in the areas of functional academics, vocational interest, and specific aptitudes (Botterbusch, 1978). Rather than viewing them as an alternative to work simulations, psychometric tests can be an effective evaluation procedure to supplement and complement work simulations within the vocational evaluation process.

Special education is taking increasing responsibility for the vocational planning and outcome of more severely and multiply handicapped special education students. Unfortunately, as the level of severity increases, fewer and fewer psychometric tests are directly applicable to the student. This is particularly true for students with hearing impairments and visual and perceptual disabilities.

This chapter highlights the common psychometric tests available in vocational evaluation for use with special needs students as well as how each may be used to maximize the acquisition of vocational information.

ADVANTAGES AND DISADVANTAGES OF PSYCHOMETRIC TESTS

Generally speaking, there are specific advantages and disadvantages in using psychometric or paper and pencil tests for purposes of vocational assessment in special education.

Advantages of psychometric tests include:

1. The administration of the tests may be accomplished quite rapidly, especially compared with the time required by most work samples and job simulations.
2. The administration of the tests is usually uncomplicated and routine if the administrator is careful in following standardized instructions.
3. Psychometric tests can be quite inexpensive compared with most work samples.
4. The tests usually provide a great amount of objectivity in that it is easier to control the relatively few variables when compared to work sample evaluations.
5. Psychometric tests generally have proven to have a high level of internal reliability and acceptable validity.

In addition to these advantages, there are several limitations to psychometric tests with severely handicapped students. Test characteristics that particularly limit their use with severely disabled students in evaluating vocational areas include the following:

1. Most paper and pencil tests require a higher level of verbal fluency, reading or academic ability, and intellectual capacity than many special needs students may have. Standardized administration methods using written or verbal instruction and/or multistep directions are inappropriate for severely disabled students and may result in unrepresentative performance. Individuals with disabilities such as severe hearing impairments and deaf-blindness have isolated educational experiences and often demonstrate inadequate educational and communication skills needed for many paper and pencil tests. For individuals with other developmental disabilities, including severe mental retardation, multiple and secondary disabilities such as hearing, speech, and motor coordination difficulties would limit performance evaluation.

2. Much of the content of tests currently used in schools is directed at school or home situations rather than information related to work or vocational planning.

3. Similarly, much of the content of many tests is aimed at adolescents or children rather than potential "workers."

4. Most tests provide a one-trial-learning administration format that often confounds subsequent performance measurement and does not allow the evaluator to make observations about learning ability.

5. The nature and demands of the test situation usually differ greatly from the nature and demands of the work situation (Neff, 1985), particularly as compared with the work sample's relation to a work situation. Consequently, psychometric tests usually do not offer the evaluator as much information for vocational choice and decision making as does the work sample approach; nor is the information usually as meaningful to the student and the teacher (Jewish Employment and Vocational Service, 1968).

6. Due to the relatively short period of time during which a person is in a test situation, internal factors, such as anxiety level, motivation, concentration, and sensory and perceptual ability, which often are not controlled, have a more serious effect on the test situation than they would have in the longer period of the simulated work evaluation situation.

Similarly, the paper and pencil testing situation is very familiar to the student and usually represents negative or failure experiences rather than positive experiences.

7. Psychometric tests are built upon norm group interpretations that are not well suited to developing vocational curricula or program planning objectives.

8. Modifications of testing procedures usually are not stated clearly in test manuals and evaluators are hesitant to modify tests, due to heavy reliance on norm group interpretation.

TEST MODIFICATIONS AND ADAPTATIONS

Many of the limitations and restrictions of psychometric tests used with students having more severe disabilities can also be applied to work samples and other simulated work situations. Because of the level and type of disability, either the *content, format,* or *administration procedures* make the test activity inappropriate for the student. Without accounting for how the disability impacts performance within standardized test administration practice, evaluators, teachers, and the student could conclude that the student does not have the particular skill potential or aptitude to learn, or is too disabled to participate in a particular training activity.

The evaluator is encouraged to explore how modification and adaptive assessment practices may be developed, but with care and consideration for the subsequent interpretations that are to be made.

As with other vocational assessment tools, modification in psychometric test administration procedure may alter either the method of instruction or task performance. For example, the individual may better understand test expectation if instructions are modified to include verbal and written direction, coupled with demonstration, or perhaps involving practice to criteria levels. Similarly, performance evaluation may begin with single step tasks and increase to multistep tasks, may use pictures or other physical performance cues or compensatory aids, or may build in check steps to assist the student in monitoring task performance.

The goal of test modification is to change a testing format that has potential for excluding individuals from a program because of the disability and to develop adaptations or incorporate work aids that promote maximum performance and allow the evaluator to validly assess performance ability.

Test modifications must not be made indiscriminately and the evaluator is charged with understanding the impact of altering testing procedures for a specific test with a specific disability. Most importantly, the evaluator must consider how similar modifications may be applied in the work-related environment for the student.

Many testing specialists view modification of testing situations as disturbing; the creative evaluator views modification of evaluation activity as an opportunity to assess how maximum performance of the individual may be enhanced. Typical modifications are:

1. Using pre-trials/practice
2. Repeating instructions—having the student repeat verbal instructions
3. Oral instruction versus written instruction
4. Relaxing time limits
5. Color coding tasks
6. Demonstrating performance activity
7. Individual rather than group testing

Modifications can be developed that accommodate a specific disability, for example, large print text or Braille for students with visual handicaps, using signs or an interpreter with hearing–impaired students, using low literate or pictoral test forms with poor readers.

A strength of vocational evaluation is the wide range of formal and informal tests, activities, and resources available to the evaluator. In order to obtain maximum results from the evaluation process, the evaluator will use certain tests in a standardized format and develop modifications that respond to the unique needs of the individual student.

The flexible use of tests and testing procedures is reflected in the following description of psychometric tests.

APTITUDE AND ACHIEVEMENT TESTS

Aptitude and achievement tests have assumed a primary role in vocational evaluation due to their practical utility in identifying a student's performance level or potential in functional academics and vocational areas (Bolton, 1976; Fower, 1984). *Aptitude* is defined as the student's capacity to benefit from training in a certain area (mechanical aptitude, clerical aptitude, verbal aptitude, etc.). Achievement tests measure the level of skill or proficiency the student has gained in a particular area (math, spelling, reading, etc.).

Achievement tests, especially in the area of functional academics, are able to provide measures of student gain or progress while in a training program. In addition, achievement tests may help the evaluator and teacher formulate learning objectives against specific criterion levels in the IEP or in vocational transition planning. Achievement tests traditionally have the highest reliability of all paper and pencil tests, ranging between .80 and .90.

Aptitude tests may provide relatively quick screening information in such areas as spatial, mechanical, or clerical aptitudes. However, the evaluator must supplement information gained through aptitude tests with information gained through simulated or hands-on work samples. A student may not demonstrate proficiency in mechanical ability on traditional paper and pencil tests, but may be able to work through mechanical tasks that are presented in a more realistic format.

Achievement and aptitude tests that have utility in special education are outlined here.

WIDE RANGE ACHIEVEMENT TEST—REVISED (WRAT)

The WRAT is designed to measure basic skills of reading, spelling, and arithmetic. The test combines oral directions and written testing. The math section is timed and consists of basic addition, subtraction, multiplication, and division. It also involves decimals, fractions, and written computations. The WRAT takes from 15 to 25 minutes to administer and provides useful screening information about basic academic skills.

A gasoline pump registers in gallons and in tenths of gallons. What will this pump register when another *tenth* of a gallon of gas is pumped out of it?

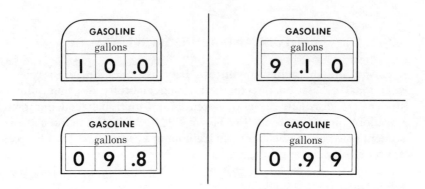

Figure 7-1. Peabody Individual Achievement Test. Reproduced by permission of American Guidance Service, Inc. Peabody Individual Achievement Test by Lloyd M. Dunn and Frederick C. Markwardt. Copyright 1970. Rights reserved.

PEABODY INDIVIDUAL ACHIEVEMENT TEST (PIAT)

The PIAT is a widely accepted academic achievement test that provides measurement of mathematics, reading recognition, reading comprehension, spelling, and general information (Figure 7-1). The test is normed on over 3,000 students from kindergarten through twelfth grade. All test items are presented orally and scores are given in grade

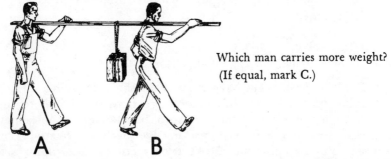

Which man carries more weight? (If equal, mark C.)

A   B

Figure 7-2. Bennett Mechanical Comprehension Test. Reprinted from Bennett Mechanical Comprehension Test by G.K. Bennett with permission of The Psychological Corporation.

scores, age scores, percentile rank, and standard scores. The PIAT is useful with most disabled students, although limited in usefulness with blind and hearing–impaired students.

BENNETT MECHANICAL COMPREHENSION TEST

The Bennett Mechanical Comprehension Test measures the ability "to perceive and understand the relationship of physical forces and mechanical elements in practical situations." The reading requirement of the test is relatively low and involves test items dealing with gears, pulleys, hydraulics, acoustics, gravity, weights, and motion. The test is timed, but can be considered a power test. There are several norm groups of adequate size with student, industrial applicant, and industrial employee norms. This test is a highly visual test, having relatively detailed pictures, thus making it inappropriate for individuals who are blind. Instructions may be modified to allow for practice and/or discussion without jeopardizing performance. The construct of mechanical aptitude is relatively difficult and may not be realistic for some special needs students. The test complements work samples for mechanical or technical jobs (Figure 7–2).

REVISED MINNESOTA PAPER FORM BOARD

The Revised Minnesota Paper Form Board measures the mechanical aptitude needed to visualize and manipulate objects in space. The test consists of 64 two-dimensional diagrams cut into separate pieces. This is a 20-minute timed test with educational and industrial norms of adequate size and description. Acceptable reliability and validation studies are reported. Since the task requires visual ability, the test is not appropriate for blind individuals. The instruction format requires reading ability but can be supplemented with oral instructions. This

Look at the problems on the right side of this page. You will notice that there are eight of them, numbered from 1 to 8. Notice that the problems go DOWN the page.

First look at Problem 1. There are two parts in the upper left-hand corner. Now look at the five figures labelled A, B, C, D, E. You are to decide which figure shows how these parts can fit together. Let us first look at Figure A. You will notice that Figure A does not look like the parts in the upper left-hand corner would look when fitted together. Neither do Figures B, C, or D. Figure E does look like the parts in the upper left-hand corner would look when fitted together, so E is PRINTED in the square above [1] at the top of the page.

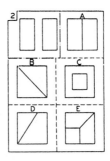

Figure 7–3. Revised Minnesota Paper Form Board Test. Reprinted from the Revised Minnesota Paper Form Board Test by R. Likert & W.H. Quasha with permission of The Psychological Corporation.

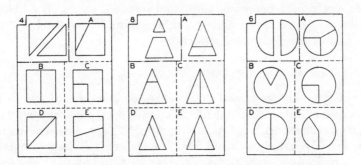

test is similar to other spatial aptitude tests and has had wide usage in testing batteries for mechanical and technical jobs. Because of the abstract nature of the task, certain individuals may have difficulty relating the test to vocational aptitudes (Figure 7–3).

MINNESOTA CLERICAL TEST

The Minnesota Clerical Test was designed to evaluate clerical speed and accuracy in number and name comparisons. The student's task is to identify and check identical parts of similar and dissimilar pairs of names and numbers. The test is normed on clerical applicants and employees as well as student groups. Adequate correlations have been reported between scores and supervisor ratings. As the test is highly visual, it is not suitable for individuals with a visual handicap. Although it is called a clerical test, the test measures only a very circumscribed ability, but may be a useful first step in evaluating a wider range of clerical abilities (Figure 7–4).

GENERAL APTITUDE TEST BATTERY (GATB)

The GATB is a battery-oriented aptitude test that assesses a range of aptitudes related to the Guide for Occupational Exploration (GOE) Work Groups, including: General Learning Ability, Verbal, Numerical, Spatial, Form Perception, Clerical Perception, Finger Dexterity, and Manual Dexterity. There are 12 subtests that take about 2.5 hours to administer. The test is standardized on both general working population and student norms. Results are directly related to specific job requirements or jobs within specific Occupational Aptitude Patterns (OAP).

The evaluator is cautioned that the GATB is a highly standardized and formal test battery with strict time limits. The test battery is controlled and administered through the state employment services.

THE NON-READING APTITUDE TEST BATTERY (NATB)

The NATB is a nonreading adaption of the GATB and is suitable for learning–disabled individuals and others with limited reading skills. Both batteries use the same worker trait aptitude format for test interpretation. The NGTB takes a longer time than the GATB to administer and score.

Other achievement and aptitude tests are described in Appendix I.

VOCATIONAL INTEREST INVENTORIES

Exploration and discussion of vocational interest is a developmental process occurring at elementary levels and continuing through middle and high school. Not only does it serve to stimulate consideration of vocational options, it also creates a growing awareness of the role the individual will play as a productive worker. As such, interest exploration plays an important yet subtle role in the developing vocational maturity of the student. Formal vocational interest inventories can be productive tools to

- stimulate initial exploration of vocational options;
- compare individual skills and abilities with the requirements of specific areas of interest;
- begin narrowing job choices and alternatives.

Interest inventories should not be used to identify specific job choices or to establish a specific vocational objective. Throughout vocational and transition planning they are the first step to compare testing interest with expressed interest. Expressed and tested interest can be compared with the student's outside activities, hobbies, and interests.

As the individual progresses in vocational decision making, interest inventories aid in organizing occupational information, identifying additional testing needs, and prompting exposure to more concrete work samples and simulated work activity.

John Holland (1970) developed a model of vocational and occupational preference that is widely accepted and forms the basis for many vocational interest tests in use today. Holland organized occupations and occupational preferences within six groupings as depicted in Figure 7–5.

The occupational environments identified by Holland include:

- Realistic
- Investigative
- Social
- Artistic

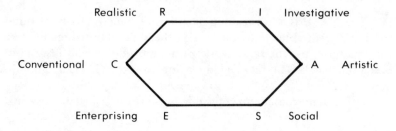

Figure 7-5. A hexagonal model of Holland's occupational scales.

■ Enterprising
■ Conventional

The occupational divisions provide a useful and understandable format for organizing information about vocational interest and work environments.

Formal vocational interest tests are not always the most appropriate interest exploration technique. All too often, interest exploration has not been an organized or structured activity through middle and high school. Students may have had very limited exposure to the world of work or may have been influenced by significant others about "appropriate" job choice. Results of interest testing would point to a narrow vocational choice, not reflecting knowledge of available opportunities. It is often more appropriate to provide such an individual with a range of vocational experiences to stimulate vocational exploration.

The following vocational interest tests are appropriate for formal interest exploration with severely disabled students.

WIDE RANGE INTEREST AND OPINION TEST (WRIOT)

The WRIOT is a picture interest inventory measuring interests in areas ranging from unskilled through professional occupations. The WRIOT presents a series of three illustrations of individuals performing a work activity and the student selects the most- and least-preferred activities. The inventory requires no reading, covers a wide range of the occupational spectrum, and is appropriate for many types of disability. Because of the reliance on pictures, it is inappropriate for blind individuals (Figure 7-6).

A **B** **C**

Choose the picture which shows best what you would like to do.
Next, indicate the picture you don't like to do.

Figure 7-6. Wide Range Interest-Opinion Test. Reprinted from the Wide Range Interest-Opinion Test by Jastak and Jastak with permission of Jastak Assessment Systems.

REVISED READING-FREE VOCATIONAL INTEREST INVENTORY (RFVII)

The RFVII is a nonreading picture interest inventory that directs the student to make a choice from three illustrations. The inventory was normed on a national sample of retarded and learning–disabled students in schools, workshops, and vocational training centers. Scoring and interpretation is easily understandable and the occupational areas include unskilled, entry level, and nontechnical positions.

GORDON OCCUPATIONAL CHECKLIST

The Gordon Occupational Checklist is an occupational interest inventory for non-college-bound individuals interested in unskilled, semiskilled, or technical jobs. Students read a list of job activities and underline and circle activities of interest and then of great interest (Figure 7-7). Results are interpreted through business, outdoors, arts,

Read the list slowly, and when you come to an activity that you would like to do as part of a full-time job, underline it.

1. sort and deliver mail, messages and packages
2. do routine sorting, numbering and stapling
3. operate a duplicating machine
4. file letters, bills and receipts
5. type routine letters and statements

Figure 7–7. Gordon Occupational Checklist. Reprinted from the Gordon Occupational Checklist by L.V. Gordon with permission of Harcourt Brace Jovanovich, Inc.

technical, and service occupations. Reading level requirement is approximately sixth grade, but the checklist could also be administered orally. Occupational areas have a strong relationship to the DOT and GOE interest group.

SELF DIRECTED SEARCH (SDS)

The Self Directed Search (SDS) was developed by John Holland after two decades of career development research. The SDS was one of the first theory- and reseach-based inventories that guides the student through a self-exploration and self-interpretation process. Two booklets are used by the student. In one, the student identifies Occupational Daydreams, Activities, Competencies, Occupations, and Self Estimates. This process results in a Summary Code based on Holland's occupational category types, for example, RIE = Realistic, Investigative, and Enterprising Themes. The individual then uses the Occupations Finder to identify specific jobs under this code. The student and counselor are encouraged to use different Summary Code combinations (REI, IRE, ERI) to explore additional jobs and compare interest with job activities.

The SDS requires a sixth-grade reading level, but has a FORM E that requires only a fourth-grade level. Although the SDS is useful for independent self administration and exploration, the evaluator is encouraged to "work" through the inventory with the student. This process functions to further increase self exploration and self evaluation on the student's part.

The SDS is also available on computer software, allowing further interactive exploration between the student and the computer's occupational data base.

Other vocational interest inventories include:

■ *Higher reading level* (Sixth-grade level)
   Career Assessment Inventory (CAI)
   Strong Vocational Interest Inventory

Kuder Vocational Interest Inventory
Ohio Vocational Interest Survey
Vocational Preference Inventory
Interest Checklist
Vocational Interest, Experience and Skill Assessment (VIESA)
■ *Picture Interest Inventories*
Vocational Interest and Sophistication Assess (VISA)
Geist Picture Interest Inventory
Picture Interest Inventory

Each of these instruments have specific uses with severely disabled youth. A brief description of some of these tests can be found in Appendix I.

PERFORMANCE TESTS

Performance tests are hands-on evaluation tools used to measure dexterity, coordination, and tool use. Although inappropriate norm groups and restrictive administrative procedures may limit standardized administration of performance tests with severely handicapped students, valuable information may be gained through modified testing formats and systematic observation. The evaluator may alter instruction procedures and assess the student's response to different verbal or demonstration cues, and evaluate the person's performance in both structured and unstructured settings.

Performance tests are relatively quick, specialized, concrete activities that allow the evaluator to vary the testing conditions to explore under what conditions the individual best learns. Along with the specific information that the test is developed to obtain, the evaluator may gather additional information, such as:

■ Learning/response style
■ Visual motor ability
■ Fine finger dexterity
■ Coordination
■ Short-term sequential memory
■ Gross motor ability
■ Use of basic tools
■ Sequencing ability

CRAWFORD SMALL PARTS DEXTERITY TEST

The Crawford Small Parts Dexterity Test is a hands-on performance test that measures fine-finger eye-hand coordination. In the first section, the student uses tweezers to pick up a pin and place it in a hole and then to pick up a collar to be placed over the pin. In the second section, the student uses a flat head screwdriver to turn a threaded screw in a hole using both hands. Performance is timed. Norms are provided for students, employed workers, adults in a vocational training program, and mentally retarded adults. Sample size for norm groups and reliability and validation estimates are small. The test lends itself to modification in testing procedures, and also provides valuable observational information. The test tends to be routine and frustrating for individuals with poor dexterity and for many mentally retarded individuals (Botterbusch & Michael, 1985).

BENNETT HAND-TOOL DEXTERITY TEST

The Bennett Hand-Tool Dexterity Test measures gross motor ability, coordination, and proficiency with basic hand tools. The individual must use an adjustable wrench and hand tools to remove nuts, bolts, and washers from the left side of a wood frame to the right side. Performance is timed and takes between 5 and 25 minutes. Norms include job applicants, mechanics, welders, and educational norms, but are quite dated and not well described. Reviewers often advise that the test should be used with caution due to questionable norms and inadequate validation. The value of the Bennett does not rest on psychometric principles or its ability to compare performance with a related norm group. More important is the opportunity to systematically modify the instructions and performance procedures and to use observation procedures to identify individual learning styles (follow verbal instructions, demonstrations, etc.); and the ability to chain multiple step activities, organize a work area, plan and sequence motor tasks, and sustain work activity; as well as to observe ability to use tools and to demonstrate dexterity and coordination.

Used with the Crawford Small Parts Dexterity Test, the Bennett provides the evaluator with a relatively quick estimate of fine finger and gross motor manual dexterity, coordination, and ability to use small and/or basic tools.

PENNSYLVANIA BI-MANUAL WORK SAMPLE

The Pennsylvania Bi-Manual Work Sample is not a true work sample but a performance test that measures integration of motor tasks such as fine finger dexterity, gross movements of both arms, and eye-hand coordination. The first part of the test involves turning a nut on a bolt and placing it on a board. Disassembly of the nuts and bolts is the second part. Performance time ranges between 10 and 25 minutes and the test is timed to completion. Norm groups consist of separate male and female norms in two age groups and an industrial group. The test has been normed on blind and partially blind individuals. The Pennsylvania is a very old test, but retains value in its applicability to many handicapped individuals.

PURDUE PEGBOARD

The Purdue Pegboard is a performance test that measures fine finger dexterity and coordinated movement of hands, fingers, and arms. Different parts of testing involve right hand only, left hand only, both hands, and multistep assembly. Performance involves placing pins, collars, and washers into holes on the test board. Time periods for each task are short and the entire test takes between 10 and 15 minutes. Norms include male and female industrial workers as well as job applicants and college students. The Purdue presents unusually low reliability and validity coefficients in the manual as well as dated norm groups. The test has value as a performance test that may be administered in a flexible manner with relatively short time limits to make specific behavioral observations.

As can be noted from the previous descriptions, performance tests are of value in vocational evaluation as they are hands-on tests, although involving more abstract work activity, that can be administered in a relatively short period. Although the psychometric principles are weak, the tests derive value from being able to modify the testing procedures and make observations about behavioral characteristics of the student.

Although the test manufacturers often make claims relating the usefulness of performance tests in selection and placement directly into assembly, packing, or inspecting jobs, the tools are used best as an initial activity to introduce hands-on testing and as a preliminary testing activity leading to more complex work samples. An additional value of performance tests is that extensive training is not needed to administer them and they are portable enough to be used by classroom teachers.

SUMMARY

Psychometric tests will continue to have a place in vocational evaluation with severely disabled students, despite the limitations of individual tests noted throughout this chapter. When the evaluator is able to relate the tests to specific work factors or demonstrate the relatedness of test performance and results to worker trait characteristics, the test becomes a valuable part of the vocational evaluation

TABLE 7-1.
General Aptitudes and Related Tests.*

	WRAT	PIAT	Revised Minnesota Paper Form Board Test	Bennett Mechanical Comprehension Test	Minnesota Clerical Test	GATB	Crawford Small Parts Test	Bennett Handtool Dexterity Test	Penn Bi-Manual Test	Purdue Pegboard Test
G (General)		X	X			X				
V (Verbal)						X				
N (Numerical)	X	X				X				
S (Spatial)			X	X		X				
P (Form Perception)			X			X				
Q (Clerical Perception)					X	X				
K (Motor Coordination)						X	X	X	X	X
F (Finger Dexterity)						X	X	X	X	X
M (Manual Dexterity)						X		X	X	
E (Eye-hand-foot coordination)										
LS (Learning Style)							X	X		
FA (Functional Academics)	X	X								

*Listed above are 10 work aptitudes related to worker trait requirements, and a chart identifying ability and aptitude tests covering different traits. The practitioner may choose the most appropriate evaluation tool—one that measures aptitudes needed for individual occupational training program.

process. Table 7-1 identifies aptitudes evaluated by the paper and pencil tests identified in this chapter. It is important for the evaluator to use tests that are appropriate to the student, that relate to job characteristics from the student's perspective, that provide results in behavioral terms, that are understandable to the student, and that contribute information that facilitates vocational decision making.

CHAPTER 8

Simulated Work Evaluation: Work Sample Evaluation

The uniqueness of vocational evaluation as an evaluation process derives from placing the individual in practical, concrete, simulated work activities to determine vocational potential. Simulated work activities may range from informal observation of the student in unstructured work situations to highly structured and formal standardized work simulations. Work samples, as examples of the latter, have come to represent the primary tool of the vocational evaluator, although less-structured simulated job stations and/or on-the-job evaluations are of equal value.

A work sample is a structured and standardized simulation of a job, or part of a job, that incorporates some or all of the activities or performance requirements of the job and that is closely observed by the evaluator.

Work samples have been used as job simulations for many years. Pruitt (1986) stated that the Institute for the Crippled and Disabled (now the International Center for the Disabled) developed and used the first standardized and normed work sample battery, the TOWER system, in the 1930s. However, over the last 15 to 20 years there has been a tremendous growth in the development and utilization of commercial work sample systems, and there are over 20 systems available today.

The reasons for this rapid growth are varied, and appear to support a continuing refinement and utilization of work sample methodology.

Rehabilitation legislation has mandated that vocational rehabilitation serve an increasing number of eligible clients, including priority services to more severely disabled persons. Vocational education legislation has placed increased priority on vocational planning at early ages and, with recent legislation (the Carl Perkins Act), has made vocational evaluation a mandated service for special education students involved in vocational education. These initiatives promote individualized planning (IWRP, IEP, ISP) and have emphasized the need for valid, timely, and individualized methods of assessment.

At the same time, vocational evaluation as a profession has experienced rapid growth, expansion, and demand for evaluators. When higher education institutions could not provide sufficient evaluators to satisfy the demand, commercial work sample system developers trained staff through short-term seminars.

Although vocational evaluation has its roots in the expansion of public vocational rehabilitation, it also is expanding rapidly as a separate professional field, providing service in public schools, vocational schools, manpower programs, hospitals, and private rehabilitation. There has developed an ever-increasing assessment market that commercial work sample systems have eagerly filled.

As vocational evaluation becomes more a part of special education planning, questions arise about the place of work samples in vocational evaluation planning.

- What work samples are appropriate for the particular special needs student?
- What abilities or aptitudes can best be measured by work samples?
- Are work samples necessary for special needs students?
- Who should administer work samples to the student?

The purpose of this chapter is to orient the reader to work sample evaluation in special education, to discuss the advantages and disadvantages of work samples with particular students, and to offer guidelines on selecting and using work samples as part of a vocational evaluation process.

WORK SAMPLE EVALUATION DEFINITION

The final report of Task Force Number 7 of the Vocational Evaluation Project defines the various categories of work samples. In general, a work sample is described as:

A well-defined work activity involving tasks, materials, and tools which are identical or similar to those in an actual job or cluster of jobs. It is used to assess an individual's vocational aptitude, worker characteristics, and vocational interests.

The work sample evaluation process derives value as an evaluation tool from its strong reality orientation, involvement in concrete work activity, as well as through standardized sampling of work behavior.

The Task Force identified four categories of work samples:

1. Actual job samples
2. Simulated work samples
3. Single trait samples
4. Cluster trait samples

Actual job samples and simulated work samples use the tasks, material, equipment, and supplies that would be commonly found in a job or work activity. The difference between the two is found in the relatedness to specific jobs found in the community.

Actual job samples are replicated directly from specific jobs in industry, in their entirety, and include the equipment, tasks, raw materials, supplies, procedures, and exacting standards found in the industry setting.

The simulated work sample replicates a segment of the essential work factors and tasks, materials, equipment, and supplies that may simulate one or more jobs to be performed in the community.

An example of a simulated work sample is the tools utilized for certain aspects of plumbing activity (862.381–030). The DOT number following this job title is that of a construction plumber. A work sample based on this plumbing job could entail the use of certain tools such as a pipe cutter, a pipe threader, a reamer, a file, and a vise to hold the pipe. Materials might consist of galvanized pipe and oil to lubricate the pipe threader. Sequential instructions for this plumbing or pipe fitting operation would be read by the evaluee, or read or verbalized to the evaluee by the vocational evaluator. The latter would time the evaluee and make observations on the behaviors and performance during the construction and completion of the work sample.

An actual job sample based on the same DOT plumbing job is more likely to be indigenous to a particular plumbing job in the community. In addition to the mentioned tools, supplies, and equipment, the evaluator would bring in copper tubing and a torch and flaring tools, as well as some PVC pipe, glue, hacksaw, pipe wrenches, and other tools If the job sample were to be even more representative of the actual job in the community, a sink with faucets and even the wall studs through which the pipes were to run would be provided. Although all of this could be in a simulated work sample, the job sample is a more exact duplicate of a job in the community and may be set up to the exact specifications of that job. The simulated work sample may be simpler and less detailed than the actual job sample, whereas the latter would bring with it the standards and norms associated with the job in industry.

There is not always a complete distinction made between a simulated work sample and an actual job sample. Anastasi (1976) was probably speaking more of a job sample when she said, "In such tests, the task set for the subject is similar to the work he is to perform on the job. The representativeness of the behavior sample and the closeness with which the task duplicates actual job conditions are essential considerations" (p. 424). However, it is the duplication of the components of the job that applies to the simulated work sample, whereas the actual job sample, per se, is more apt to have a closer approximation of the specific job conditions.

In reality, there are certain components of an actual job, or cluster of jobs, which should be integrated into the work sample. Nadolsky (1977) noted that "a work sample is a practical, realistic instrument of assessment which incorporates the important features (i.e., tasks, activities, tools, equipment and other procedures) of an occupation or a group of closely related occupations into its format" (p. 8).

The single trait work sample. often called the isolated trait work sample, assesses a single worker trait or characteristic. It may have relevance to a specific job or many jobs, but it is intended to assess a single isolated factor. Some would argue that in measuring only a single or isolated trait, we do not have a work sample, but only a psychometric test. Roberts (1970) argued that the isolated trait work sample, in assessing a specific trait such as finger dexterity, or sorting ability traits common to a number of jobs, is similar to psychometric performance tests. However, the redeeming factor of the isolated trait work sample is that it has a greater "degree or element of reality" than does the psychometric test (Roberts, 1970).

In contrast to the single trait work sample, the cluster trait work sample is designed to assess a group of worker traits. The work sample contains a number of traits inherent in a job or variety of jobs and is intended to assess the student's potential to perform various jobs (Kulman, 1975). Nadolsky (1977) recognized that the "worker traits" or job factors are not inherent in the work sample, and we must add that the work sample is merely the medium for bringing out both traits and factors when the person "acts upon" the work sample.

In essence, a work sample is a simulation of a job or an aspect of a job, which, when acted upon by the evaluee, and when such performance is observed and measured by the evaluator, enables the evaluator to observe and measure performance. Measurement of both worker traits and work factors of the evaluee is more feasible when standardized instructions are given and when companion data is utilized for assessment measurement.

WORK SAMPLES: ADVANTAGES AND DISADVANTAGES

The rapid development and use of work samples to evaluate vocational potential has resulted from the distinct advantages of work samples over other forms of testing. These advantages include:

1. Work samples use tools, material, equipment, and supplies that are used in the competitive work world, thus, testing approximates "real life" activity more closely than paper and pencil tests. Similarly, the evaluation environment more closely resembles the normalized demands, noise, and distractions than does the "testing room" environment of psychoeducational testing.

2. The structure of the work sample, in terms of standardized administration, demonstration, and production, allows opportunity to observe behavior in a relatively controlled setting. This allows the evaluator to compare performance against a criteria; identify specific skill deficits and strengths that limit or enhance production; identify vocational traits or behaviors beyond standardized scores or productivity measures.

3. As work sample tasks have high face validity, individuals respond more naturally to testing activity. As individuals see that they are "working on" practical tasks, they accept the testing activity as significant to their vocational planning. This results in greater acceptance of evaluation outcome and subsequent program involvement.

4. Work samples emphasize psychomotor ability and skills rather than verbal ability (Wehman & McLaughlin, 1980). This is a significant point for the more severely disabled students who may have more limited verbal or interpersonal skills, but are better able to perform hands-on tasks.

5. Work sample evaluation is usually a time-limited process. The individual experiences and is exposed to a wide range of jobs in a relatively short period of time. For students who have not had exposure to different work environments and are not aware of vocational alternatives, the work sample introduces many opportunities, challenges, and choices to promote vocational exploration and to develop vocational interest.

6. Performance on the concrete tasks provides direct and immediate information to the evaluator and, in turn, immediate feedback to the individual about his or her performance. The student is able to readily acknowledge the tools he or she was able to use well, the work activity that was most difficult, the tasks that were most interesting. The facilitative counselor is able to use the work sample activity as a direct stimulus to promote counseling and further vocational exploration.

In summary, work samples present a particularly valuable evaluation activity for the special needs student, as the evaluation process is basically a carefully structured hands-on process using real tools, equipment, supplies, and products. The work sample serves to orient the individual to the world of work, involve the student with applied work tasks, provide exposure to a variety of tasks, and provide opportunity for observation, feedback, practice, and adjustment. This is particularly important for students who may have had only limited exposure to jobs, tools, or equipment. Students also benefit from the structure, immediate encouragement, and opportunity for guided exploration with the evaluator.

Although work samples demonstrate potential for vocational evaluation with special needs students, there are also several cautions that the evaluator must consider, including:

1. Although an advantage of work samples is thought to be that they represent a standardized assessment tool that is founded on psychometric principles, in fact, the norming, validity, and reliability characteristics frequently have been rightfully criticized (Botterbusch, 1980; Kulman, 1975; Power, 1984). Often, the norm groups are inadequate or poorly represented and the work sample manuals do not provide reliability estimates or validation studies.

2. The evaluator must be aware that performance on the work sample does not reflect or predict performance in competitive environments. The work sample is a simulation of work tasks and is not intended to contain the range of social and physical demands of real work. This caution is not a criticism of the work sample as much as it is a caution to the evaluator not to read more into work sample performance than is present. Work sample evaluation is not a complete evaluation tool in special education.

3. Work sample evaluation represents a relatively short evaluation process that frequently involves standardized and timed evaluations. As such, the evaluation process penalizes individuals who may require longer periods of time to learn a task before skill may be demonstrated to potential. All too often, a conclusion of work sample evaluations is that the person cannot perform, when, in actuality, insufficient time has been provided to learn a task.

4. Work samples may become obsolete in today's rapidly changing technology.

5. Work samples represent a large initial expense, one that is often too large for individual school systems or agencies. It is important that practitioners examine work sample characteristics important to their school population and community before purchase is made. Work sample selection criteria are offered at the end of the next chapter.

There are often disadvantages specific to individual work samples that are of particular concern to special needs students.

■ A work sample carrel or work station may be filled with tools, hardware, equipment, supplies, and material that can overwhelm students with selected perceptual or organizational deficits.

■ Other work samples may instruct the student through visual or slide tape formats that students have difficulty following due to visual, auditory, or motor handicaps.

■ Some work samples may rely heavily on strict timing procedures or handicap the student through penalties for early performance errors.

Evaluators often place value on work samples because of the structure, standardization, and norming practices, not realizing that it is this dimension that actually diminishes the value of the process for many students.

WORK SAMPLE OUTCOMES

Maximum utilization of work samples is made through flexible use of the work simulations, based on an understanding of the person's disability. Instruction methods may vary, but essentially should provide opportunity for:

■ orienting the person to the task, tools, materials, and equipment;
■ demonstrating tools, procedures, and outcomes;
■ providing time for the person to practice.

The benefits of work samples for special needs students are similar to benefits for other individuals. The person has experience with a variety of realistic work demands to promote interest exploration and skill identification in a supported setting. The evaluator has the opportunity to observe vocational skill, systematically alter performance expectations, and observe organization, sequencing, problem solving, and decision making. The student and evaluator are able to discuss impressions of performance immediately and determine how a task may be performed differently. The work sample may be used in a flexible way to recognize and compensate for skill deficits and to systematically alter work sample tasks to evaluate potential.

Through flexible use of work samples, the evaluator is able to obtain more information than from a norm-based comparison of the individual's performance. Work samples should also function to provide:

1. Job-related outcomes in terms of aptitudes, abilities, and ability to use tools. (Note that the work sample may not accurately evaluate individuals requiring even longer periods to learn a skill.)
2. Exposure to a variety of vocational experiences within a relatively short period. Work samples can effectively promote interest exploration.

3. Assessment of learning style. Work samples are especially powerful tasks to vary instruction strategies and to present different learning situations to determine under what situations the individual best learns.
4. Evaluation of problem-solving and decision-making abilities in more realistic hands-on vocational situations.
5. Organization of occupational information about job duties, requirements, employment outlook, and available training opportunities on jobs in the community that relate to specific work samples.
6. Assessment of the modifications, accommodations, and compensations that may support independent productivity. Modifications made to support work activity on a work sample should be replicable in a competitive work environment.

IN-HOUSE WORK SAMPLES

Because of the severity or specificity of many disabilities served by special education (e.g., hearing impairments, deaf–blind disabilities, or severe developmental disabilities), commercial work samples do not always provide the functional information that is needed by the educator. Commercial work samples may be limited by the instruction or administration format used (verbal, visual, or slide/tape format), may not account for the type of disability being evaluated (specific perceptual disability), or may not be sensitive to the specific skill or skill level of the student. When the evaluator finds that gaps exist in information provided by commercial systems, or that systems are not useful due to the performance demands placed on the specific disability, "in house" work samples may be developed to complement selected commercial work sample systems. The range of commercial systems are described in Chapter 9.

JOB ANALYSIS IN DEVELOPING WORK SAMPLES

While evaluators or special educators may not consider statistical analysis or formal test development procedures within the range of their expertise, the potential benefit of in-house work samples as an individualized assessment procedures should encourage the evaluator to explore work sample development more carefully. Test development can be a highly technical activity, as well as a highly creative process, far less "painful" than the evaluator may have expected. The following considerations are to be used as guidelines in developing in-house work samples.

JOB ANALYSIS

Professional evaluation procedures dictate that work samples be based on job analysis procedures (Commission on Accreditation of Rehabilitation Facilities, 1982; McCray, 1979) to ensure that the skills and traits assessed can be related to a specific area of work. Through job analysis procedures, work samples can be standardized with regard to tasks, activities, materials, equipment, tools, instructions, and scoring procedures.

As discussed in Chapter 5, the primary tool of job analysis is the *Handbook for Analyzing Jobs*, published by the Department of Labor. To perform a job analysis correctly, the evaluator must observe a job site and work area to identify the work activity, job requirements, and environmental conditions that are important to job performance. The *Handbook for Analyzing Jobs* outlines the following systematic study of the worker on the job to be analyzed:

1. What the worker does in relation to data, people, and things (Worker Functions)
2. The methodologies and techniques employed (Work Fields)
3. The machines, tools, equipment, and work aids used (MTEWA)
4. The materials, products, subject matter, or services which result (MPSMS)
5. The traits required of the worker (Worker Traits)

STUDENT CHARACTERISTICS

The evaluator will next review the specific assessment questions and student disability characteristics that must be taken into account and that must be evaluated through the work sample. If the student population is visually impaired, Braille directions may be printed to aid in instructing, orienting the student, or in sequencing the work tasks. Similarly, the outcome of work sample evaluation activity may be organized around specific student traits (tactile perception, dexterity, sound localization, cognitive/perceptual ability, coordination, awareness of work space organization) that may be important to performance of the work task by the student.

Modifications to the work sample instruction, orientation, and performance may be required to compensate for the student's disability. Student characteristics will dictate how instruction and administration formats are developed to maximize subsequent performance potential. For example, opportunity for familiarization to tools and equipment is important to visually impaired students. Similarly, work aids such as color coding may be necessary for mentally retarded students for more complex assembly activity. To be useful to the student, the modifications or work aids must also be suitable to the work task and work site in industry.

NORMING THE WORK SAMPLE

Without a standard for comparing behavior, performance on a work sample cannot be understood and is not useful to the student or evaluator. At this stage of work sample development, the evaluator is presented with a decision about how to make comparisons and interpret performance. Usually, two methods are used to evaluate an individual's performance on a work sample. The first method is called Methods-Time-Measurement (MTM). MTM is performed by industrial engineers who evaluate the time in motion of fingers, hands, arms, and body, and assign a specific time value to the motion(s). MTM time standards are based on experienced workers from an industrial setting, a format which is not always appropriate when examining inexperienced handicapped students.

The second method for establishing normative data involves psychometric principles. These principles have been reviewed in Chapter 6. The evaluator must choose between different norm group options including:

- Student norms
- Disabled student norms
- Training norms
- General population norms
- Competitive employment norms

It is not necessary to obtain norm groups from all categories. Determining which norm group and norm group standards to use is governed by the questions to be answered through assessment. If questions involve how the student would perform in a particular job, competitive norms would be needed. If the work sample is used to select students for a vocational training program or supported work program, training norms would be most useful.

GATHERING NORMATIVE DATA

Once the justification or rationale for the work sample has been identified, job analysis identifies the equipment, tools, and machines to be used. Next, the equipment and work aids have to be designed and constructed, and the test administration procedures and instruction format have to be developed. Decisions are then made about the characteristics of the norm group. Once these tasks have been completed, the work sample is ready for field testing. The evaluator is then able to begin the process of gathering normative information about the sample.

As reviewed in Chapter 6, norms are developed in order to measure the student's performance on the work sample against a group of other persons who have also taken the work sample. How then, are the norms set up for the work sample? First, what is meant by the word "norm"? When raw data are compiled on the number of errors each person makes when taking the work sample, they tell us very little unless there is some way of measuring what the raw data mean. Thus, norms are measures used to describe the test performance of specified groups of people who have taken the work sample under standardized conditions. The norm group is a group of people with whom the student is compared. Norms compare the students responses to the responses of the norm group, whose characteristics (e.g., job, age, education, disability, geographic location) are known and recorded.

In developing norming procedures the distinction between *sample* and *population* should be maintained. Anastasi (1976), notes that "the former refers to the group of individuals tested. The latter designates the larger, but similarly constituted, group from which the sample is drawn" (p. 89). So, if we are fortunate enough to be able to secure entry level carburetor mechanics as a sample, these individuals would represent a population who work in craftsmanship and related worker trait group. Generally, it is difficult to engage the services of workers in the field, and evaluators usually ask individuals in the facility to take the work sample in order to establish the normative sample. This could include staff members, students, or clients.

An important aspect of the norming process is the matter of *standardization*. The final report of Task Force 7, VEWAA Project (Ehrle, 1975), describes standardization as "A uniformity of procedures used in administering and scoring of a measuring instrument" (p. 91). The concerns of Anastasi (1976), regarding standardization on psychological tests are applicable to work samples:

> If the scores obtained by different individuals are to be comparable, testing conditions must obviously be the same for all. Such a requirement is only a special application of the need for controlled conditions in all scientific observations. In a test situation, the single independent variable is usually the individual being tested. (p. 25)

Some of the aspects of work sample administration that must be standardized are (1) detailed directions for administration, (2) materials and equipment used, (3) time limits, (4) error count, and/or number of units produced, (5) oral, written, filmed, and taped instructions, (6) and methods and content of performance and behavioral observations.

How does the evaluator go about norming the work sample? In either developing a new work sample, or in developing expanded norms on a commercially produced work sample, the evaluator may use procedures that do not entail overly complex record keeping. Probably the simplest yet most effective method is that presented by Dunn (1970). This method places student performance in one of three categories: Above Average–75th percentile and above; Average–26th through the 74th percentiles; Below Average–the 25th percentile and under. Dunn recommends the following five-step procedure for estimating the cut-off scores for 25th and 75th percentiles:

Step 1. Use a separate 3 x 5 card for each person for recording the score obtained on the work sample performance. Recorded information should be standardized; time taken to complete the task, number of units produced, number of errors made, and demographic information such as age, sex, grade, source of referral, etc.

Step 2. Arrange the cards in order from the lowest to the highest score. A low score means high performance if the evaluator is using task completion time or number of errors as the score; a low score means low performance if the score is the number of units produced.

Step 3. Count the cards and divide the number by four. Any fractions should be rounded off to the nearest whole number. This shows the number of cards, or cases needed to make up 25 percent of the total.

Step 4. Using the number found in Step 3, start with the lowest score, and count off the required number of cards. Check to make sure that cards with the same score have not been separated. If this happens, determine if there is a more natural breaking point by looking at the next highest and next lowest scores. In this step the lowest 25 percent of the scores has been ascertained.

Step 5. Starting with the highest score, count off the required number of cards, using the number found in Step 3. Check again to make certain that cards with the same score have not been separated. In this step the highest 25 percent of the scores has been determined. In Step 2 the meaning of a high score in terms of performance was ascertained.

The cut-off scores found in Steps 4 and 5 should now be recorded. Scores between these cut-off scores define the middle 50 percent of the cases, or the average group.

The evaluator is able to record and check the student score on the work sample against the scores for the average range of performance. Scores falling within this range rate the student as average, and outside this range as either above or below average—depending on which side of the middle range the scores fall.

DEVELOPING RELIABILITY AND VALIDITY DATA

Reliability and validity estimation has been discussed in Chapter 6 in relation to psychometric tests. However, establishing the reliability and validity of a work sample is a more complex task than with traditional paper and pencil tests, and many authors raise legitimate questions about the extent to which either can be realistically established.

ESTIMATING RELIABILITY

The primary characteristic of reliability in a measurement instrument, including a work sample, is consistency. Can the evaluator trust that the test is stable and will evaluate performance consistently over time?

The issue in work sample development is that reliability is difficult to establish, because learning is expected to take place on each task performance and most students are expected to perform better on the second and subsequent trials (Pruitt, 1986). Most work samples do not lend themselves to split-half reliability estimations, where one-half of the tasks are performed at one time, then compared to performance on the other half.

One method to take actual and expected performance changes into account is to examine the student's performance change (scores on a second trial) against the distribution of scores within a group of students. When a group of students are evaluated on assembling a 12-piece bicycle lock, the performance speed and error rate may decrease from trial to trial. Assumptions about reliability or consistency are possible if the students' relative standing within the group remains the same (Botterbusch, 1981).

ESTIMATING VALIDITY

The most widely used validation procedure in work sample development is content validity. Content validity relies on job analysis procedures (*Handbook for Analyzing Jobs*) to compare work sample activities to the tasks, requirements, and equipment found in a particular job or occupational cluster. As validation is performed through a review of job descriptions in the DOT, as well as direct observation of work activities, it is the most expedient validation procedure and serves to link the work sample to work expectations. However, the evaluator involved in developing in-house work samples is encouraged to use multiple validation procedures in order to respond to the many questions raised about student potential.

If content validity is the only validation method used, only questions asked about the work sample being an accurate measure of the job tasks required for a particular job are possible. With other validation procedures, more informative questions are possible, such as "Can the student perform well as a clerical aide?" "Will the student complete the technical training course?" "Is the student able to assemble electrical components well enough to perform competitively?" Depending on the assessment need, the evaluator will want to develop criterion, predictive, or concurrent validity.

While procedures to validate the work sample are relatively straightforward, the statistical procedures to develop the validity coefficient are complex and should involve a statistician. The important point to understand is that validation may be a lengthy procedure, but is not overly complex. The increased capability to understand student potential makes validation efforts necessary in developing a work sample.

MANUAL DEVELOPMENT

If the vocational evaluator is to use standardized procedure and methodology for administering a work sample and understanding work performance, then a work sample manual is essential. All commercial work sample systems provide manuals, and all have basically similar formats. The manual allows any evaluator to administer the work sample, score performances, interpret results, and understand how the behavior may generalize to training or competitive settings.

The work sample manual is the key to standardization of assessment. It should contain information on the purpose of the test; a description of the narrative group, data collected about the normative sample(s), identification of the equipment, material, tools, and supplies to be used, reliability and validity estimates, administration and scoring directions, as well as any studies that have been performed using the work sample.

A flow chart representing work sample development steps is provided in Figure 8-1.

SUMMARY

The work sample approach offers special needs students a direct opportunity to gain insight into their vocational aptitudes, worker characteristics, and vocational interest. The time spent in evaluation makes possible more definitive scrutiny of the student's functioning, and promotes a clearer understanding of vocational potential.

Step 1. Develop a Work Sample Rationale

    a. Identify Need for Assessment

    b. Identifying Population(s) to be Served

Step 2. Perform Job Analysis

    a. Identify Worker Function Information

    b. Identify Worker Trait Characteristics

Step 3. Identify Student Characteristics and Assessment Needs

    a. Modifications to Enhance Instruction and Performance

    b. Accommodations and Work Aids to Maximize Student
       Performances

Step 4. Standardize Work Sample Activities

    a. Equipment, Tools, Materials Used

    b. Instruction and Administration Format

    c. Measurement, Scoring, and Interpretation Procedures

Step 5. Develop Norming Procedure

    a. Characteristics of Normative Sample(s)

Step 6. Gather Normative Data

    a. Field Test Instrument

Step 7. Establish Reliability and Validity Procedures

Step 8. Develop and Disseminate Work Sample Manual

Figure 8-1. Steps in developing work samples.

By observing and organizing information about work performance, adjustment behaviors, physical functioning, vocational interests, and learning styles, a Qualifications Profile is created on the student. Thus the evaluator is able to measure the student's work sample performance against U.S. Department of Labor standards on such factors as General Education Development, aptitude, and interest levels.

Occupational exploration is a related advantage in the work sample approach; a student may become more aware of the world of work, job duties, and requirements. By varying instruction strategies on the work samples, the special needs teacher is supplied with insight into the student's learning styles. As the student learns about his or her vocational interests and aptitudes as they relate to jobs in particular worker trait groups, the teacher is able to relate classroom academic instruction to the functional math and language factors involved in those job duties, as well as to the general work behaviors required to satisfy an employer.

Work samples assess actual job skill activity. Consequently the students respond more readily and naturally to the testing activity. Also, the concrete information based on work sample performance provides direct, immediate, and usable information for the evaluator, as well as reinforcing feedback to the student.

Although standardized administration procedures often limit the information that may be obtained, the advantages of a flexible work sample approach still outweigh the disadvantages when working with special needs students.

CHAPTER 9

Commercial Work Sample System

$\mathbf{A}$s noted in Chapter 8, the earliest formal work sample system was the TOWER system developed by the Institute for the Crippled and Disabled (now called the International Center for the Disabled) in the 1930s and 1940s. During the 1950s and 1960s commercial work sample systems experienced a tremendous growth that continues to the present day.

Commercial, or industrial work evaluation systems, are primarily designed and produced by a company (e.g., Singer Education Division), or by an institution (e.g., ICD Rehabilitation and Research Center). The system may be sold as a complete package (e.g., VIEWS), by the component(s) desired (e.g., Valpar, Singer, COATS), or by the purchase of the manual alone (e.g., TOWER, SAVE), leaving the purchaser to buy and/or construct the work sample.

This chapter will review several commercial work samples and identify how each may provide information useful to the special educator. Table 9–1 identifies the aptitudes evaluated by several of the work samples identified in this chapter and in Appendix J. The Materials Development Center at the University of Wisconsin-Stout has produced slide/tape presentations of many commercial systems, and the reader who is interested in additional information about a specific work sample is encouraged to contact the Center.

With the advent of the Carl D. Perkins Act of 1984, many school systems have become interested in purchasing commercial systems, but are hesitant because of the relative high cost. This chapter will review considerations important to special education in evaluating whether one commercial system is more appropriate than another.

COMMERCIAL WORK SAMPLE SYSTEMS

TESTING ORIENTATION AND WORK EVALUATION IN REHABILITATION (TOWER)

The TOWER system was the first formal work sample battery, developed after years of preliminary experiences and research. The

TABLE 9-1.
General Aptitudes and Related Work Samples.*

Aptitude Ability	Work Sample Systems										
	TOWER	Singer	JEVS	Valpar	Tap	VIEWS	WREST	Sage	Apticom	MESA	McCarron-Dial
G (General)	X			X				X	X	X	X
V (Verbal)		X	X	X				X	X	X	X
N (Numerical)	X	X	X	X		X		X	X	X	X
S (Spatial)	X	X	X		X	X		X	X	X	X
P (Form Perception)	X	X	X		X	X		X	X	X	X
Q (Clerical Perception)	X	X	X	X		X	X	X	X		
K (Motor Coordination)	X	X	X	X	X	X	X	X	X	X	X
F (Finger Dexterity)	X	X	X	X	X	X	X	X	X	X	X
M (Manual Dexterity)	X	X	X	X	X	X	X	X	X	X	X
E (Eye-hand-foot coordination)	X	X		X			X	X	X	X	X
LS (Learning Style)											X
FA (Functional Academics)	X	X	X	X		X		X	X	X	X
Job Simulation	X	X	X	X		X					

*Listed above are 10 work aptitudes related to worker trait characteristics and a chart identifying work samples covering different traits. The practitioner may choose the most appropriate evaluation tool—one that measures aptitudes needed for individual occupational training programs.

135

system originally was developed for physically disabled individuals, but is presently used for many types of disabled persons.

The TOWER system is based on job analysis and its 93 work samples are categorized under 14 job training areas:

---

1. *Clerical*
   Business arithmetic
   Filing
   Typing
   Payroll computation
   Use of sales book
   Record Keeping
   Correct use of English

2. *Drafting*
   T square, triangle
   Compass
   Working drawing
   Drawing to scale
   Geometric shapes

---

3. *Drawing*
   Perspective
   Forms, shapes & objects
   Shading, tone & texture
   Color
   Free hand sketching

4. *Electronics Assembly*
   Color perception &
   sorting
   Running a 10-wire cable
   Inspecting a 10-wire
   cable
   Lacing a cable
   Soldering wires

---

5. *Jewelry Manufacturing*
   Use of a saw
   Use of needle files
   Electric drill press
   Piercing & filing metals
   Use of pliers
   Use of torch in soldering
   Making earrings & broach
   pin

6. *Leather goods*
   Use of ruler
   Use of knife
   Use of dividers
   Use of paste & brush
   Use of scissors & bone
   folder in pasting
   Constructing picture
   frame
   Production task

---

7. *Lettering*
   Lettering aptitude
   Alphabet & use of T-
   square
   Use of pen & ink
   Use of lettering brush
   Brush lettering

8. *Machine Shop*
   Reading & transcribing
   measurements
   Blueprint reading
   Measuring with a rule
   Drawing to measurement
   Metal layout & use of
   basic tools
   Drill press operation
   Fractions & decimals
   Measuring with the
   micrometer caliper
   Mechanical understanding

9. *Mail Clerk*
   Opening mail
   Date-stamping mail
   Sorting mail
   Delivering mail
   Collecting mail
   Folding & inserting
   Sealing mail
   Mail classification
   Use of scale
   Postage calculation

10. *Optical Mechanics*
   Use of metric ruler
   Use of calipers
   Lens recognitions
   Lens centering & marking
   Use of lens protractor
   Hand beveling & edging

11. *Pantograph Engraving*
   Introduction to the
   pantograph
   Setting up & centering
   copy
   Adjustment of cutter
   Running off a job

12. *Sewing Machine Operation*
   Sewing machine control
   Use of knee lift &
   needle pivoting
   Tacking & sewing curved
   lines
   Upper threading
   Winding & inserting
   bobbin
   Sewing & cutting
   Inserting, lacing, &
   typing
   Art paper banding

13. *Welding*
   Measuring
   Making a working
   drawing
   Identifying welding
   rods
   Use of acetylene torch
   Use of rods & electrodes
   Use of torch & rod
   Measuring & cutting
   metal
   Soldering

14. *Workshop Assembly*
   Counting
   Number & color
   collation
   Folding & banding
   Weighing & sorting
   Counting & packing
   Washer assembly
   Inserting, lacing,
   & tying
   Art paper banding

As the work samples have high face validity, there is ample opportunity for vocational exploration. Recommendations are more training oriented than job oriented and are limited to jobs that are directly related to the work sample.

The TOWER system has served as a model for the development of subsequent simulated work samples as well as "home-made" work samples. The system is a flexible, open-ended, work-oriented system where individuals work at their own pace and are provided with ample opportunity for work exploration. Since the actual tasks of the trade are used, there is significant carry-over into the world of work. The TOWER system takes two weeks to complete, but the evaluator may choose work samples more pertinent to training or job opportunities.

THE SINGER CAREER SYSTEM

The Singer Vocational Evaluation system is a series of independent, hands-on work samples. Presently, there are over 30 work samples available, including bench assembly, drafting, electrical wiring, soldering and welding, cooking and baking, cosmetology, soil testing, photo lab technology, sample making, and information processing.

The student is presented with the tools, material, equipment, and supplies necessary to perform the work sample and is instructed through an audiotape and slide format. Although many of the work areas are physically and cognitively demanding, several are suitable for special needs students.

The work samples use both the USOE Career Cluster Classification, the DOT Occupational Group Arrangement (OGA) and related DOT job titles. By presenting hands-on experience with industry-related tools and material and by relating closely to the DOT, the work sample promotes career exploration and exposure to different job demands. Over 25 work factors are incorporated into the system and the results can be related to more than 1,000 job areas in the DOT.

Each work sample activity requires from 1.5 to 2 + hours to complete, and work sample selection is important. Each unit offers three types of norms: participant, employed worker, and MTM. Reported test-retest reliability coefficients are in the .61 to .71 range for a mentally retarded population. Content validity is based on the job-task matrix and the job analysis for each work sample.

PHILADELPHIA JEWISH EMPLOYMENT AND VOCATIONAL SERVICE WORK EVALUATION SYSTEM (JEVS)

The Jewish Employment and Vocational Service began development of its work sample system during the late 1950s. Originally developed for use in WIN and CEP Programs, the JEVS has a wide distribution as an assessment tool for special needs populations. The system is based on the Work Trait Group Arrangement of the DOT and is also related to the Guide for Occupational Exploration. The 28 work samples are arranged under 10 worker trait groups:

Areas of Work, Worker Trait Groups, and Work Samples	*DOT (4th Ed.) Worker Function Number*			

ELEMENTAL WORK

1. *Handling*:	.667	.687		
Nut, Bolt, Washer Assembly				
Rubber Stamping				
Washer Threading				
Budgette Assembly				
Sign Making				

CLERICAL WORK

2. *Sorting, Inspecting,*	.484	.485	.487	
Measuring and Related Work			.584	
Tile Sorting	.585	.587		
Nut Packing	.684	.685	.687	
Collating Leather Samples				

MACHINE WORK

3. *Tending*:				
Grommet Assembly	.685			

CRAFTS

4. *Manipulating*:	.484	.574	.584	
Union Assembly	.664	.684		
Belt Assembly				
Ladder Assembly				
Metal Square Fabrication				
Hardware Assembly				
Telephone Assembly				
Lock Assembly				

CLERICAL WORK

5. *Routine Checking & Recording*:	.562	.567	.587	
Filing by Number	.687			
Proofreading				

6. *Classifying, Filing, & Related Work*:	.362	.367	.382	.387
Filing by Three Letters				
Nail & Screw Sorting				
Adding Machine				

Payroll Computation
Computing Postage

7. *Inspecting & Stock Checking*:	.364	.367	.382
Resistor Reading	.384	.387	.484
	.487		

CRAFTS

8. *Craftsmanship &*	.261	.281	.361
Related Work:	.381		
Pipe Assembly			

9. *Costuming, Tailoring,*	.261	.361	
and Dressmaking			
Blouse Making & Vest Making			

ENGINEERING

10. *Drafting & Related Work*:	.161	.261	.281
Condensing Principle			

The work sample manual presents photographs depicting how the work sample should appear to the evaluee before beginning to work with it, or the correct assembly, as well as types of errors affecting the score. The sequence of administration follows generally from the simplest worker trait groups and work samples through the more complex traits and samples.

Most instructions are presented orally with a demonstration. Written instructions are used only when reading is required for the occupational area being sampled. Twenty specific and four global work performance factors (size discrimination, form perception, accuracy, neatness) and 20 work behaviors are specified as observational criteria.

The work samples may be considered to be abstract enough that they do not allow for as much vocational exploration as do the more moderately and highly complex samples. The excellent tie-in with the DOT worker traits, however, makes for a much more logical approach to final determinations of job recommendations.

The norm group was expanded nationally in 1975 to provide a normative data base of over 1,100 clients and students. There is no published reliability data available at this time. Although there have been no validation reports since the system was revised, Nadolsky's (1973) research indicates that the system has validity for assessing immediate employment potential. One week is required to complete all work samples. The severely disabled may be able to complete only half of the work samples, depending on the extent and type of disability.

VALPAR COMPONENT WORK SAMPLES

The Valpar Component Work Sample series was developed by the Valpar Corporation and represents a trait and factor approach to vocational evaluation. The manual for each work sample relates performance to different worker trait group arrangements as well as to specific occupations. Although Valpar work samples were originally developed for injured workers, there are now several norm groups, including the mentally retarded, the deaf, and employed workers.

Currently, there are 16 work samples in the series. The work sample manual lists a wide range of DOT titles for each work sample. The samples include the following:

  (1)   Small Tools (Mechanical)
  (2)   Size Discrimination
  (3)   Numerical Sorting
  (4)   Upper Extremity Range of Motion
  (5)   Clerical Comprehension and Aptitude
  (6)   Independent Problem Solving
  (7)   Multi-Level Sorting
  (8)   Simulated Assembly
  (9)   Whole Body Range of Motion
 (10)   Tri-Level Measurement
 (11)   Eye-Hand-Foot Coordination
 (12)   Soldering and Inspection (Electronics)
 (13)   Money Handling
 (14)   Integrated Peer Performance
 (15)   Electrical Circuitry and Print Reading
 (16)   Drafting

The evaluator may decide which component to purchase and use and the order of work samples to be administered. The manual for each work sample, in addition to listing related DOT job classifications, describes and illustrates the work sample, gives instructions for administration and scoring, instructions to the student, normative data, and a bibliography.

Instructions are given orally and by demonstration. Reading is required only to perform certain tasks. The 17 defined worker characteristics, on which the evaluee is rated on a 5-point scale, are identical for each work sample. The work samples do not allow for formal practice to allow the client to reach an established criteria level (separation of learning from performance), but the evaluator is strongly encouraged to ensure a thorough understanding of the task before timing begins.

Since the work samples are compact (as well as sturdily built) and portable, space requirement is kept at a minimum. Although face validity may not be as high with reference to the work samples looking like the jobs whose factors they purport to be assessing, evaluee motivation generally is high due to the work samples being interesting. Test-retest reliability coefficients for the work samples are quite high, but no validity information is provided.

Students generally find the work samples appealing and interesting. The appeal to the evaluator is that components can be chosen based on student characteristics and evaluation need. Most evaluators find that the components can be incorporated easily into an overall evaluation program. Most work samples require 30 minutes or more to complete.

VOCATIONAL INFORMATION AND EVALUATION WORK SAMPLES (VIEWS)

The VIEWS system was developed by the Philadelphia Jewish Employment and Vocational Service especially for mildly, moderately, and severely mentally retarded individuals. VIEWS contains 16 work samples based on six worker trait groups within four broad areas of work in the third edition of the DOT and the Dictionary of Worker Traits (DWT). (Worker function codes for each of the samples have been converted to the fourth edition of the DOT and DWT.)

Areas of Work and Worker Trait Groups	*DOT (4th Ed.) Worker Function Numbers*	
ELEMENTAL WORK		
1. *Handling*:	.667	.687
Tile Sorting		
Nuts, Bolts, & Washers Sorting		
Paper Count & Paper Cutting		
Collating & Stapling		
Stamping		
Nuts, Bolts, & Washers Assembly		
Screen Assembly		
2. *Feeding-Offbearing*:	.686	
Machine Feeding		
CLERICAL WORK		
3. *Routine Checking & Recording*:	.562	.678
Mail Sort		
Mail Count		

4. *Sorting, Inspecting,*	.484	.485	.487
Measuring, & Related:	.564	.567	.584
Nut Weighing	.585	.587	.683
Valve Disassembly	.684	.685	.687

MACHINE WORK

5. *Tending*:	.685
Drill Press	

CRAFTS

6. *Manipulating*:	.484	.664	.684
Budgette Assembly			
Valve Assembly			
Circuit Board Assembly			

The *VIEWS Evaluator's Handbook* presents administrative details, such as setting up each work sample, instructions for the evaluator and client, and procedures for scoring.

The work samples are administered from least to most complex. The work sample developers have built into administration a process to separate learning from performance. Administration is performed in the following phases:

1. *Demonstration Phase*: The standardized instructions are read and the correct procedures are demonstrated by the evaluator.
2. *Training Phase*: The evaluator instructs the evaluee until the prescribed criterion of mastery is achieved. Mastery entails the evaluee's performance of a specified number of units, or consecutive operations, without requiring assistance or making errors.
3. *Production Phase*: The evaluee works independently, after training is completed, in the production phase. The production goal is to perform a set number of units or cycles on the work sample.

The evaluator uses oral instructions and modeling during the demonstration phase, thus, reading is not required for any of the work samples. There is extensive student involvement in the training and subsequent sessions.

Ten work performance factors (e.g., finger dexterity, motor coordination) are to be observed, as are certain work behaviors (e.g., attendance, communication). The final report format includes such items as general observations, interpersonal relations, and worker characteristics, as well as job and training recommendations within the six worker trait groups. There is some opportunity for vocational exploration on the work samples although several tasks are more abstract in nature.

One week is required to complete the system. The VIEWS 1979 norms are based on the performance of 452 mentally retarded persons (mean I.Q. = 53, ages 15 to 61). In addition to a 3-point rating scale, MODAPTS (Modular Arrangement of Predetermined Time Standards) are available.

McCARRON-DIAL WORK EVALUATION SYSTEM (MDWES)

This system was designed and developed by Dr. Lawrence T. McCarron and Dr. Jack G. Dial as a predictive approach to work evaluation for the mentally retarded and chronically mentally ill, using a neuropsychological theoretical base. The MDWES is probably more accurately classified as a work evaluation system than as a work sample battery. The system is organized around the following five neuropsychological factors and testing procedures:

1. *Verbal-Cognitive*—Wechsler Adult Intelligence Scale or the Peabody Picture Vocabulary Test. In many instances, an achievement test such as the Wide Range Achievement Test (WRAT) or the Peabody Individual Achievement Test (PIAT) is also given.

2. *Sensory*—Bender Visual Motor Gestalt Test (BVMGT) and the Haptic Visual Discrimination Test (HVDT). For visually disabled clients, the Haptic Memory Matching Test (HMMT) is used in place of the HVDT and the BVMGT.

3. *Motor*—McCarron Assessment of Neuromuscular Development (MAND). Fine Motor Skills Assessment: Beads-in-Box; Beads-on-Rod; Finger Tapping; Nut-and-Bolt Task; Rod Slide. Gross Motor Skills Assessment: Hand Strength; Finger-Nose-Finger Movement; Jumping; Heel-Toe Tandem Walk; Standing on One Foot.

4. *Emotional*—Observational Emotional Inventory (OEI).

5. *Integration-Coping*—Dial Behavior Rating Scale (BRS) and the Street Survival Skills Questionnaire (SSSO).

The administration of the tests is sequential from factor one through five. Although the first three factors may be assessed in one day, the emotional and integration coping factors require a minimum of one week of systematic observation. Instructions are oral and by demonstration.

Little opportunity is afforded for the evaluee to engage in vocational exploration, partly because the system offers little by way of face validity related to actual jobs. However, the system appears to be useful in fulfilling its intended purpose of assessing the student's ability to function in one of the following five areas: Day Care, Work Activities, Extended Sheltered Employment, or Community Employment.

The norming practice, validation, and determination of reliability is very thorough. In addition, the developers have had a consistent program of research and detailed study with the instrument.

WIDE RANGE EMPLOYMENT SAMPLE TEST (WREST)

The WREST was originally developed at the Opportunity Center, Inc. to aid in assessment of mentally retarded and physically handicapped individuals. Today, the WREST is marketed by Jastak Associates, Delaware.

The 10 work samples are listed in the order in which they are administered:

1. *Single, Double Folding, Pasting, Labeling, and Stuffing*
   Handling and folding paper envelopes. Requires some degree of dexterity and orderliness.
2. *Stapling*
   Using hand stapler. Requires ability to use small mechanical devices. Requires spatial judgment and accuracy.
3. *Bottle Packaging*
   Assembling eight pegs in bottle-shaped enclosure. Requires color perception, dexterity, and coordination.
4. *Rice Measuring*
   Filling vials in various measurements with fine material. Requires judgment of quantities, speed, and accuracy.
5. *Assembling*
   Assembling assorted screws and nuts on board to match sample row. Requires speed and accuracy in fine finger dexterity and manipulation and ability to recognize pattern and pattern construction.
6. *Tag Stringing*
   Inserting string through hole in card, forming loop, and placing ends of string through loop. Requires ability to work with both flexible and semiflexible materials.
7. *Swatch Pasting*
   Placing paper swatches accurately on lines of standard swatch sheet. Requires neatness, some judgment of spatial relations, dexterity, and accuracy.
8. *Collating*
   Placing different colored sheets of paper in proper order and collating and cross-filing them. Requires color perception, accuracy, dexterity, and speed.
9. *Color and Shade Matching*
   Matching squares and rectangles of various colors of leather swatches and matching them to same shapes and colors on sample sheet. Requires both color and form perception.
10. *Pattern Matching*
    Inserting various colored wooden pegs in holes in a block to reproduce a pattern. Requires color and form perception.

These work samples are administered in sequence, although each work sample is independent of the others. The WREST may be administered to an individual, or to groups of three to six persons (with duplicate sets). Around 1.5 hours are required for administering to one person, and about 2 hours are required for three to six persons. Little student involvement is involved due to the resemblance of the WREST to a formal testing situation.

Instructions are oral and by demonstration, and no reading is required. Each work sample has a practice period prior to testing to separate learning from performance. The simple nature of the work sample activity makes the WREST of little use in job exploration.

Normative information is provided in the manual for men and women, but the source and demographic information is not given other than age and that some are employed workers. Reliability coefficients are very high, based on 428 employed workers, with correlations exceeding .90 for the various work samples. Validity data on the 428 workers yields correlations of .86 (time) and .92 (quality).

The 10 work samples in the WREST are short and thus provide the evaluees with short-term rewards or reinforcement. The samples assess primarily the dexterity and manipulative abilities for individual assignment to workshop vocational activity.

APTICOM

Apticom is a system produced by the Vocational Research Institute of the Philadelphia Jewish Employment and Vocational Service. Apticom is a desktop microcomputer designed specifically for assessing an individual's aptitudes, job interests, and language and mathematics skill levels.

The Apticom unit consists of a portable instrument with a slanted front containing a built-in display and keyboard. A panel for each subtest is placed on the front, allowing red lights to show as the user inserts a probe to indicate multiple choice answers. The evaluator moves control switches at the rear to set Apticom for the various subtests and activities and to activate the printer.

Apticom assesses for the same subtests as the General Aptitude Test Battery (GATB) and adds eye-hand-foot coordination. Correlational studies between Apticom and the GATB show extremely high validity correlations with the General/Verbal/Number (GVN) scores, strong relationships with the Spatial/Form Perception/Clerical Perception (SPQ) scores, and acceptable moderate relationships with the Finger Dexterity (F) and Manual Dexterity (M) scores of the GATB. The reliability coefficients display a mean correlation for GVN of .86, SPQ of .82, while KRM is .70.

There are six panels of multiple choice questions covering the 12 interest areas of the *Guide for Occupational Exploration* (GOE). Based on correlation with the USES Interest Inventory, ten areas have a validity coefficient above .75, while nine areas have test-retest correlations above .80. The Educational Skills Development Battery not only ranks the student's language and math skill levels, but breaks down the level of functioning in various skills.

The final printed report lists jobs under the GOE Interest Area and OAP number and critical aptitudes. Jobs within the evaluees assessed capabilities are listed with DOT title and code, as well as GED and SVP requirements. The Data Entry Panel enables the evaluator to choose various report options if the comprehensive report is not required. Around 90 minutes are required to complete the system. Although reading may be a problem for some special needs students, Apticom measures vocationally related aptitudes that often are difficult to measure due to the evaluatee's limited cognitive ability or lack of reading skills.

MICROCOMPUTER EVALUATION AND SCREENING ASSESSMENT (MESA)

MESA was developed by Valpar International in Tucson, Arizona. It is a vocational screening program that can be supplemented by Valpar's component work samples for those students who need a more comprehensive assessment. MESA is linked to the worker traits profile of the DOT, and applies a Methods Time Measurement (MTM) process to the timed hardware work samples.

MESA contains 23 subtests, work samples, and inventories. Thirteen use an interactive computer format to evaluate the student: academic skills (reading, math, vocabulary, and spelling); size, shape, and color discrimination; eye-hand coordination; eye-hand-foot coordination; reasoning; visual memory; and vision screening. There are 10 subtests that use hardware, audio visuals, and paper/pencil tests: vocational awareness; vocational interest; perceptual screenings, talking/persuasive screening; physical capacity and mobility; hardware exercises/tool use; finger dexterity; assembly; instruction following, and problem solving.

One significant benefit to the evaluator working with special education students is that there are no reading requirements for assessment activity on the computer terminal. This is especially useful for learning disabled students who may have reading problems but for whom information in discrimination, sequencing, and problem solving is important.

The MESA comprehensive access profile relates students performance to local job and training programs. The report writer records evaluee performance using a screening profile, a qualifications profile, and an access profile report.

There is more opportunity for evaluator/student interaction in MESA than in other screening systems, both during testing and explanation of the worker traits qualifications profile. The student uses paddles, or small wheels, rather than the computer keyboard, and uses a foot pedal for the eye-hand-foot test. There are both student and adult worker norms. Test–retest reliability coefficients range from .79 to .96 on the subtests. Validity is based on the performance relationships of the various subtests and the requirements of the DOT worker traits qualifications profile.

Completion time for the entire system is four to five hours, depending on the ability of the student. The MESA package makes possible the testing of four students simultaneously.

SYSTEM FOR ASSESSMENT AND GROUP EVALUATION (SAGE)

SAGE was developed originally by Schabacher and Associates and Creative Development Associates, Inc., owned by the Train-Ease Corporation, and marketed by Progressive Evaluation Systems Corporation (Pesco), Pleasantville, NY. It is directly linked with the Fourth edition DOT and the GOE.

SAGE consists of four components covering 14 tests, work samples, and inventories:

- Vocational Interest Inventory (VII)—paper and pencil testing format, linked with GOE.
- Vocational Aptitude Battery (VAB)—paper, pencil and other instruments; 11 aptitudes linked with DOT and GATB.
- Cognitive and Conceptual Abilities Test (C-CAT)—reading, math, and language sub-tests, results linked with DOT/GED levels of functioning.
- Assessment of Work Attitudes (AWA)—paper and pencil; 20 work attitudes categories.

There is reasonable evaluator/student interaction during explanation of the profile form, although minimal interaction during testing. Each test can be self-administered (instructions at fourth grade reading level), or instructions may be read aloud by the evaluator. The norms for VAB and C-CAT are the number of correct responses converted to DOT/GED and Aptitude levels. The AWA uses a Likert-type scale from one to four in scoring. In the VII, responses chosen in each of the 12 GOE interest areas are totalled and compared with set arbitrary cut-off points.

High school students and adults make up the norm base, with small samples, sometimes under 100, used. Test–retest reliability coefficients are reasonably high. Validity data based on correlations with other tests are at an acceptable level. At least four hours are required to complete the system, with the possibility of assessing up to 23 students simultaneously with the aptitude battery.

TALENT ASSESSMENT PROGRAM (TAP)

TAP was developed by Talent Assessment Programs of Des Moines, Iowa, and is marketed by Talent Assessment, Inc., Jacksonville, Florida. Reading is not required since instructions are given orally by the evaluator. Ten different tests are administered: (1) structural and mechanical visualization; (2) size and shape discrimination; (3) color discrimination; (4) tactile discrimination; (5) fine dexterity without tools; (6) gross dexterity without tools; (7) fine dexterity with tools; (8) gross dexterity with tools; (9) flowpath visualization; and (10) retention of structural and mechanical detail.

Administration entails separation of learning and performance with a practice period prior to timing. There is acceptable opportunity for evaluator/student interaction. A hand-scored profile shows the percentile rating of each of the 10 tests, and the highest three test scores form the basis for looking up jobs in the manual. If job titles are selected by use of the computer, a readout is given for the jobs, physical requirements, environmental conditions, SVP, and GED math and language levels. A coefficient of stability of over .85 in test–retest studies is noted.

TAP stresses measurement of perceptual and dexterity tests, tactile discrimination, and retention of details. It does not claim to assess all vocationally significant behaviors. Up to eight students may be tested simultaneously. The tests are very compact and transportable. One evaluator could test eight evaluees in the morning and the same number in the afternoon.

BASIC CONSIDERATIONS FOR THE SELECTION OF A COMMERCIAL WORK EVALUATION SYSTEM

In the preceding pages of this chapter we have taken a cursory look at 11 systems—not all strictly work sample systems. Some, as they stand now, are more in the nature of work exploration systems. Some are not purely commercial, because they are produced by private, non-profit organizations. This list of systems is representative and is not meant to be complete. Other systems could be included which are primarily training and/or work exploratory in nature. A brief description of other work evaluation systems can be found in Appendix J.

With so many commercial systems available, the evaluator and special education administrators can easily become confused about which system or systems would best satisfy their assessment needs. Staff should contact company or institutional representatives, visit other centers which use various systems, look over brochures, and if possible, talk with clients and students who went through the different systems.

With these systems as a basis for consideration, the following outline is offered as a point of departure in evaluating and assessing work evaluation systems. In general, consideration must be given to matters specific to special education that we have discussed to some extent previously, before we look at the points in this outline. Brolin (1973) suggested that the following questions be asked when selecting a work sample system:

1. Does it provide opportunity for success by the student?
2. Does it penalize the student for low academic achievement?
3. Does it penalize for low verbal skills?
4. Does it take into account limited past experience?
5. Does it provide a practice or orientation period?
6. Are testing conditions conducive to testing and does it use spaced rather than massed testing?
7. Does the system have norms for the handicapped as well as for a random sample of the population employed in that occupational area? Does it have reliability and validity studies?

Pertinent questions to ask about system costs would be: What is the cost of the total package? Is it necessary to buy the whole package, or can one or more components be purchased? What are the extra, or incidental costs involved (e.g., training for the evaluator, audio-visual equipment, carrels, tables, expendable items of materials and supplies)? What is the cost of any data processing and print-outs, and what is the turn-around time required for the print-outs? Also related to cost is the length of time required for the average person to take the work samples in the system, and the evaluator/student ratio (e.g., from a one-to-one to a one-to-five, etc.).

Space requirements, durability, and mobility of the work samples must be considered. Can some of the components be stored compactly when not in use? Although experience and professional opinion have shown that between 100 and 125 square feet per student/client usually is adequate for evaluation purposes (Pruitt, 1986), this may vary according to the center, the population, and the length of time in evaluation.

The durability of the work sample is important relative to space and maintenance.

In one sense, no one system can provide appropriate opportunities for all students and all schools. In another sense, any one or two of the systems can be both individualized and at the same time broad enough to meet these varied needs. The primary key to this individualized versus comprehensive coverage question is the vocational evaluator. This person's competencies and ability to establish rapport, and individualize the work samples, will determine the system's effective usefulness.

In view of these questions, the following points should be considered in selecting a commercial work evaluation system:

1. *Type of Classification System*
   Trait factor system
   Job Cluster system
2. *Normative Information*
   Normative population sample
   Reliability data
   Validity data
3. *Cost Considerations*
   Initial cost: System, set-up, training
   Equipment maintenance & replacement
   Expendable materials & supplies
   Computer time & print-outs
   Space requirements
   Evaluator/evaluee ratio
4. *Logical Consistency of the System*
   Is it sequential in nature?
   Is it interrelated?
   Are measures identified clearly?
      Behavioral measures
      Performance measures
      Physical capacity measures
5. *Student Involvement*
   Are there opportunities for work exploration?
   Are there opportunities for vocational counseling?
   Are there appropriate forms for recording and reporting observations and recommendations?

Other considerations could be made which would be important in considering a commercial evaluation system. In order to determine how well any system meets the needs of a particular school or facility, the administrator and/or vocational evaluator should write the system's manufacturer for current information; talk with evaluators in other facilities who are using various systems; talk with clients who have gone through the system; try out the system; view the sound/slide presentation available through the Materials Development Center (Menomonie, Wisconsin) on many of the systems; and read pertinent literature on the systems and on the comparisons of systems (e.g., Botterbusch, 1987).

CHAPTER 10

Situational Assessment
and Job Site Evaluation

Situational assessment is an evaluation process that places the student in a simulated job situation that represents as closely as possible actual jobs in the community. As such, situational assessment provides a direct, realistic, and immediate process for assessing a range of work-related skills and behaviors without placing the individual in a competitive employment environment. In contrast, job site evaluation exposes the student to the range of social, environmental, and production demands of a competitive work environment in a business or industrial setting. Both evaluation procedures provide opportunity to systematically observe behavior in order to identify the student's learning and performance potential. The usefulness of simulated or actual job sites in evaluation rests with their relatedness to the outcome criteria: actual employment in competitive employment settings.

As described in the last two chapters, the goal of work sample evaluation is assessment of work skills and skills potential through structured involvement with actual tasks and equipment over a relatively short period of time. The process of situational assessment is very different; it places the student in actual job situations for longer periods, perhaps a week or more. The goal of situational assessment is assessment of technical ability to perform work tasks, as well as assessment of the impact of the interpersonal and psychosocial aspects of the work environment on work behavior. Observation in situational assessment focuses on the interaction between the student and co-worker, and between the student, the work environment, and work production demands.

Recently, several authors have noted that classroom "prevocational training," classroom job simulations, or work experience in school or sheltered settings, have little utility for individuals with more severe disability (Bellamy, Rhodes, & Albin, 1986; Kiernan & Stark, 1986). These observations are based on findings that individuals with severe

---

disabilities do not easily generalize or transfer work behaviors from a training setting to a job setting. Also, the traditional skills taught in a prevocational curriculum (such as ability to follow instructions, ability to attend to a task, or skills in completing a job application) are not always prerequisite skills for future performance in a competitive work setting. Students could be more efficiently evaluated (and subsequently trained) in the environment or work setting where they would eventually be expected to perform (Hursh, 1987).

These observations raise several important questions about the relevance of situational assessment practice in special education settings:

- Is it realistic to use classroom or school-based job simulations, or should all evaluation sites be community based in order to improve efficiency and provide more functional behavior assessment?
- Can school-based situational assessment be structured to generate student information relevant to curriculum, program development, and/or job placement?
- How are decisions made about when situational assessment should be used, for what student population group, and within which particular simulated work setting?
- Is more research needed about the usefulness of situational assessment with special education populations before schools perform costly market analyses to develop comprehensive situational alternatives?

This chapter responds to these questions and identifies characteristics of situational assessment and job site evaluation important in special education settings. Methodology is prevented for developing situational assessment procedures that provide a continuum of transitional vocational evaluation opportunities to better evaluate and prepare students for employment.

SITUATIONAL ASSESSMENT AND JOB SITE EVALUATION CHARACTERISTICS

Utilization of real or simulated job activities in the school or community settings has long been a common practice in education. In many schools, situational assessment is an informal process of having students work in a school cafeteria, office, maintenance department, or landscaping department. The general goal of the placement is to determine whether the student can "make it" or not. In these situations, little standardization is used to measure actual performance, and the evaluator often relies on the supervisor's judgement about work performance.

The use of situational evaluation sites becomes a tool of vocational evaluation when:

- The evaluation process is standardized to make the evaluation activity consistent for all students
- The student's performance is measured against an objective standard on criteria
- The process yields information about the student and his or her potential or progress

With these broad guidelines considered, however, confusion still exists about what exactly constitutes situational assessment and about how it is performed.

SITUATIONAL ASSESSMENT DEFINED

The Vocational Evaluation Project Final Report (Kulman, 1975) defines situational assessment in a general way as:

A clinical assessment method utilizing systematic observational techniques in established or created environments. Situational assessment includes, but is not limited to:

- Evaluation in a vocational training setting
- Job tryout
- On-the-job evaluation
- Production work evaluation
- Simulated job station
- Work samples. (p. 91)

By definition, situational assessment may incorporate activities in the school or agency setting, as well as in an industrial or competitive work setting.

Pruitt (1986) defines situational assessment as ". . . a systematic method for observing, recording, and interpreting work behavior" (p. 136). As such, situational assessment is appropriate to any work situation, including work samples, laboratory, or vocational training classroom, when observation may be systematized.

From these definitions, it appears that job site evaluation is a form of situational assessment that takes place in a competitive industry or business setting where the student is evaluated by the employer.

As schools increasingly become more involved in developing industry linkages, increased vocational training alternatives, and community-based training, emphasis is placed on examining the procedures and benefits of school-based and community-based programs independently of each other. Situational assessment encompasses the various job simulations available to the student in the school setting, while job site evaluation involves activities in an actual industrial job site. In examining the procedures and benefits of situational assessment and job site evaluation, this distinction will be maintained throughout the chapter.

Situational assessment consists of:

1. Placement in a real, yet controlled, work situation in the school
2. Supervision of the student by employees of the school who may have responsibility for school functioning, but may or may not be trained evaluators
3. Students working with other student co-workers, as well as employees of the school on production or service activities
4. The tasks and work activities important to the performance or purpose of the school or work area (maintenance, clerical, horticultural, etc.).

The purpose of situational assessment is to systematically observe the individual's performance in relation to the characteristics of the work environment, and to systematically adjust work characteristics (tasks assigned, relations to others, amount and type of supervision, production demands) in order to identify the social and environmental factors that may promote or hinder work performance. Situational assessment recognizes that successful performance is a result of the interaction between the student and his or her environment. Situational assessment is not only a process of observing behavior, but is also a dynamic process of systematically altering work characteristics to observe work adjustment and performance.

JOB SITE EVALUATION DEFINED

Job site evaluation consists of:

1. Placement of the student in an actual competitive job setting in the community
2. Supervision of the student by an employee of the job site
3. The student working with employees of the industry or business, as well as a limited number of student co-workers
4. Job tasks or activities that involve real work of the particular industry or business
5. Payment of the student, if production occurs, conforming to wage and hour regulations of the Department of Labor.

The purpose of job site evaluation is to evaluate the student's ability to acquire a job and perform successfully in a competitive employment situation.

OUTCOMES OF SITUATIONAL ASSESSMENT
AND JOB SITE EVALUATION

Although situational assessment and job site evaluation place the student in actual work environments and involve the student with real work activities, there are significant differences in assessment objectives and desired outcomes. Situational assessment is a *proactive* tool that allows the evaluator to immediately and directly adjust or manipulate student activity. Situational assessment is also a *programmatic* tool that is used to provide recommendations for teaching and learning objectives as well as program placement. In contrast, job site evaluation is more *placement oriented*, designed to assist the evaluator and student in identifying the characteristics of the optimal work environment in a business or industry setting.

SITUATIONAL ASSESSMENT

Situational assessment objectives, like all vocational evaluation objectives, are highly individualized and dependent on the student, his or her disability, and present vocational or transitional stage. However, there are specific objectives and assessment outcomes common to all students.

Situational assessment identifies the *skill and ability levels* that the student demonstrates in specific work environments. Four categories of behavior are assessed:

■ *Work Adjustment Behavior.* Does the student demonstrate adequate ability to cope, adjust, adapt, and conform to the roles, rules, "customs," and expectations of the job? Important behaviors include arriving on time, being neat and clean, observing safety rules, returning from breaks or lunch on time, using the time clock, caring for tools, equipment, and work area.

■ *Interpersonal Skills.* Does the student demonstrate adequate interpersonal and social skills to work cooperatively with co-workers, supervisors, and the public? Is he or she able to take directions, ask for help, respond to constructive criticism, or interact appropriately with the supervisor? Does the student demonstrate basic interpersonal skills to promote cooperative work with coworkers? Is the student able to understand role expectations when interacting with and serving the public?

■ *Productivity Behavior.* Does the student demonstrate the emotional and physical tolerance to work steadily and consistently through the work period (3, 4, or 6 hours)? Is the student able to adjust to work demands that may vary throughout a work period? (For example, food service has "busy" and "slow" periods throughout the day.) Is the student able to cope with supervisors who may not state qualitative or quantitative production standards clearly? Does the student perform tasks that are both enjoyable and at times boring?

■ *Occupational Job Skill.* Does the student demonstrate job skills important to the work area, such as ability to inspect, code, assemble, clean, wash, or file? Is he or she able to use the equipment, tools, or materials and/or can the student perform services that the job requires? Are skills demonstrated in a manner that reflects a balance between speed and accuracy?

Situational assessment identifies critical *work setting characteristics* that may promote or limit successful work performance. Work performance does not occur in a vacuum, but as a result of the complex interaction between the student and his or her environment. Situational assessment is an active process that attempts to systematically modify work environment elements to identify the work situations that promote effective worker production. Supervisor attention and short cycle production tasks may be developed for the student who may need immediate and concrete reinforcement to sustain activity. Similarly, assessment may find that the student works best independent of others on repetitive and routine activity; jobs such as coding, filing, or inspection may satisfy these worker requirements.

Poor performance or lack of demonstrated work skill is examined from more than one perspective. First, if the student does not perform a job task correctly, it may be that he or she does not have the particular skill or group of skills needed. The student may not have learned how to assemble, how to code by number, how to measure or weigh, or how to use particular hand tools. The student has not learned the requisite skills, and demonstrates *skill acquisition deficits.*

In contrast, the student may know how to perform the job and demonstrate skill, but the behavior is not performed because the student may not know where to begin, the activity is not reinforced (no incentive to work), the work setting is too confusing, crowded, noisy, or distracting, or the student does not know what standard is to be met to measure job completion. Rather than a task acquisition deficit, the student demonstrates a *skill performance deficit.*

If situational assessment identifies inadequate performance as resulting from a lack of job skills, the assessment recommendation will focus on a *training objective* and *curriculum or program format* to develop the skill(s). For example, the student may need to learn functional academics in areas of linear or liquid measurement, change making, or completing inventory or purchase order forms. Recommendations may also focus on specific job skills (using soldering gun, chronological filing, or transplanting seedlings), and identify the training program (skills training, supported work, or on-the-job training) that would facilitate learning.

If the student demonstrates performance deficits, situational assessment may make recommendations to a vocational instructor, job coach, or job developer about using specific instructional methods, incorporating natural reinforcers or cues into work activity, developing job modifications or accommodations, or using other supports that maintain more independent and sustained work.

Situational assessment also *stimulates exploration of vocational interest*. This is especially true for students who have had limited exposure to the world of work and who may not be able to benefit from paper and pencil interest tests.

For many students, work samples provide opportunity to explore a wide range of job areas in a relatively short period. However, for many special needs students, work samples do not provide adequate time to adjust to the work sample, to learn what is expected, or to familiarize themselves with the tools and equipment. The timed format is not conducive to interest exploration for students such as mentally retarded or learning disabled individuals. These and other students may benefit from the situational assessment approach that provides a longer period of adjustment, self-paced exploration, and multiple instruction and performance options.

Situational assessment also identifies and recommends specific *program alternatives* needed to increase the students' vocational development. These program recommendations may include:

- Occupationally related functional academics;
- Developmental career education;
- Direct occupational skill training (food service, soldering, typing, etc.);
- Community-based options such as:
    Work-study
    On-the-job training
    Supported work
    Enclave
    Student-run business

Program recommendations are based on the student's career development stage (career preparation will use direct skill teaching; transition planning will use enclave and supported work models; career placement will use supported work and work-study), as well as the student's level of skill.

JOB SITE EVALUATION

Situational assessment is a flexible vocational evaluation process; the evaluator is able to adjust the students time in a work area, his or her duties and responsibilities, as well as the physical demands and work environment characteristics. In contrast, job site evaluation places the student in a competitive work environment and the student is expected to meet the production demands of the particular business or industry. With little opportunity to change work patterns, the objectives for job site evaluation involve assessing the student's performance level and the supports that may be used to sustain successful work performance.

Specific objectives of job site evaluation include the following.

1.   Evaluation of *job readiness*. Is the student able to transfer job skills learned in vocational training programs to the competitive setting? Does the student demonstrate skill and aptitude to benefit from instruction on the job? Does the student demonstrate physical tolerance to work for the necessary time periods? Does the student enjoy the work, the people, and the setting? What job-seeking skills is the student able to use in obtaining employment (completing applications, calling employers, interviewing, following up on the job).

2.   Evaluation of *job modifications* and *work environment accommodations*. While situational assessment *identifies* needed job modifications, job site evaluation assesses how the modifications can be *implemented* in a job situation.

Job modifications and accommodations to the individual's disability may take the form of *environmental adjustments*, such as diffused or improved lighting; *physical accommodations*, such as raising or lowering a seat or work table, enlarging print on a computer screen, installing a jig or guide to inspect or measure, or color code assembly bits in a multi-step task. *Job restructuring* may be possible, especially if the business will allow job sharing, flex time, or task sharing.

The evaluator makes modifications that are reasonable, that contribute to productivity, and that do not interfere with the work of other employees.

Job site evaluation also identifies natural cues and reinforcers that may be present in the competitive work environment. The student may use other workers to model work speed for pace, may use clocks, breaks, or counters to self-monitor production rate, or may use break time, lunch, co-workers, or supervisors as reinforcers for completed work.

3.   Evaluation of *supports used to sustain employment*. Not all special needs students will be able to function at competitive levels in the work place. However, most students are able to be productive in competitive settings if assessment is able to identify the supports needed to accommodate the student's disability. Supports may be in the form of people,

such as using job coaches to provide extended training and supervision. Supports may also take the form of transportation to get back and forth to a site, mobility aides to walk from one location to another, or back-up workers if the worker is not able to handle personal stressors for a day or two.

Job site evaluation does not limit itself to information about worker productivity alone. As job site evaluation usually occurs when plans are being developed for competitive placements, evaluation should identify and involve adult community service agencies that are able to provide needed support services. This may involve an Office of Vocational Rehabilitation for job placement assistance or supported employment placement, community agencies to assist in integrating the student into recreation or leisure activity groups, or peer support groups for civic and community functioning.

Identification of a support system on the job and in the community is often the critical difference between successful and productive functioning on a job, or placement in more sheltered settings that are below the student's capability.

SITUATIONAL ASSESSMENT AND JOB SITE EVALUATION TECHNIQUES

As situational assessment examines both student performance and student performance requirements, two independent evaluation techniques are used throughout the assessment process. *Behavior analysis* is a structured observation procedure that measures the student's work behaviors in relation to the work environment characteristics of the specific setting. The purpose is to assess how the elements of the work environment function to support and sustain, or to limit or interfere, with successful performance.

Critical function analysis is an evaluation planning approach to job analysis that studies the job duties and work environment characteristics that relate directly to the student's level of skill and work adjustment behaviors.

BEHAVIOR ANALYSIS

Behavioral observation procedures using behavior rating scales or checklists have been documented in vocational research as useful procedures to identify work skills and adjustment behaviors related to job simulation activity (Hursh & Dellario, 1981; Watts, 1978).

The major limitations of behavioral observation techniques in program planning for special needs students are that they do not link behaviors to specific situational or environmental characteristics and that the scaling procedure used in the rating forms often obscure the specific nature of the behaviors being observed. A typical behavior rating scale is shown in Figure 10-1.

A behavior rating scale may use different scaling measures to assess behavior. *Appropriate interaction with co-workers* may be scaled as "Always, Sometimes, Never," or may be rated on a five point scale from "good" to "poor." However, with these scaling procedures, the characteristics of the behavior that make it important to work performance are not clearly identified.

Behavior analysis is a more functional approach in situational assessment. This approach uses systematic behavior observations that identify how adjustment behaviors, interpersonal skills, and production performance interact with the social, technical, and production demands of the work environments. Behavior analysis not only identifies the specific behavior(s), but links the behavior(s) to known "events" or work environment components that may be contributing to productive or nonproductive performance.

Key ingredients to effective behavior analysis involve:

1. Developing a hierarchy of behaviors that are important to the work environment
2. Developing "behavioral keys," or operational definitions of behavior(s) that have been identified (e.g., student turns off soldering gun when finished using; student will identify current job skills and vocational goal)
3. Linking behaviors to work performance conditions–or identifying *when* and *where* the behavior occurred, *how* often and the duration of the behavior, or the frequency, *who* was involved (if co-workers, supervisor, or the public were present).
4. Identifying the behavior or performance standards: how does the behavior relate to the criterion established; is it performed 50 percent of the time; is it appropriate to industry standards; is the student able to demonstrate the behavior or skill upon request.

CRITICAL FUNCTION ANALYSIS

Job analysis is a systematic and comprehensive process used to study the job tasks and duties as well as the worker requirements needed to perform a specific job. The job analysis process is a lengthy process to perform and educators often find that job analysis procedures are beyond their expertise. More important, information that is identified through job analysis is often too generally defined and does not highlight the essential skill and performance requirements important for the special needs student.

Figure 10-1. Behavior rating scale.

Vocational Skill	Behavior is	
The Student:	Present	Absent
1. Is punctual		
2. Sustains work effort		
3. Organizes work independently		
4. Conforms to shop rules		
5. Follows instructions		
6. Follows sequence of multiple step task		
7. Able to read written instructions		
8. Accepts criticism		
9. Willing to accept new jobs		
10. Responds well to increased work demands		
11. Is courteous and well-mannered		
12. Demonstrates self-confidence		
13. Interacts with co-workers on break		
14. Initiates greeting to co-worker/ supervisor/public		
15. Demonstrates good grooming and hygiene		

Critical function analysis (CFA) is a structured evaluation planning approach to job analysis that identifies job functions and work characteristics that are important to student job performance. The benefits of the critical function analysis process include the following points.

■ The CFA process does not involve an extensive time commitment or high level of expertise by the evaluator or special educator. Very often a complete analysis of a new situational assessment or industrial job site can be performed in one day.
■ The CFA process is goal oriented, examining specific functions that relate to student abilities, limitations, and assessment needs. The functional descriptors are developed with the special needs student's performance level as a guide.
■ The CFA process is program specific, in that not all job tasks or environmental characteristics are included. The student may not be required to perform a full range of job tasks or demonstrate complete job knowledge to perform successfully in a particular work area.

CRITICAL FUNCTION ANALYSIS DEVELOPMENT

The development of a critical functional analysis work sheet may utilize several occupational information resources. Most frequently, the process begins by reviewing written material about a job and listing the typical job duties noted. Most companies or businesses have detailed job descriptions that will identify the employee duties and responsibilities, abilities and skills needed, experience or training needed, and the work hours or schedule. In addition, the evaluator should review resources such as:

■ Dictionary of Occupation Titles and Worker Traits
■ Guide to Occupation Exploration
■ Occupational Outlook Handbook

Rarely do job descriptions or occupation information resources provide information that can describe the range of unique activities, the work atmosphere, or the characteristics of the work environment and building in which a specific job occurs. The next step in developing the critical function analysis is to interview work supervisors and employees about the job. It is important at this stage to identify the supervisor's and employee's opinion about what may be essential job duties and skills.

Finally, the evaluator must visit the potential assessment site and observe workers performing the specific job function. Observations must include information about the job activities and work space, as well as the physical characteristics of the plant, including cafeteria, rest rooms, lounges, parking facilities, and potential architechtural barriers.

CRITICAL FUNCTION ANALYSIS INFORMATION

Information to be used in situational assessment or job site evaluation can be organized in the following categories:

1. Job Duties and Activities
2. Work Devices
3. Social and Physical Demands
4. Work Environment Conditions

The information that has been gained during the analysis activity is evaluated against student characteristics and is incorporated into the job site assessment checklist. Figure 10-2 is an example of a typical Critical Function Analysis Checklist for a clerical aide position.

JOB SITE DEVELOPMENT PROCESS

Situational assessment and job site evaluation are essential vocational evaluation tools in special education. For many students, because of the nature of the disability, placement in actual job simulations is the evaluation methodology of choice when identifying behaviors related to vocational outcome. With more severely disabled students, a valid evaluation of training potential and performance is best obtained in the actual setting in which they will be expected to perform.

Unfortunately, few special education programs use on-site job simulations, and fewer still use industrial job sites as part of a vocational evaluation process.

Often schools have not developed direct relationships with industry because they do not know how to judge which job(s) will be marketable in the future, which industry to contact in their community, who to contact within the company, or what criteria are important in developing a job site.

The following steps are important to choose, develop, and maintain industry based sites that offer evaluation and training opportunities with a positive employment outlook (Shrey, Mitchell, & Hursh, 1985).

LABOR MARKET ANALYSIS

The objective of the labor market analysis is to identify job and career areas that represent a present and continuing opportunity for special needs students within a targeted community. The primary goal

Job Title: _Clerical Aide_   D.O.T. _219.362-010_

Site Address: _____

Evaluator: _L.C. Hawk_

Dates of Evaluation: _12-2-87 through 12-22-87_

Job Duties and Activities

E	I*	
E		1. Sorting mail
	I	2. Preparing mailings
E		3. Copying documents
E		4. Sorting, collating, and stapling reports
E		5. Answering telephone and taking messages
	I	6. file by alphabet
		7.
		8.

Work Devices
(Machines, equipment, tools, work aids)

E	I*	
E		1. telephone
E		2. copy machine
	I	3. electric stapler
E		4. scales
	I	5. stamp pad
		6.
		7.

*E = Essential, I = Important

Functional Academics Required:

Requires functional reading - names, alphabetizing.
Clear writing skills.
Needs to weigh items.

Figure 10-2. Critical function analysis form.

Social/Physical Demands

Student	Activity	% of Time
	Lifting - light	10%
✓	Sitting	50%
✓	Interaction with coworkers	50%
✓	Interact with public by phone	50%

Work Environment Conditions

Student	Condition	Support Action
	DOOR	
	DESK	Adjustment on desk
✓	TOILET AREA	height
	ACCESS WAY	
✓	CAFETERIA	May need assistance
		locating

Work Atmosphere: Student must work with frequent short periods of high production demands (described as "frenzied"). Co-workers very supportive, promote team orientation in clerical activities.

Figure 10-2. Critical function analysis form (*continued*).

in any labor market analysis is not to identify a specific job or job site, but to identify work fields that demonstrate stability or growth in employment potential. This procedure goes beyond examining want ads in local and regional newspapers, resources that may actually mislead rather than assist in labor market analysis or job forecasting. Information sources that should be consulted include:

- Chamber of Commerce publications
- State Employment Division, Job Market Research Division
- State Office of Vocational Rehabilitation, Placement Records
- Occupational Information Coordinating Committee
- *Occupational Outlook Handbook* (National employment outlook)
- Department of Labor publications:
     Monthly labor reviews
     Area wage surveys
     Industry wage surveys

The labor market analysis should identify the occupational clusters that have present employment openings and potential for continuing growth.

INDUSTRIAL ANALYSIS

Once the special educator is better informed about the work fields in the local area that demonstrate employment potential, decisions about choosing a specific employer and job site are made. Shrey, Mitchell, and Hursh (1985) have described an *Industrial Analysis* process that results in a better understanding of industry by the special educator and a positive working relationship between the two.

CHOOSING EMPLOYERS. Preliminary considerations in choosing an industry or business to contact are:

- Employers having the broadest range of jobs at the student's level of functioning
- Largest employers in the community
- Employers that have hired disabled workers in the past (contact the local Office of Vocational Rehabilitation)
- Employers that demonstrate involvement in community issues (funding closed-captioned television, sponsoring Special Olympics, etc.)

PRIOR INVESTIGATION. Prior to contacting an employer, the educator should become informed about the company. What are the employer's products? What is the organizational structure? Is the company local, national, international? Do they have local subsidiaries? The information can be obtained from company annual reports, from state manufacturing associations, or reference resources available at a local library.

WHOM TO CONTACT. There is no one "right" person to contact for all companies, although time can be wasted "selling" the wrong person. While most sources may suggest starting with personnel departments, the Affirmative Action or Equal Employment Officer would make a more appropriate contact. These individuals, by training and experience, are more informed about the needs of the disabled and how it may benefit the company to work closely with special needs students. If the company does not have an Affirmative Action or Equal Employment Officer, the next best step is to ask for individuals who have responsibility for hiring workers who may have a disability.

The goal of the initial meeting is usually to establish a relationship and determine whether there is a foundation for further discussion. Most importantly, if the employer and educator appear to have a basis for working together, additional meetings should be scheduled at that time.

INDUSTRIAL ANALYSIS. During subsequent industrial visits, the educator will gather both broadly based information, to become familiar with the company's overall operation, as well as specific employment based information that will result in evaluation, training, or potential job placement sites.

Information should include:

- Employers experience with disabled persons in the work force.
- Employers experience with school systems (vocational education, special education).
- Employment practice, including:
    Recruitment procedures (internal posting, affirmative action policy, use of want ads, etc.)
    Application procedures (ask for copy of application, ask how questions of physical/mental disability are considered)
    Interview procedures (multiple interviews, who makes hiring decision, what do they look for)
    Prerequisite testing, if any
    Hiring decisions
- Existence of employee support systems
- Attitude of management, supervisors, co-workers toward disabled workers
- Which are stable and which are high turnover jobs
- What characteristics are valued by employer, looked for during interview

■ What are most common reasons for worker being terminated; how is it handled
■ Access to job descriptions

Once an evaluation of the employment characteristics has been gathered, a job site analysis of work areas identified as having particular need, both from the employer's perspective (high turnover), and from the special education student's perspective (potential success), is performed.

JOB SITE ANALYSIS. The job site analysis is more thorough than the critical function analysis described above (although similar information may be gathered). The purpose of the job site analysis is to determine how the site may have potential as an evaluation and/or training site for all special needs students. Critical function analysis is more individualized, identifying evaluation components for a selected student. Job site analysis identifies:

■ *What* an employee would do on a job, including a description of the job tasks involved.
■ *How* the employee performs the tasks, including the methods, equipment, tools, and supplies used.
■ *Why* an employee performs the tasks, and what service or product results.
■ *When* and *how often* each task is performed
  The general or technical *knowledge, skills, and abilities* needed to perform the tasks.
■ The *physical activities* required to perform the job e.g., climbing, lifting, pushing, pulling, carrying, etc.
■ The *environmental characteristics* of the job, including the degree to which the worker will be required to perform under specific environmental hazards such as noise, heat, dust, adequate ventilation, lighting, etc.

Job site analysis organizes a wealth of information about a specific job that is oriented around specific work characteristics and requirements. The information obtained is useful for determining readiness for job placement, performance objectives for school-based training, matching students to specific jobs, or developing in-house work samples or other assessment procedures. Appendix K provides a functional form to organize job site analysis information for use in counseling students, developing transition IEP objectives, as a data base for curriculum development, and as the first step in establishing an evaluation or training site in an industrial setting.

SUMMARY

Situational assessment and job site evaluation represent important vocational evaluation procedures for all special needs students and essential opportunities for many. Chapters 11 and 12 will demonstrate how both techniques can be applied to learning-disabled and emotionally disturbed students.

Special educators have begun to realize the importance of stronger alliances with industry, business, and the community. As this process continues, special educators will develop the organizational, marketing, and business skills needed to work cooperatively with employers, with the result being more varied evaluation and training sites and increasing vocational opportunities for the student.

CASE STUDY

Johnny M.

Johnny had been working as a part of the work-study program in a fast food restaurant at the counter. He enjoyed operating the cash register when there were not a lot of people in line and he could take his time ringing up the sales. He did not care for taking orders or placing sandwiches and french fries in bags for the customers, but he did enjoy keeping track of sales slips and making sure that items would match with the items on the tickets. Johnny always dressed neatly and liked to keep things orderly in the work place.

In the vocational evaluation center he was given *interest tests* which indicated an interest in working with things and objects (1a); in routine, concrete, organized work (3a); and in nonsocial processes, machines and techniques (4b). These interests were noted also in his approach to subsequent work samples.

Through both observation and interview it was noted that Johnny's temperament indicated a preference for repetitive or short cycle operations carried out by set procedures (R) rather than a variety of duties and change. Likewise, his temperament showed a preference for evaluating information against measurable or verifiable criteria (M), and a moderate amount of concern for the precise attainment of set limits, tolerances, or standards (T).

Profile of Johnny M.

Demographics and Diagnostics
Age 17
Emotionally Disturbed (E.D.)
Low back injury

Education / IEP
GED: R, M, L—S (L—1, H—6)

Vocational Evaluation
Aptitudes: (L—5, H—1)

G—3	S—3	K—3	E—4
V—3	P—2	F—2	C—3
N—4	Q—3	M—4	

Interests
1a   Things and objects
3a   Routine, concrete, organized

Temperament
R   Repetitive or short cycle operations carried out by set procedures
M   Evaluating information against measurable or verifiable criteria

Physical Demands
Sedentary and Light only. No climbing (2). No stooping, kneeling, crouching, or crawling (3). Reach, handle, finger, feel (4) OK Talk and hear (5) and Seeing (6) OK

Environmental Condition: I or B OK Noise and vibration (5) not good for E.D.

Johnny's vocational assessment indicated that he functioned at a medium level on time in Worker Trait Group (WTG) 024, classifying, filing, and related, but had some difficulty with the quality of work at a Worker Function Numbers (WFN) level 3 (compiling). Also, in the lab he was able to do jobs in WTG 105, e.g., Valpar 06, Independent Problem Solving, and Valpar 14, Integrated Peer Performance, but only by incurring quite some emotional strain, especially on the latter in working with others. This confirmed his dislike of working with the public under pressure during his work-study program at the restaurant (WTG 029). See Chart 1.

Case Study Chart 1

GOE- 07–Business Detail
GOE- 07.5 = Records Processing
28% of jobs (25) 07.05.03 Records Preparation and Maintenance
024 = Classifying, Filing & Rel.
Total Jobs = 88

MSC. Personal Service Work
(Food Serving, Ordering, Valeting and Rec.)
105–Msc. Personal Service Work
Total Jobs = 66

	024 = Classifying, Filing & Rel. (Total Jobs = 88)	105–Msc. Personal Service Work (Total Jobs = 66)	Student
WFN	.362(10/11.4%),. 367(34/38.6%), 387(35/39.7%)	.474(3/4.5%) .477(13/19.7%),. .674(8/12.1%),. .677(30/45%)	364
GED	R : 3(58/65.9%) M: 1(12/13.6%), 2(38/43.2%), 3(36,40.9%) L : 2(12/13.6%), 3(65/73.9%)	R : 2(38/57.6%), 3(26/39.4%) M: 1(26/39.4%), 2(39/59.1%) L : 1(10/15.2%), 2(43/65.2%), 3(13/19.7%)	3 3 3
SVP	3(19/21.6%), 4(32/36.4%), 5(21,23.9%), 6(13/14.8%)	2(28/42.4%), 3(33/50%)	6
APT	G: 4(3/3.4%), 3(82/93.2%) V: 4(5/5.7%), 3(82/93.2%) N: 4(35/39.8%), 3(48/54.5%)	4(41/62.1%), 3(25/37.9%) 4(44/66.7%), 3(22/33.3%) 4(57/86.4%)	3 3 4
	S : 87(99%) of jobs level 3 or lower P : 4(47/53.4%) Q: 3(52/59.1%)	4(54/81.8%) 4(56/84.8%) 82% of jobs at level 4 or lower	2 2 3
	K : 4(57/64.8%), 3(26/29.5%) F : 4(50/56.8%), 3(35/39.8%) M: 4(66/75%), 3(20/22.7%)	4(42/63.6%), 3(22,33.3%) 4(54/81.8%), 3(9/13.6%) 4(19/28.8%), 3(44/66.7%)	2 2 4
	E : 5(83/94.3%) C : 5(62/70.5%), 4(20/22.7%)	91% of jobs at level 4 or lower 92% of jobs at level 4 or lower	4 3
INT	1a:(35/39.8%), 1b:(29/33%), 2a(24/27.3%) 3a:(81/92%), 4b:(19/21.6%)	1a:(14/21.2%), 2a(51/77.3%) 3a:(52/78.8%)	1a
TEMP	V : (7/8%), R(31/35.2%), P(10/11.4%) J : (16/18.2%), M: (37/42%), T: (62/70.5%)	V : (21/31.8%), R(26/39.4%) P : (60/90.9%)	
P.D.	S(49/55.7%), L(36/40.9%), 3(6/6.8%) 4(73/83%), 5(19/21.6%), 6(61/69.3%)	L(50/75.8%), M(13/19.7%), 3(19/28.8%) 4(64/97%), 5(51/77.3%), 6(17/25.8%)	
E.C.	I(81/92%), B(6/6.8%), 5(3/3.4%)	I(59/89.4%), 5(7/10.6%)	

Although he was given a number of work samples to do, he came out higher in those included in *Worker Trait Group 029, Routine Checking & Recording*. On a rating scale of 1 (low) to 5 (high) his performance was as follows:

WFN: .567, .587, .687	Time	Quality
Valpar		
Numerical Sorting	3	4
Upper Extremity Range of Motion	4	5
Clerical Comprehension & Aptitude	4	3
Independent Problem Solving	3	4
JEVS		
Filing by Numbers	4	5
Proof Reading	3	4
TOWER		
Clerical (Selective)	3	3
Mail Clerk	4	4

Note Chart 2, indicating Johnny's performance compared with the number and percentage of jobs by factor (e.g., GED, Aptitude) for which he could meet the level requirements. On Chart 3 some specific jobs are listed from WTG 029 showing factor levels and comparing Johnny's performance with them. Note that the jobs are sedentary or light, and do not require climbing and balancing (2), or stooping, kneeling, crouching, crawling (3), so would not have an adverse affect on his low back injury.

Case Study Chart 2

CLIENT/DOT (WTG) QUALIFICATIONS PROFILE

Agency/Center_____

Johnny M._____

WTG Title_Routine Checking and Recording 029_____

Worker Function Number(s)_.567 (10/19%); .587 (31/58%)_____

GOE: 05.09.03–Verifying, Recording, and Marking (21% of jobs)
        07.05.03–Records Preparation and Maintenance (19% of jobs)

Elements	DOT/WTG LEVEL: JOBS/%	Student/Client Level
GED	R – 2(18/34.0);3(32/60.4) M – 1(20/37.7);2(30/56.6) L – 2(30/56.6);3(19/35.8)	R, M, L – 3
SVP	2 (18/34.0) 3 (19/35.8)	4 (3–6 months OK)
APT: G	4 (13/24.4) 3 (38/71.7)	3
V	4 (25/47.2) 3 (26/49.1)	3
N	4 (36/67.9) 3 (17/32.1)	4
S	5 (10/18.9) 4 (38/71.7)	3
P	4 (39/73.6) 3 (11/20.8)	2
Q	3 (45/84.9)	3
K	4 (42/79.2) 3 (10/18.9)	3
F	4 (36/67.9) 3 (15/28.3)	2
M	4 (39/73.6) 3 (11/20.8)	4
E	5 (52/98.1)	4
C	5 (36/67.9) 4 (16/30.2)	3
INT	1A (31/58.5) 2A (8/15.1) 3A (51/96.2)	1A 3A
TEMP	R (39/73.6) M (8/15.1) T (27/50.9)	R M
PHYS. DEM.	S (21/39.6) L (31/58.5) 6 (26/49.1) 4 (49/42.5)	S & L only; No climbing No stoop, Kneel etc. Reach Handle (4), OK, & 5&6
E.C. WORK COND.	I (50/94.3)	I Avoid noise vibration (5) & Hazards (6) bec of E.D. 2,3,4,7 OK

This person would _____ would not _____ qualify for this WTG.
Rationale:

Case Study Chart 3

Client Information Name_____ Referred by_____ DOT WTG GOE D.O.T. Title Code Page Code (Industry)	Work fields	M.P.S.M.S.	Physical Demands						Working Conditions (Environment)								GED			SVP	
			Strength (SLMHV)	Climb/Balance	Stoop/Bend	Reach/Handle	Talk/Hear	Vision	I/O/B	Cold	Heat	Wet/Humid	Noise/Vibs	Hazards	Fumes/Dust/Odor	Reasoning (1…6)	Math (1…6)	Language (1…6)	Duration (1…9)	(NPT, V, T, C, or G) TRG
Past Work Experience_____			1	2	3	4	5	6	1	2	3	4	5	6	7	R	M	L	D	T
_____																				
_____																				
_____																				
_____																				
Work Experience Level Maximums (WELM)																				
Current Performance Profile (CPF)																				
Job Possibilities																				
_____																				
_____																				
_____																				
_____																				
Vocational Outcome																				

Significant Vocational Information (educational, vocational, medical, psychological, social)

Aptitudes			Interests			Temperaments		
			Work Activities			Work Situations		

Aptitudes: (low) 5 4 3 2 1 (high)

Temperaments: (1) (2) (3) (4) (5) (6) (7) (8) (9) (0)

Intelligence	Verbal	Numerical	Spatial Perception	Form Perception	Clerical Perception	Motor Coordination	Finger Dexterity	Manual Dexterity	Eye/Hand/Foot Coord.	Color Discrimination	Things 1a	People/Ideas 1b	Business with People 2a	Science/Technology 2b	Routine/Organized 3a	Abstract/Creative 3b	Social/Helping 4a	Non-Social/Machines 4b	Prestige/Esteem 5a	Tangible Productivity 5b	Varied Duty/Change V	Short Cycle/Repetition R	Close Instructions	Control over Task D	Dealing with People P	Working Alone	Influencing Others I	Stress/Risk Taking S	Subj. Eval. of Info. J	Obj. Eval. of Info. M	Interpret Feelings F	Meet Precise Standards T
G	V	N	S	P	O	K	I	M	E	C	1	6	2	7	3	8	4	9	5	0	1	2	3	4	5	6	7	8	9	0	X	Y

Rows (first block): 1 2 3 4 5 6

Rows (second block): 1 2 3 4 5 6 7

Final row: 1

CHAPTER 11

Vocational Evaluation Issues with Learning Disabled Students

Over the past 20 years, attention to the learning and academic problems of learning-disabled students has increased dramatically. Researchers and clinicians such as Cruickshank (1977; 1984), Kirk (1966), Hammill (1976), Hammill & Bartel (1978), and Wiig & Semel (1980) have enlightened educators about the unique capabilities of learning-disabled students, as well as the complex perceptional difficulties that interfere with traditional education methods.

Extensive research in the area of assessment and teaching technology (Hammill & Bartel, 1978; Wiig & Semel, 1980) have resulted in gains in functional academic skill and achievement, to the extent that many learning-disabled students graduate from high school and enter college. More impressive is the growing number of more severely learning-disabled students for whom graduation from high school is becoming a reality.

Unfortunately for students with more severe learning disabilities, training advances in vocational education have not kept pace with gains in traditional academic education.

Studies reveal that over 75 percent of learning-disabled students leave high school unemployed and without plans or resources for employment (Tyrell, 1986; Washburn, 1975). The disabling aspects of the disability dramatically interfere with the process of seeking and maintaining a job. The developmental, perceptual, and social problems experienced during school are amplified in vocational environments that are unsympathetic to the "invisible" disability, to the "accident prone" new kid, or the "forgetful," "disorganized," "rude," or "spaced out" worker.

Specific learning disabilities represent the highest incidence rate of any disabling condition in special education, over 1,741,000 students (U.S. Department of Health and Human Services, 1985). The figures represent an unacceptable waste of individual potential and productivity.

This chapter will discuss the particular vocational evaluation challenges presented by learning-disabled students in special education.

DEFINITIONS AND STUDENT CHARACTERISTICS

Specific learning disability has been defined by the Department of Education as

> A disorder in one or more of the basic psychological processes involved in understanding or in using language, spoken or written, which may manifest itself in an imperfect ability to listen or think, speak, read, write or to do mathematical calculations. The term includes such conditions as perceptual handicaps, brain injury, minimal brain dysfunction, dyslexia and developmental aphasia. The term does not include children who have learning problems which are primarily the result of visual, hearing, or motor handicaps, or mental retardation, or disturbances, or emotional of environmental, cultural, or economic disadvantage. (U.S. Office of Education, 1977, p. 65083)

Note that the definition emphasizes the "psychological processes" that are involved in specific academically related functions.

A definition more related to how specific learning disabilities interfere with functional ability in all life areas is:

> A disorder in one more of the central nervous system processes involved in perceiving, understanding, and/or using concepts through verbal language or nonverbal means. This disorder manifests itself with a deficit in one or more of the following areas: attention, reasoning, processing, memory, communication, reading, writing, spelling, calculating, coordination, social competence and emotional maturity. (Vocational Rehabilitation Center of Allagheny County, 1984, p. 1)

This definition recognizes that within the group of individuals diagnosed with specific learning disabilities there is wide variation in how an individual may "process" information and how difficulties may result in one or more functional problems. One student may have difficulty performing a specific work task due to deficits in understanding verbal directions. Another student may have difficulty performing the same task because of a need to coordinate multistep tasks, or because of visual distractions in the work place.

There are several behavioral concomitants to specific learning disabilities that interfere with work production and could result in loss of a job:

MOTOR PROBLEMS

■ *Coordination*—may bump into work tables or people; may trip over stair or curb; may have balance problems on a ladder; may have difficulty coordinating eye-hand movements (following a pattern); may demonstrate behavior typical of "accident prone" individual.

■ *Handwriting*—may demonstrate labored handwriting; may have difficulty completing job application.

■ *Impulsiveness*—may respond too quickly; may interrupt co-workers or interviewer; may rush into job activity before instructed.

■ *Voice modulation*—may speak too quickly or too loudly; may perseverate in a conversation.

COGNITIVE DEFICITS

■ *Attention to task*—may look around when performing task or talking to supervisor; may lose place in work sequence; may be easily startled by outside noise.

■ *Disorganization*—may have difficulty organizing information (i.e. making career choice, decision making in general); may not be able to orient self in new work environment; may be unable to organize tools to perform a specific task; may upset easily with multiple instructions.

■ *Memory*—may not remember task sequence from day to day; may forget customer request; may forget directions to get from point A to point B; may have memory deficits ranging from short term to long term, auditory or visual sequential memory.

■ *Visual perceptual problems*—may have difficulty identifying errors, monitoring errors, using visual cues to understand when work is completed; may have difficulty understanding memos, job duties, orders; may have difficulty separating essential from nonessential detail.

■ *Time and space*—may have difficulty estimating when a task will be done, when to report for an assignment; may have poor ability to estimate whether it was one week or two months since he or she talked to someone; may be unable to plan day's activities or use time efficiently.

SOCIAL/INTERPERSONAL DEFICITS

■ *Interpersonal relationships*—may have few friends, may not know how to make friends; may be isolated from other workers;

■ *Communication ability*—may appear immature in social situations; may have difficulty understanding long sentences when instructed;

may use similar social problem-solving strategies in different situations (using what works with co-worker also with supervisor); may have "word finding" expressive ability problems; may use words incorrectly or speak in halting, brief sentences; may have problems organizing verbal expressions such as story telling; may forget the punch line in a joke.

■ *Role problems*—may not understand social uses of boss/employee relationship or customer/worker role differences; may respond to job interviewer as a friend or teacher.

■ *Social cues*—may misinterpret facial cues (anger, sadness, concern); may misinterpret verbal cues; may not be aware of how others view him or her;

■ *Emotional limitations*—may have very labile emotional reactions; may be unable to label own feelings; may be depressed or confused; may have low self esteem.

Few definitions incorporate the emotional overlay that is often associated with specific learning disabilities, especially in adolescents and young adults. Emotional components are so much a part of adolescent learning disability, and so critical to successful performance, that they must be considered as equal in importance to the perceptual/cognitive deficits that contribute to vocational success (Cruickshank, 1984; Hursh, 1984). Research by the Vocational Rehabilitation Center in Pittsburgh (1984) found that over 50 percent of individuals exhibited emotional or interpersonal problems that interfered with job performance.

ASSESSMENT CHALLENGES

Current evaluation models used with specific learning–disabled students are not useful in determining vocational characteristics of special needs students. Psychoeducational diagnostic tests (Hammill & Bartel, 1978) have an academic orientation and are diagnostic in nature. Neuropsychological tests (Luria-Nebraska Neuropsychological Battery, Halstead-Reitan Battery) are appropriate diagnostic tools and accurately identify central nervous system dysfunction. However, they have limited ability to provide information about vocational outcome and are difficult to understand by educators.

The difficulties that learning–disabled individuals face with traditional testing (including vocational evaluation) are similar to difficulties faced by other disabled students. Specific problems are created through administration procedures requiring reading, multiple-step instructional tasks, and lack of opportunity to explore, practice, or fully understand performance expectations. In addition, testing and training experiences in the past have resulted in frustration, confusion, and feelings of helplessness. Testing highlights failure, and teaching or training confronts learning–disabled students with their limitations.

Vocational evaluation has a wide range of tools and techniques but few specific tests that are directly appropriate for learning–disabled students (Hursh, 1984). With specifically learning–disabled individuals, evaluation must explore modifications and adaptive assessment practices to attain valid information (Commission on Accreditation of Rehabilitation Facilities, 1982).

VOCATIONAL EVALUATION PLANNING

ORIENTING THE STUDENT TO EVALUATION

As the evaluator initiates testing and evaluation activity, an awareness of the individual's past testing experience must be developed. All too frequently, the student has had little explanation about the purpose of specific tests, less understanding of the evaluation process itself, and has been confused over poor test performance.

As the evaluator and student begin evaluation, the evaluator must make special effort to discuss how vocational strengths and deficits of the student will be identified, the types of testing and simulated work experiences in which the student will be involved, and what he or she would expect to get out of evaluation. Similarly, the evaluator must identify the limitations of testing and evaluation activity that may be present.

Rather than being a passive recipient of evaluation services, the learning–disabled student must be encouraged to be actively involved in the evaluation process. The student works with the evaluator to:

- Assist in choosing the evaluation activity (interest testing, identification of remedial areas, matching worker trait characteristics with a particular job, etc.);
- Assess how useful a particular test may be;
- Discuss how difficult, easy, interesting, or challenging a particular evaluation activity may have been;
- Evaluate how helpful a particular compensatory aid may have been;
- Identify vocational alternatives resulting from the evaluation experience and to specify a particular vocational objective for the student to explore further.

In this way, the student contributes to the evaluation process and is involved in evaluating its results in a more direct way than in the past, learns how to evaluate and discuss strengths, and gradually assumes responsibility for the positive outcome of vocational evaluation. Most importantly, the student begins to develop useful methods of self evaluation and decision making that can be useful in ongoing career planning activity.

ORIENTING THE STUDENT TO THE EVALUATION PROCESS

In addition to anxiety, tentativeness, and concern about taking tests, the learning–disabled student often has practical questions about his or her value as a worker and potential to perform adequately in competitive work environments.

Tests and evaluation activity become valid if the student is able to understand how the tests and the potential testing outcome may be important. If vocational evaluation activity is able to demonstrate a direct relationship with the individual's ability to perform real work, then the value of the evaluation activity is enhanced. What makes this process a difficult one for the learning–disabled student is his or her inability to "match" or relate evaluation activity to a job, or to organize the information to better understand the world of work. It becomes important for the evaluator to organize the world of work in a way that is understandable to the student and to ensure that the student understands how the testing activity and evaluation results are able to relate to his or her potential to perform successfully in a job.

Prior to testing, the evaluator will explain how the world of work is organized and what kind of information is needed to determine potential for a particular job or cluster of jobs. The Department of Labor classification of jobs that has been discussed earlier is particularly useful for this process.

It is not necessary at this time to review with great detail the organizational complexities of the work world. The objective in the initial stage of introducing vocational evaluation is to demonstrate that the evaluation process is based on concrete and practical information needs and that the outcome of evaluation is information and decision making related to the student's vocational potential.

To orient students to how information about jobs is organized, the evaluator should review:

- Occupational clusters and related work groups (GOE)
- Significant work aptitudes
- Work situations related to worker trait characteristics
- Work activities related to worker trait characteristics

STEP ONE

The first step in orienting the evaluation process to the work world is explaining how the world of work is organized according to occupational clusters (the *Guide for Occupational Exploration* [GOE] is

useful for this process). As noted earlier, the occupational clusters and
the range of work groups include the following:

Artistic occupations
Scientific occupations
Plant and animal occupations
Security, safety and law enforcement occupations
Mechanical occupations
Industrial occupations
Business and management occupations
Sales occupations
Customer service occupations
Humanitarian occupations
Leading and influencing occupations
Sports and physical occupations

The GOE is a very readable and informative resource for both the
student and evaluator to use at this stage of evaluation.

STEP TWO

The second step in demonstrating how the world of work is
organized is to introduce the significant work aptitudes that are
necessary for particular jobs. Specific aptitudes required for a job can
be defined and discussed to demonstrate to the student how he or she
may have a constellation of strengths important to a range of jobs or
occupational clusters.

These aptitudes and a short description are found in Appendix F.

STEP THREE

The third step in orienting the student to the work world is io
demonstrate how jobs may be organized according to work situations
and work activities. For example, the evaluator may identify how certain
work situations such as

■ Performing duties that change frequently,
■ Working under pressure, or
■ Dealing with people

may be difficult with particular visual, organizational, or attentional
problems, but that

■ Making decisions using standards, or
■ Influencing people's opinions

may be more suited to the individual (and to his or her particular
interests or experiences). Again, the goal for the evaluator is to

demonstrate to the student that, although he or she may not be able to perform many activities (for whatever reason), there are also many work activities and work situations in which the student may be successful.

The evaluator uses these parameters to demonstrate that evaluation activity may examine different aspects of the work world through an organized approach, and that the student can understand that

- Different duties and requirements exist in the work world;
- A set of skills can be used in a variety of work settings;
- The purpose of evaluation is to identify how his or her skills interact with different work possibilities.

VOCATIONAL EVALUATION INSTRUMENTS AND PROCEDURES

Vocational evaluation has a wide range of tools and techniques available, but few are directly applicable to learning–disabled students. To obtain maximum results from the various formal testing strategies, the evaluator will use relatively few tests in the standardized test administration format but will explore how modifications may be developed to respond to the unique and individualized assessment and performance needs of the student.

Observations of test performance are directed more to the level, type and characteristics of behavior on, or resulting from, the testing activity. This type of information is far more useful in developing teaching or training objectives for vocational IEPs.

CURRICULUM-BASED VOCATIONAL ASSESSMENT

Curriculum-based vocational assessment (CBVA) is particularly useful to screen individuals for learning disabilities as well as to develop information about functional characteristics related to the student. Typical observations that would alert the teacher or guidance counselor to the possibilities of a specific learning disability would include:

- Wide variation between achievement levels and school grades
- Wide variation on aptitude or cognitive ability tests
- Poor writing ability
- Easy distraction, restlessness, poor listening skills
- Clumsy appearance in gym, recess, and class

Assessment should focus on gathering information about

1. Family history
   - any history of learning disability in family

2. Medical history
   ■ unusual illnesses, accidents
3. Psychological history
   ■ any treatment for emotional problems
   ■ periods of depression
4. Vocational history
   ■ involvement in job tryouts
   ■ stated vocational interests/goals
   ■ hobbies, leisure and recreation activities
   ■ after-school activities
5. Educational background
   ■ involvement in special education
   ■ any repeated school grades
   ■ attitude toward school
   ■ grade variations

The teacher or guidance counselor should next observe the student in school and nonacademic activities; for example, recess, lunch, and school sports. Does the student demonstrate friendships, a range of affect, and appropriate affective responses? Does he or she listen well to instructions, or do directions need repeating? Is the student able to follow through an assignment? Does the student maintain eye contact, respond in a mature manner, recognize a teacher/learner relationship?

The teacher will explore how the student views his or her vocational potential, what interests, skills, abilities he or she feels are assets, and whether the student has a vocational goal.

During middle school, the student will be more involved in community-based exploration, involving community, vocation, and training environments. The teacher or staff involved in CBVA should identify job tryout experiences; what the student enjoyed and disliked; which activities were performed well and which ones were difficult; what adaptations or coping behaviors were developed.

FORMAL VOCATIONAL EVALUATION

More formal vocational evaluation techniques evaluate how the student's perceptual abilities and limitations enhance or hinder vocational performance. During middle and high school, the student should explore vocational alternatives to develop a tentative vocational objective and initiate vocational training. If the student has a well-defined vocational goal that appears consistent with his or her abilities, vocational assessment will concentrate on identifying skill training objectives, methods for compensating for functional difficulties, or areas for remediation.

Work samples represent a particularly valuable evaluation activity for the learning–disabled student. The work sample functions to involve the student in functional work tasks, orient the individual to occupations available in the work world, and provide supervised exposure to tasks, tools, equipment, and work situations.

Commercial work samples such as the Singer, COATS, JEVS, Valpar, and WREST provide hands on experiences that are important to the student as well as the evaluator. Although they have great potential in evaluation, there are also cautions that the evaluator must practice. Work sample stations are often filled with tools, equipment, and material and may present an overwhelming organizational task for the student. Adaptations to instructions may be needed to provide a multisensory approach to task instructions and performance, allowing the student to practice and become familiar with all equipment before testing. Instruction methods and directions must be made in small increments, with the student allowed to orient, practice, view demonstrations, and repeat steps before production measurement.

Information from work sample evaluation should be structured around the individual's cognitive, perceptual, and motor abilities. The evaluator should determine if the individual was able to follow verbal (visual) instructions, organize his or her work, plan a task, sequence multiple steps, discriminate between large/small or small/rough or acceptable/unacceptable, solve mechanical problems, and make decisions. Work samples are useful tools to identify, develop, and try out work aids such as visual or auditory cues, pacing structure, motor guides, tape recorders, and so forth.

The usefulness of work samples is a result of the flexible and immediate control the evaluator is able to maintain over the work sample activity. If the evaluator notes confusion in understanding instruction, multiple input can be developed. If task sequencing results in disorganization, the sequence may be altered or adjusted. If the work environment presents too many distractions, cueing aids may be developed. If the task emphasizes instructional or performance activity in a disability-related perceptual mode, other tasks or samples may be attempted. The evaluator is able to gather rich information about learning, performance, and modifications while providing a successful experience for the student.

Situational assessment places the student in a real work situation, where the student is working with co-workers, under supervision of an employee of the school. The major benefit of situational assessment is that the student's social and interpersonal skills are evaluated as well as his or her ability to perform the work activity. Whereas work samples are a relatively short evaluation activity, situational assessment allows opportunity for more extended observation of work performance.

Behavior analysis, as a primary technique of situational assessment, assesses the interaction between the student and the supports, demands, and characteristics of the social and physical elements of the work environment.

Many learning–disabled students have no difficulty being hired for a job, as the disability is not readily apparent or visible. However, disorganization, motor difficulties, distractibility, and/or other functional difficulties may result in their being fired. Situational assessment should focus on the factors that promote sustaining and maintaining work production and positive social adjustment. The focus of situational assessment activity is on social skills and social judgment needed to get along with co-workers, interact appropriately with a supervisor, and/or provide courteous service to the public.

Role-playing techniques are a component of situational assessment that are used to practice, refine, and adjust social and work role situations. Situations such as introducing self, initating "small-talk," listening to directions, asking for assistance, and serving a demanding public can be rehearsed.

Visual cues, tape recorders, timing clocks, and auditory aids can be developed to manage perceptual deficits. A final focus of situational assessment is to identify accommodations that may be needed along with the recommendation for supported work placement, before the individual attempts competitive employment. Transitional work activities are essential training activities for the learning–disabled student and assessment must develop recommendations that identify the supports and accommodatlons that will be used.

CASE EVALUATION

Peter is a 19 year old man who has recently graduated from high school. He is approximately 5'9" tall with a slight build. He is neatly dressed, well groomed, and appears intent and interested in discussing available services and work possibilities.

He describes his school experiences as "average" and notes that he had to repeat grades "once or twice." He is not very specific about why he had to repeat grades and appears hesitant about describing school experiences and related difficulties. School experiences that are discussed with greatest interest and excitement involve carpentry and construction shops. Although he states that these courses were very interesting, he apparently performed only C-level work. However, this appears to be the area of greatest interest for him and the area in which he would like to find employment.

Peter's available test scores are as follows:

WAIS-R

Verbal Tests		*Performance Tests*	
Information	10	Picture Completion	14
Digit Span	11	Picture Arrangement	7
Vocabulary	10	Block Design	6
Arithmetic	5	Object Assembly	12
Comprehension	12	Digit Symbol	7
Similarities	16		

Verbal I.Q.	101
Performance I.Q.	94
Full Scale I.Q.	97

Wide Range Achievement Test

	Grade Rating	*Percentile*
Reading	9.2	55%
Spelling	7.8	39%
Arithmetic	4.5	13%

Peter participated in work-study jobs during school and, after discussion, related the specifics of his most recent experience. Although he was satisfied with his first position, he had especially looked forward to his new position waiting on tables at a local restaurant. The opportunity for good tips was also available. Typical experiences on this job were as follows:

Ben, his boss, introduced him to the restaurant and explained how best to request orders from customers and write them up for the cooks to prepare. He began working with Ben during the first few training days. Ben gave him an order booklet and indicated where they would be working. Peter was unable to follow where he indicated. Peter tried to see how Ben put together the order, but couldn't get close enough to see what was written.

Ben spent the day talking him through the job and explaining detail after detail. Peter listened but was continuously distracted by the other workers, customer noise, and general noise of kitchen activity. When Peter worked the following day, he had his own section to cover. He took an order from a man and a woman but did not know where to get the prices. He asked Ben, but had not asked whether coffee was black or regular. He could not remember how to make set-ups of salads and only approximated amounts of food. He would bring the order to the customer, but would forget to bring the hot items. It was hard to differentiate between large and small drinks. Ben became upset when

Peter would take his item to replace the items he had forgotten to order. Peter would forget to give bills and often would not have them itemized when he did remember.

The first few times using the cash register, he would forget how it worked. Ben became upset when asked to show him again how to use it. Understandably, Ben was not happy when Peter rang up incorrect prices and Ben had to repeatedly void the transaction. Peter's overall boss was understanding, but other co-workers were frustrated with Peter's endless questions. He had difficulty remembering prices even when studying the menu at home. He would forget where utensils, napkins, and dispensers were. Often, he would ask where something was only to find it appear right in front of him when Ben pointed it out. It was difficult to remember left from right, whether an item took a large amount of this and a small amount of that, or vice versa. He also had trouble navigating the crowded floor, often bumping into others or the tables. Most embarrassing, he had difficulty remembering faces and would often confuse orders. He took to writing down brief descriptions of the people. The tax tables were a particular problem and he would rather leave off the taxed items than ask co-workers.

In spite of all this, he liked the job, was friendly, reliable, eager, and would try to help others. Although he often made mistakes, his friendliness made up for his errors. Co-workers were not as forgiving as his boss or as the customers. They had to answer his frequent questions and either correct or put up with his frequent errors. They appeared to put up with him, probably because he would stay late or come in early to clean or prepare the floor. He liked working at his own pace when no one else was around.

Peter wondered why he had to try so hard with what were simple tasks for others. Why did others not need attention or training from supervisors and why did he have to spend break, lunchtime, and after work reviewing or reworking assignments?

CASE CRITIQUE

1. Note the specific learning-disability characteristics of similar students with whom you have worked. What characteristics appear to be most significantly related to vocational outcomes?

2. What additional information and functional characteristics would you like to determine? How would you gather this information?

3. Identify potential strengths, assets, and vocational barriers or limitations as presented by this individual as you begin career/vocational planning activity.

4. What resources are typically available and typically unavailable for your "composite" student?

5. What would be the next three (3) management decisions/plans/service components you would forsee this individual? What may happen to assist or hinder you in completing this plan?

CHAPTER 12

Vocational Evaluation of
Severely Emotionally Disturbed Students

Determination of the vocational potential of students with severe emotional disturbances is important to teachers and special educators, mental health practitioners, and a range of professionals in the rehabilitation field. Unfortunately, traditional diagnostic tools and practices do not provide information relevant to the student's present or future ability to perform vocational tasks in competitive work settings. Although adequate for establishing diagnostic labels, these methods, including psychiatric interview, psychometric tests, and clinical observation, consistently fail in predicting vocational outcome or future vocational performance. Similarly, many vocational evaluation tests and procedures have not been found useful in decision making or determining employability of individuals with psychiatric disabilities.

The challenge for vocational evaluators in special education is to identify the behaviors and characteristics of seriously emotionally disturbed students that are important to vocational potential as well as the techniques and procedures to evaluate these factors.

This chapter will provide an overview of the usefulness of vocational evaluation tests and tools with severely emotionally disturbed students as well as specific methodology useful in middle and high school settings.

STUDENT CHARACTERISTICS

Students who are described as emotionally disturbed may range from those who demonstrate very specific and circumscribed behaviors or characteristics, such as school phobias, to those who exhibit more generalized symptomatology, including depression, mood swings, withdrawal, or lack of reality orientation. In addition, the severity of the disability can range from fear or anxiety surrounding a specific situation or setting, such as taking tests or participating in an industrial arts course, to significantly more serious behaviors such as aggressive outbursts, extreme manic behavior, hallucinations, or failure to communicate with others. In addition, the problems manifested by students can be demonstrated during random and isolated periods of time, followed by a period of remission for several months to more chronic and consistent maladaptive behavior. This chapter considers the more complex, multifaceted, and chronic emotional disorders and the challenges placed on vocational evaluation and subsequent vocational and training planning.

Often it is difficult to agree on what is meant by *emotionally disturbed behavior* as well as by the label, *severely emotionally disturbed student*. Perhaps the definition is confounded by confusion over what may or may not be considered "normal" behavior (Brolin & Kokaska, 1979), as well as the negative stigma attached to the label by both family and society. Critical to our purpose is how the dysfunctional behavior may interfere with, limit, or prevent learning.

The Education for All Handicapped Children Act of 1976 (Public Law 94–142) identifies students as seriously emotionally disturbed if the students demonstrate one or more of the following characteristics over a period of time and to an extent that educational performance is adversely effected:

- Inability to learn which cannot be explained by intellectual, sensory, or health factors
- Inability to build or maintain satisfactory interpersonal relationships with peers and teachers
- Inappropriate type of behavior or feelings under normal circumstances
- General pervasive mood of unhappiness or depression
- Tendency to develop physical symptoms or fears associated with personal or school problems

The definition includes students who are schizophrenic or autistic, but not socially maladjusted students, unless it is determined they are seriously emotionally disturbed.

Behavioral characteristics of seriously emotionally disturbed student may include:

- Extreme fluctuations in emotion from day to day or week to week
- Temper outbursts or mood swings
- Aggressive actions toward people or property
- Depression/apathy toward others, toward school
- Irrational beliefs about teacher, students, principal, self, etc.

■ Extreme sensitivity about topical area; hyperreactive to specific events, situations
■ Perseverances in behaviors, conversation

These behaviors may represent typical symptoms or presenting problems, one or more of which may prompt a teacher to refer the student for evaluation and may raise questions about the vocational potential and performance of the student.

INCIDENCE OF DISABILITY IN PUBLIC EDUCATION

Standardized behavioral descriptions are alleviating the confusions surrounding what constitutes "maladaptive," "disturbed behavior," or "mental illness." As definitions become more widely accepted, special education is able to acquire a more accurate picture of the extent of the handicapping condition.

Estimates suggest that approximately .79 percent, or between 270,000 and 288,000 students, experience serious emotional disturbances and require professional intervention (U.S. Department of Health and Human Services, 1985). Of those requiring specialized education services, 56 percent receive services outside of regular classrooms or in a separate education facility. Other survey research indicates that there are over 1,100,000 emotionally disturbed students and that 85 percent of these students are not receiving needed attention (Gearheart & Weisholm, 1978). An accurate estimate is that between one and two percent of school-aged youth have emotional difficulties that interfere with learning and performance and that require ongoing intervention (Kelly, Bullock, & Dykes, 1977).

EDUCATIONAL PROGRAMMING

Most students who are emotionally disturbed are able to participate and learn in a regular classroom if support, teaching modifications, and program adaptations are provided. The benefits of keeping the student in the classroom are that the stigma of mental illness or psychiatric disability is minimized and the student is able to observe and model appropriate student and adult behaviors. Also, the teacher and special education practitioner are able to adapt and modify teaching accommodations that may be useful models or techniques in a future job site. Regular classroom placement satisfies requirements for a least restrictive environment and provides natural feedback and reinforcement in a normalizing environment.

Although there have been significant advances in the research and development of medication as an effective control of symptomatology, the structure and characteristics of the learning environment and the skills of the special education teacher continue to be the significant variables in teaching and training emotionally disturbed students. The teacher must be able to establish learner guidelines and clear limits and use behavioral techniques that have been found successful in modifying dysfunctional behavior. Behaviors and symptomatology vary widely from student to student, and to work effectively with each student, the teacher must be both consistent and flexible as well as be able to incorporate a variety of existing external resources.

In an innovative approach toward working with chronic emotionally disturbed young adults, Unger and Anthony (1984) have developed a skills training approach to education and career planning for emotionally disturbed students. They view skill deficits in the areas of living, learning, and working, rather than symptomatology, as the teaching and training focus. For example, in training the student in the vocational area, training objectives highlight the behaviors needed to choose, get, and keep a job, as well as the resources and supports needed to sustain successful work behavior.

EMPLOYMENT SUCCESS OF INDIVIDUALS WITH A PSYCHIATRIC HISTORY

Research examining the success of vocational performance and community integration clearly demonstrates the problems that confront individuals with emotional and psychiatric disability. Studies consistently show that no more than 20 to 30 percent of individuals who have emotional or psychiatric history are involved in competitive employment (Anthony, 1979). More recent survey research suggests that a lower rate of 10 to 15 percent may be more accurate, with some studies yielding employment figures between 0 to 10 percent (Zipple & Spaniol, 1984).

Review of state and federal vocational rehabilitation caseloads shows that, although individuals with a psychiatric diagnosis make up from 25 to 50 percent of an active caseload, successful employment case closure is lower than for any other disability population (Danley, 1987).

ASSESSMENT OF VOCATIONAL POTENTIAL

Traditional methods of assessment and evaluation used with individuals demonstrating emotionally disturbed behavior have not been found useful in identifying characteristics important to future vocational performance. In addition, several vocational evaluation procedures used to reflect measures of vocational potential appear to have little relationship to the student's vocational potential.

PSYCHOMETRIC TESTS

Anthony (1979), in reviewing paper and pencil tests used with psychiatrically disabled adults, found that psychometric tests were poor predictors of employment and community adjustment. In a recent study, Ciardello and Turner (1980) attempted to assess how several widely used psychometric tests may be used to improve vocational programming efforts with individuals labeled psychiatrically disabled. Results indicated that the reliability and validity of several widely used tests, including the Differential Aptitude Test, Rosenberg Self-Esteem Scale, and the Career Maturity Index could not be established. In addition, the Strong-Campbell Interest Inventory, widely used in school settings, was unable to discriminate interest patterns, and the General Aptitude Test Battery (GATB) had unacceptably low validity to be used in a vocational evaluation process.

WORK SAMPLE

Hursh and Anthony (1983) have identified several benefits of work samples for evaluating the vocational behaviors of individuals with a psychiatric disability:

- The student is able to respond in a more natural way to concrete and realistic tasks, tools, and materials when compared to paper and pencil tests;
- As an assessment tool, work samples provide a measure of the individual's ability in a wide range of tasks in a relatively short period of time;
- The individual is provided with a wealth of occupational information in order to facilitate vocational exploration;
- A variety of behavioral observations is obtained about the interactions with peers and instructors, individual learning style, ability to sustain effort, concentrate, problem solve, or invest in a vocational activity.

Although work samples appear to be a useful approach in evaluating specific vocational characteristics of the student, there are also several concerns. First, there are no published norms on any commercial work samples for students who have emotional or psychiatric disabilities. Second, work samples are not developed to evaluate the specific characteristics of emotionally disturbed students that appear to relate directly to vocational success. A final consideration is the brevity of the work sample process. One skill limitation for the student is consistency over time. Although a student may perform well for one week, he or she may not perform well the next. Typically, work samples are unable to evaluate such factors as consistency, reliability, and perseverance, as they do not involve the individual for extensive time periods.

SITUATIONAL ASSESSMENT

Fortunately, there have been empirical studies that indicate what variables are predictive of career and vocational outcomes, as well as how these critical variables can be most effectively measured. Results of several studies suggest that systematic observation in a work setting is the most viable tool in vocational evaluation and that work adjustment and interpersonal skills are the characteristics most closely related to vocational success or failure for individuals labeled emotionally disturbed or psychiatrically disabled (e.g., Griffiths, 1983, 1974). Similarly, interpersonal skills and the ability to interact with peers on the job or in other social situations are significantly related to future vocational performance (e.g., Watts, 1978).

Survey research (Hursh, 1983) gathered information from vocational evaluators, rehabilitation practitioners, and vocational program administrators about the usefulness of vocational evaluation tools and procedures with psychiatrically disabled adults and working-age youth. The data from the survey indicate that all practitioner groups find that:

- Work adjustment behaviors and interpersonal skills are the critical characteristics related to vocational success for individuals who are psychiatrically disabled
- Symptomatology and diagnostic labels are poor predictors of overall vocational potential and future vocational performance
- Paper and pencil tests, including intelligence, aptitude, interest, and personality tests do not provide adequate measures of either work adjustment or interpersonal skills
- Situational assessment is the preferred procedure to evaluate work adjustment and interpersonal behaviors
- Situational assessment is the preferred procedure with individuals who have a psychiatric disability to evaluate overall vocational behaviors and future vocational success

PRINCIPLES OF THE SITUATIONAL ASSESSMENT WITH EMOTIONALLY DISTURBED STUDENTS

Employability is a function of interpersonal skills and work adjustment behaviors. Productivity and work skills do not appear to be the critical factors that determine whether an emotionally disabled person will succeed or fail on a job. More important is whether the student is able to interact appropriately on the job with co-workers, supervisors, and, if necessary, with the public. Equally important are work adjustment behaviors such as attendance and punctuality, concentration, consistency, the ability to adjust to changes in assignment and production needs, and the ability to maintain energy and alertness. These two major factors are the variables that vocational evaluation must assess in determining vocational potential of students with psychiatric disability.

The best way to evaluate the critical vocational strengths and limitations of emotionally disturbed students is to place the individual in a simulated situational work setting and systematically observe his or her work behavior over time. The traditional approach to assessment that emphasized interviewing and testing may be useful for diagnostic purposes, but is unable to gather information about work adjustment and interpersonal skills. Work samples, a traditional approach in vocational evaluation, focuses on technical ability to perform a task and usually does not provide a long enough period to evaluate adjustment behaviors over time. Situational assessment relies on a realistic work setting and the evaluator's ability to make systematic observations about behaviors critical to vocational functioning. Unfortunately, observation practice is not always a standardized and objective practice in situational assessment. Often, evaluators use behavior rating scales and behavior checklists that do not always provide information that accurately describes individual performance.

Involvement of the student in his or her own assessment is critical to an accurate assessment of vocational potential. The evaluator must facilitate the student's understanding of the goals of assessment activity. Evaluation results are validated by having the person involved in planning, implementing, and evaluating assessment activity from middle school through high school.

Situational assessment is responsive to the student's developmental progress. As with other students, severely emotionally disabled students experience career maturity as a developmental process. Situational assessment recognizes the developmental goals of the student by providing opportunity for worker role identification, vocational exploration, crystallization of work and personal values, decision making and personal responsibility during the middle school years.

During the transition from middle to high school, the focus is on establishing specific interpersonal and work adjustment behaviors. During high school, the student uses situational assessment to learn specific work skills, and to identify the support and accommodations needed to function in an employment setting.

A student's work behavior is a result of individual characteristics, such as vocational interest, work values, and previous experiences, as well as environmental characteristics such as the demands and support systems present in the environment. Work behavior is viewed as a complex set of interactions between the student and his or her environment. To accurately determine the individual's present ability and vocational potential to function in competitive employment, the relationship between the person and his optimal work environment must be assessed.

To be effective, situational assessment must use the range of occupational opportunities that are reflected by the student's interest and experience. Evaluation must be responsive to the needs of the student and provide a simulated work setting that reflects the work situations, activities, and level of complexity that make work interesting and satisfying. If evaluation does not take into account individual needs, the individual may be placed into a work environment that actually highlights disability. By individualizing the environment of choice, the evaluator increases the likelihood that motivation to perform well in the setting will be reasonably high.

The function of assessment is to provide information that will aid in decision making. Evaluation results should be descriptive, purposeful, and goal oriented. Evaluation must be used to:

■ Aid in determining employability
■ Determine transitional program placement
■ Aid in developing supports and interventions

A personal support system, as a component of situational assessment, facilitates information gathering and decision making. Students benefit from individual and/or group support during the assessment process in many ways. An interactive support system allows for exchange of information, facilitates reflection of feelings and concerns, and promotes the development and refinement of specific interpersonal skills. The student is able to provide and receive feedback about the assessment process and his or her involvement in it. Vocational assessment procedures do not systematically use a group or individual feedback procedure during the evaluation process and the vocational evaluation field should develop guidelines, goals, and examples of structured group formats.

A SITUATIONAL ASSESSMENT MODEL WITH EMOTIONALLY DISTURBED STUDENTS

Situational assessment begins with the premise that there are two sets of student characteristics that account for the greatest variation in performance for the student: work adjustment behaviors and interpersonal skills (Hursh & Dellario, 1984).

Interpersonal skills include verbal and nonverbal interactive behaviors between the student and co-workers, supervisors, teachers, and/or the public. Interpersonal skills may involve interaction between one

VOCATIONAL EVALUATION IN SPECIAL EDUCATION

individual and another, or between the student and a group. For our purposes, only work-related interpersonal behavior will be assessed, but it is recognized that such behaviors may occur both on and off the job. Of interest to situational assessment are all interpersonal interactions that may facilitate and enhance, or hinder or disturb the work environment and ongoing productive work behavior.

Work adjustment behaviors are learned behaviors, involving interaction with the work environment, that support the development and implementation of work skills and work productivity. Work adjustment behaviors are closely tied to work performance and productivity. Work adjustment behaviors promote work productivity by allowing the student to identify and follow the work rules, customs, codes, and expectations of co-workers and supervisors as well as to adjust, adapt, and cope with the multiple demands of the work settings. Adjustment behaviors are closely tied to work productivity and involve behaviors such as attendance, dress, consistency, reaction to work demands, organization of work environment, reaction to criteria, reaction to disruption or changes in the work environment, and demonstration of effort in the work setting.

An individual may have work adjustment behaviors or skills that allow him or her to perform in a work environment that is very limited with respect to the range of demands present. Other individuals may have work adjustment behaviors that allow them to work within a wide range of work environments.

The student's ability to learn or perform interpersonal skills or work adjustment behaviors does not occur in isolation. There are characteristics of a work environment that place demands on the student's ability to acquire and/or perform interpersonal or social skills. For example, certain work environments promote almost constant contact with the public or with other co-workers, whereas other work situations minimize contact with one group or the other. Such differences may place changing requirements for interpersonal skills performance.

There are also characteristics of a work environment that would build in support for performance of effective interpersonal skills. For example, a facilitative reinforcing supervisor may encourage, teach, or model work-related social behaviors.

Similarly, there are characteristics of the work environment that place demands on (or provide support to) the acquisition and/or performance of a range of work adjustment behaviors. For example, if the work environment is highly structured, with constant production demands, with little decision making or judgment required, many students will be able to work consistently, maintain concentration, respond to instructions, and stay on task. Similarly, other students will work effectively when tasks vary, when they are given added responsibility for work output, or when performing more abstract tasks.

Figure 12-1 identifies how the complexity of work environment characteristics may be structured and how the characteristics may be related to interpersonal skills and work adjustment demands. Figures 12-2 and 12-3 identify the interpersonal skills and work adjustment behavior categories that would be observed in different work environments.

Effective situational assessment requires that the vocational evaluator have different simulated work environments available to respond to the varied interests of the student. It also requires that:

Level of Complexity of Situational Assessment Environment

Low		**Moderate**		**High**	
1	2	3	4	5	

Work alone . . . . work with others/ supervise others	Interpersonal Skill Demand Factors
no public contact . . . . constant public contact	
facilitative supervisor . . . . autocratic supervisor	
concrete tasks . . . . abstract tasks	
routine activity . . . . varied activity	
structured activity . . . . unstructured activity	
minimal production demand . . . . high production demand	
no decision making . . . . continued decision making	Work Adjustment Skill Demand Factors
little verbal involvement . . . . high verbal involvement	
objective task performance . . . . lack of objective measurement measures	
constant production demands . . . . varying production demands	
minimal tool or machine . . . . constant machine or tool usage usage	

Figure 12-1. Work environment hierarchy.

A – Acceptable behavior/skill performed at competitive employment levels.
A/S – Acceptable behavior/skill when support is present.
NA – Behavior is either not present, problematic, or would cause the student to be dismissed from work.
NO – Not observed.

Behavior	Acceptable	Acceptable With Support	Not Acceptable
1. Interacts with co-workers in off-work situations.	A	A/S	NA
2. Interacts with supervisor appropriately.	A	A/S	NA
3. Interactions are related to the context of the setting.	A	A/S	NA
4. Interacts with co-workers to promote work production.	A	A/S	NA
5. Initiates needed work related interactions with co-workers.	A	A/S	NA
6. Tolerates minor irritations, errors, inconveniences without interfering with others.	A	A/S	NA
7. Cooperates as a member of the work group.	A	A/S	NA
8. Expresses relevant feelings to workers and supervisors.	A	A/S	NA
9. Expresses confidence in being able to carry out work.	A	A/S	NA
10. Listens and responds to individuals providing feedback about work.	A	A/S	NA
11. Communicates accurately and expresses self clearly.	A	A/S	NA
12. Interacts with the public (only for "people" oriented work situations.	A	A/S	NA
13. Asks for help when having difficulty with a task.	A	A/S	NA
14. Initiates work related conversation with supervisors.	A	A/S	NA

Figure 12-2. Interpersonal skill assessment form.

A   – Acceptable behavior/skill performed at competitive employment levels.
A/S – Acceptable behavior/skill when support is present.
NA – Behavior is either not present, problematic, or would cause the student to be dismissed from work.

Behavior	Acceptable	Acceptable With Support	Not Acceptable
1. Arrives to work on time.	A	A/S	NA
2. Begins work on time.	A	A/S	NA
3. Returns from breaks on time.	A	A/S	NA
4. Grooms and dresses appropriate to job.	A	A/S	NA
5. Organizes and maintains a neat work area.	A	A/S	NA
6. Identifies work hazards and takes necessary precautions.	A	A/S	NA
7. Recognizes and corrects work errors or poor workmanship.	A	A/S	NA
8. Demonstrates consideration for tools, materials, equipment, supplies, and work place.	A	A/S	NA
9. Demonstrates pride in work achievement.	A	A/S	NA
10. Understands and follows instructions.	A	A/S	NA
11. Maintains energy and alertness.	A	A/S	NA
12. Follows through and completes work task or assignment.	A	A/S	NA
13. Adjusts work effort to work demands.	A	A/S	NA
14. Performs work tasks consistently.	A	A/S	NA
15. Works steadily without being distracted.	A	A/S	NA
16. Controls impulsive, offensive, and/or annoying behavior.	A	A/S	NA
17. Demonstrates effort and investment in work activity.	A	A/S	NA
18. Adjusts work activity when new work tasks are introduced.	A	A/S	NA
19. Makes realistic work judgments.	A	A/S	NA
20. Following completion of work task, initiates new work.	A	A/S	NA

Figure 12-3. Work adjustment skill assessment form.

1. The vocational evaluator systematically assess the characteristics of different work environments in order to structure observation activity
2. The vocational evaluator be able to adjust the work environment characteristics to provide a work environment that incorporates the supports, reinforcers, and work demands that promote learning and performance of interpersonal skills, work adjustment behaviors, and job skills
3. The vocational evaluator be able to identify present and needed levels of vocational skills, that is, that performance objectives be established for the student
4. Performance objectives be in the form and format to be used in transitional vocational program efforts from middle through high school

SUMMARY

Situational assessment provides the student with time to adjust to the social as well as technical elements of a work environment. Similarly, the evaluator is able to observe the individual over time and understand how the individual adjusts and reacts to different changes in work expectations. Situational assessment allows the evaluator to systematically modify different social and technical aspects of the work environment to identify the student's optimal training situation.

For the emotionally disturbed student, situational assessment promotes:

- Vocational exploration
- Opportunities to identify and develop skills in a supported setting
- Identification of work environment characteristics that support skill acquisition
- Development of vocational training objectives that related to behaviors and skills needed in competitive work settings

REFERENCES

Anastasi, A. (1976). *Psychological testing* (4th ed.). New York: Macmillan.

Andrew, J., and Dickerson, L. (1974). *Vocational evaluation: A resource manual.* Menomonie, WT: Research and Training Center.

Anthony, W.A. (1979). *The principles of psychiatric rehabilitation.* Baltimore, MD: University Park Press.

Bailey, J. (1958). The work trial method of vocational evaluation. *Journal of Rehabilitation, 24*(1), 12–14.

Barlow, M.L. (1976). 200 years of vocational education. *American Vocational Journal, 51,* 5.

Bellamy, G.T., Rhodes, L.E., & Albin, J.M. (1986). Supported employment. In W.E. Kiernan and J.A. Stark (Eds.), *Pathways to employment for adults with developmental disabilities.* Baltimore, MD: Paul H. Brookes.

Bitter, J. (1967). Using employer job-sites in evaluation of the mentally retarded for employability. *Mental Retardation, 5,* 21–22.

Bolino, L.A. (1973). *Career education: Contributions to economic growth.* New York: Praeger.

Bolton, B. (1976). *Handbook of measurement and evaluation in rehabilitation.* Baltimore, MD: University Park Press.

Botterbusch, K. (1978). *Psychological testing in vocational evaluation.* Menomonie, WI: Materials Development Center.

Botterbusch, K. (1980). *A comparison of commercial vocational evaluation systems.* Menomonie, WI: Materials Development Center.

Botterbusch, K. (1981). *Work sample norms, reliability and validity.* Menomonie, WI: Materials Development Center.

Botterbusch, K. (1987). *Vocational assessment and evaluation systems: A comparison.* Menomonie, WI: Materials Development Center.

Botterbusch, K.F., & Michael, N. (1985). *Testing and test modification in vocational evaluation.* Menomonie, WI: Materials Development Center.

Bregman, M. (1969). *Some common components in vocational evaluation.* New York: National Rehabilitation Association Annual Conference.

Brolin, D. (1973). Vocational assessment: What can be gained from it. In *Vocational assessment systems.* Des Moines, IA: Iowa Department of Public Instruction.

Brolin, D. (1976). *Vocational preparation of retarded citizens.* Columbus, OH: Charles E. Merrill.

Brolin, D. (1985). Vocational assessment in the public schools. In R. Fry (Ed.). *The issues papers: Second national forum on issues in vocational assessment.* Menomonie, WI: Materials Development Center.

Brolin, D.E., and Kokaska, C.J. (1979). *Career education for handicapped children and youth.* Columbus, OH: Charles E. Merrill.

205

Burkett, L.A. (1973). Legislating career education. In J. Magisos (Ed.), *Career education*. Washington, DC: American Vocational Association.

Ciardiello, J.H., & Turner, F.D. (1980). *Final report of the vocational assessment project*. Piscataway, NJ: Rutgers Medical Center.

Collier, C.C., Houston, W.R., Schmatz, R.R., and Walsh, W. J. (1976). *Modern elmentary education: Teaching and learning*. New York: Macmillan.

Commission on Accreditation of Rehabilitation Facilities. (1982). *Standards manual for rehabilitation facilities*. Tucson, AZ: Author.

Coun, R. (1969). *Work evaluation techniques as employed in a workshop setting for the emotionally disabled*. New York: Institute for the Crippled and Disabled.

Cruickshank, W.M. (1977). *The brain injured child in home, school and community*. Syracuse, NY: Syracuse University Press.

Cruickshank, W.M. (1984). Definition: A major issue in the field of learning disabilities. *Journal of Rehabilitation, 50*(2), 7–18.

Cubberly, E.P. (1947). *Public education in the United States* (revised ed.). Boston: Houghton Mifflin Co.

Dahl, P., Appleby, T., & Lipe, D. (1978). *Mainstreaming guidebook for vocational educators teaching the handicapped*. Salt Lake City, UT: Olympus Publishing Company.

Danley, K.S. (1987). Improving vocational rehabilitation for persons with psychiatric disability. In M.G. Eisenberg & R. Grzesiak (Eds.), *Advances in Clinical Rehabilitation*. Chicago, IL: Springer Publishing Co.

Desmond, R., & Weiss, D. (1970). *The Minnesota job requirement questionnaire*. Unpublished manuscript. Minneapolis, MN: University of Minnesota.

Dunn, D. (1970). Norming of work samples. *Informational Bulletin*. Menomonie, WI: Stout Vocational Rehabilitation Institute.

Edgar, E., Levine, P., & Maddox, M. (1985). *Washington state follow up data of postsecondary special education students*. Seattle, WA: University of Washington, Networking and Evaluation, Experimental Education Unit.

Ehrle, R. (1975). Glossary of terms used in vocational evaluation. *Vocational Evaluation and Work Adjustment Bulletin*. 8, 85–93.

Folger, J.K., Astin, H.S., & Bayer, S.E. (1970). *Human resources and higher education*. New York: Russell Sage Foundation.

Fry, R. (1978). *Occupational information in vocational evaluation*. Menomonie, WI: Materials Development Center.

Garrett, J. (1959). Current research activities in work evaluation. In May T. Morrison Center for Rehabilitation, *Institutes on Work Evaluation*. San Francisco: Author.

Gearheart, G.R., & Weisholm, M.W. (1976). *The Handicapped Child in the Regular Classroom*. St. Louis: Mosby.

Gellman, W. (1968). The principles of vocational evaluation. *Rehabilitation Literature, 29*(4), 98–102.

Goertzel, V., et al. (1967). *Coordinating hospital and community work adjustment services*. Los Angeles: Camarillo State Hospital and Jewish Vocational Service.

Goldman, L. (1971). *Using tests in counseling*. Englewood Cliffs, NJ: Prentice-Hall.

Griffiths, R. (1973). A standardized assessment of the work behavior of psychiatric patients. *British Journal of Psychiatry, 123*, 403–408.

Griffiths, R. (1974). Rehabilitation of chronic psychiatric patients. *Psychological Medicine, 4*, 316–325.

Hammill, D. (1976). Defining L.D. for programmatic purposes. *Academic Therapy*, *12*, 29–37.

Hammill, D., & Bartel. (1978). *Teaching children with learning behavior problems* (2nd ed.). Boston: Allyn and Bacon.

Harnisch, D.L. (1986). *Transition literature review on educational, employment, and independent living outcomes.* Champaign, IL: University of Illinois, Transition Institute at Illinois.

Harrington, T.F., & O'Shea, A.J. (1984). *Guide for occupational exploration* (2nd ed.). Circle Pines, MN: American Guidance Service.

Hasazi, S.B., Gordon, L.R., & Roe, C.A. (1985). Factors associated with employment status of handicapped youth exiting high school from 1979–1983. *Exceptional Children*, *51*, 455–469.

Hasazi, S.B., Gordon, L.R., Roe, C.A., Hull, M., Finck, K., & Salembier, G. (1985). A statewide follow-up on post high school employment and residential status of students labeled, "Mentally Retarded." *Education and Training of the Mentally Retarded*, *20*, 222–234.

Hendel, D., & Vessey, T. (1970). *Effects of lowered reading level and anchors on responses to Minnesota job requirements questionnaire.* Unpublished manuscript. Minneapolis, MN: University of Minnesota.

Holland, J.L. (1970). *The self directed search: A guide to educational and vocational planning.* Palo Alto, CA: Consulting Psychologist Press.

Hoppock, H. (1976). *Occupational information.* New York: McGraw-Hill.

Hursh, N.C. (1983). *Diagnostic vocational evaluation with psychiatrically disabled individuals: A national survey.* Boston: Center for Psychiatric Rehabilitation.

Hursh, N.C. (1984). Vocational evaluation of learning disabled adults. *Journal of Rehabilitation*, *50*(2), 45–52.

Hursh, N.C. (1987). *Vocational evaluation in special education.* Columbus, OH: Ohio Resource Center for Low Incidence and Severely Disabled.

Hursh, N.C., & Anthony, W.A. (1983). The vocational preparation of the chronic psychiatric patient in the community. In I. Barofsky and R.D. Budson (Eds.), *The chronic psychiatric patient in the community: Principles of treatment.* New York: Pergamon Press.

Hursh, N.C. & Dellario, D. (1984). *Situational assessment: Identifying vocational potential of psychiatrically disabled individuals.* Boston: Center for Psychiatric Rehabilitation.

Hursh, N.C., Shrey, D.E., Lasky, R.G., & D'Amico, M.L. (1982). A career education model for students with special needs. *Teaching Exceptional Children*, September, 52–56.

Institute for the Crippled and Disabled. (1967). *TOWER: Testing, orientation and work evaluation in rehabilitation.* New York: Author.

Jewish Employment and Vocational Services. (1968). *Work samples: Signposts on the road to occupational choice.* Philadelphia, PA: Author.

Karan, O.C., & Knight, C.B. (1986). Training demands of the future. In W.E. Kiernan and J.A. Stark (Eds.) *Pathways to employment for adults with developmental disabilities.* Baltimore, MD: Paul H. Brookes.

Kelly, T.J., Bullock, L.M., & Dykes, M.K. (1977). Behavioral disorders: Teachers' perceptions. *Exceptional Children*, *43*(5), 316–318.

Kennedy, D.B., & Kerber, A. (1973). *Resocialization: An American Experiment.* New York: Behavioral Publications.

Kerns, A.F., & Neeley, R.E. (1987). *Dictionary of worker traits.* Philadelphia, PA: Vocational Research Institute.

Kiernan, W.E., & Stark, J.A. (1986). *Pathways to employment for adults with developmental disabilities.* Baltimore, MD: Paul H. Brooks.

Kirk, S. (1966). *The diagnosis and remediation of psycholinguistic disabilities.* Urbana, IL: University of Illinois Press.

Kulman, H. (1975). The tools of vocational evaluation. *Vocational Evaluation and Work Adjustment Bulletin, 8,* 49–64.

Landy, F., & Trumbo, D. (1976). *Psychology of work behavior.* Homewood, IL: The Dorsey Press.

Leshner, S., & Snyderman, G. (1965). A new approach to the evaluation and rehabilitation of the vocationally handicapped. In J. Adams (Ed.), *Counseling and guidance: A summary view.* New York: Macmillan.

Levitan, S.A., & Taggart, R. (1977). *Jobs for the disabled.* Baltimore, MD: Johns Hopkins University Press.

Mangum, G.L., Becker, J.W., Coombs, G., & Marshall, P. (1975). *Career education in the academic classroom.* Salt Lake City, UT: Olympus Publishing Company.

Marland, Jr., S.P. (1974). *Career education: A proposal for reform.* New York: McGraw-Hill.

Martin, E.W. (1974). Foreword. In T.P. Lake (Ed.), *Career education: Exemplary programs for the handicapped.* Reston, VA: Council for Exceptional Children.

Mauser, A. J. (1981). *Assessing the learning disabled: Selected instruments* (3rd ed.). Novato, CA: Academic Therapy Publications.

McCray, P. (1979a). *An interpretation of VEWAA/CARF work sample standards.* Menomonie, WI: Materials Development Center.

McCray, P. (1979b). *Learning assessment in vocational evaluation.* Menomonie, WI: Materials Development Center.

McGowan, J.F., & Porter, T.L. (1967). *An introduction to the vocational rehabilitation process.* Washington, DC: U.S. Department of Health, Education and Welfare.

Mills, C. (1976). The development of the Rehabilitation Acts of 1973 and 1974. In W. Jenkins (Ed.), *Rehabilitation of the severely disabled.* Dubuque, IA: Kendall Hunt.

Mithaug, D.E., Horiuchi, C.N., & Fanning, P.N. (1985). A report on the Colorado statewide follow-up survey of special education students. *Exceptional Children, 51,* 397–404.

Nadolsky, J. (1971). Vocational evaluation theory in perspective. *Rehabilitation Literature, 32*(8), 226–231.

Nadolsky, J.M. (1973). *Vocational evaluation of the culturally disadvantaged: A comparison investigation of the JEVS system and a model based system; Final report.* Auburn, AL: Auburn University.

Nadolsky, J.M. (1976). The experiential component of vocational evaluation. *Vocational Evaluation and Work Adjustment Bulletin, 9,* 3–7.

Nadolsky, J. (1977). *The use of work samples in the vocational evaluation process.* Auburn, AL: Workshop Paper.

Neff, W.S. (1985). *Work and human behavior.* New York: Aldine.

Nelson, N. (1971). *Workshops for the handicapped in the United States: A historical and developmental perspective.* Springfield, IL: Charles C. Thomas.

Obermann, C.E. (1965). *A history of vocational rehabilitation in America.* Minneapolis, MN: T.T. Denison.

Peterson, M. (1985). School-based vocational assessment: A comprehensive, developmental approach. In C. Smith & R. Fry (Eds.), *National forum on issues in vocational assessment.* Menomonie, WI: Materials Development Center.

Plumb, B. (1965). *The Goodwill man: Edgar James Helms.* Minneapolis, MN: T.S. Denison.

Power, P.W. (1984). *A guide to vocational assessment.* Baltimore, MD: University Park Press.

Pruitt, W.A. (1986). *Vocational evaluation* (2nd ed.). Menomonie, WI: Walt Pruitt Associates.

Pucel, D.J. (1972). The individual and his choice of occupation. In A.H. Krebs, (Ed.), *The individual and his education.* Washington, DC: American Vocational Association.

Roberts, C. (1970). Definitions, objectives and goals in work evaluation. *Journal of Rehabilitation, 36*(1), 12–15.

Shrey, D.E., Mitchell, D.K., & Hursh, N.C. (1985). *Employer development and industrial exploration manual.* Dublin, OH: The International Center for Industry, Labor, and Rehabilitation.

Sitlington, P.L. (1979). Vocational assessment and programming of the handicapped. *Focus on Exceptional Children, 12*(4), 1–12.

Sitlington, P.L., Brolin, D.E., Clark, G.M. & Vacanti, J.M. (1985). Career/ vocational assessment in the public school setting: The position of the Division of Career Development. *Career Development for Exceptional Individuals, 8,* 3–6.

Skolnik, A.M., & Dales, S.R. (1976). Social welfare expenditures, 1950–1975. *Social Security Bulletin, 39*(1), 3–20.

Stodden, R.A., & Ianacone, R.N. (1981). Career/vocational assessment of the special needs individual: A conceptual model. *Exceptional Children, 47*(8), 600–608.

Switzer, M. (1969). Legislative contributions. In D. Malikin & H. Rusalem (Eds.), *Vocational rehabilitation of the severely disabled.* New York: New York University.

Tanner, D. (1972). *Secondary education: Perspectives and prospects.* New York: Macmillan.

Tyrell, W.F. (1986). *The psychosocial needs of LD adolescents in work transition.* Boston: Dissertation Abstracts.

Unger, K., & Anthony, W.A. (1984). A university-based treatment for young adult chronic patients: New directions for mental health services. In B. Pepper & H. Rugglewicz (Eds.), *The young adult chronic patient revisited.* San Francisco, CA: Jossy-Bass.

U.S. Commission on Civil Rights. (1983). *Accommodating the spectrum of individual differences.* Washington, DC: U.S. Government Printing Office.

U.S. Department of Health and Human Services, Office of Education. (1985). *Progress toward a free appropriate public education: A report to Congress on the implementation of Public Law 94–142, the education for all handicapped children act.* Washington, DC: Author.

U.S. Department of Labor, Bureau of Labor Statistics. (1984–1985). *Occupational outlook handbook.* Washington, DC: U.S. Government Printing Office.

U.S. Department of Labor, Employment and Training Administration. (1981). *Selected characteristics of occupations defined in the Dictionary of Occupational Titles.* Washington, DC: U.S. Government Printing Office.

U.S. Department of Labor, Manpower Administration. (1972). *Handbook for analyzing jobs.* Washington, DC: Author.

U.S. Offfice of Education (1977). Assistance to states for education of handicapped children: Procedures for evaluating specific learning disabilities. *Federal Register, 42,* 65082–68085.

Vocational Rehabilitation Center. (1984). *A comprehensive vocational service model for persons with specific learning disabilities: A final report.* Pittsburgh, PA: Author.

Vocational Rehabilitation Center of Allegheny County. (1984). *A comprehensive vocational service model for persons with specific learning disability.* Pittsburgh, PA: Author.

Washburn, W.Y. (1975). Where to go in vocational education for secondary LD students. *Academic Therapy, 11,* 31–35.

Watkins, A. (1959). Prevocational evaluation and rehabilitation in a general hospital. *JAMA. 171,* 385–388.

Watts, F. (1978). A study of work behavior in a psychiatric rehabilitation unit. *British Journal of Clinical Psychology. 17,* 85–92.

Wehman, P. (1981). *Competitive employment: New horizons for severely disabled individuals.* Baltimore, MD: Paul Brookes.

Wehman, P., & Hill, J. (1985). *Competitive employment for persons with mental retardation: From research to practice.* Richmond, VA: Rehabilitation Research and Training Center.

Wehman, P., & McLaughlin, P. (1980). *Vocational curriculum for developmentally disabled persons.* Baltimore: University Park Press.

Wehman, P., Kregel, J., & Seyfarth, J. (1985). Transition from school to work for individuals with severe handicaps: A follow-up study. *The Journal of the Association for the Severely Handicapped, 10,* 132–136.

Whitehead, A.N. (1929). *The aims of education and other essays.* New York: Macmillan.

Whitehouse, F.A. (1953). Client evaluation in the rehabilitation process. *Journal of Rehabilitation, 19*(6), 4–6.

Wiig, E.H., & Semel, E.M. (1980). *Language assessment and intervention for the learning disabled.* Columbus, OH: Charles E. Merrill.

Will, M. (1984). *OSERS programming for the transition of youth with disabilities: Bridges from school to working life.* Washington, DC: U.S. Department of Education, Office of Special Education and Rehabilitation Services.

Wolfe, B. (1980). How the disabled fare in the labor market. *Monthly Labor Review,* September, 48–52.

Wright, G.N. (1980). *Total rehabilitation.* Boston: Little, Brown.

Zipple, A., & Spaniol, L. (1984). *Current research on families that include persons with a severe mental illness: A review of findings.* Boston: Center for Psychiatric Rehabilitation.

Appendices

The following appendices of worker trait and worker function information includes jobs listed under 20 selected Worker Trait Groups (WTG) from *The Dictionary of Worker Traits* (DWT) (Kerns & Neeley, 1987), which updates and expands the DOT, Third Edition, Volume II, Worker Trait Group format.

A Worker Trait Group (WTG) is a cluster of jobs with similar worker functions (Data, People, Things, Relationships) and similar worker trait factors (e.g., GED, SVP, Aptitudes, and Physical Demands).

The DWT contains 109 Worker Trait Groups listed under 22 broad areas of of work.

TWENTY SELECTED WORKER TRAIT GROUPS (OUT OF 109)

WTG CODE	NUMBER OF JOBS	WTG TITLES
Clerical Work		
021	14	Cashiering (Drug Stores, Theaters, Restaurants & Related)
022	211	Inspecting & Stock Checking
024	88	Classifying, Filing & Related
027	531	Sorting, Inspecting, Measuring & Related
028	16	Typing & Related Recording
029	53	Routing Checking & Recording
030	7	Switchboard Service
Crafts		
037	21	Cooking & Related
038	865	Craftsmanship & Related
040	1315	Manipulating

Elemental Work

051	396	Feeding-Offbearing
052	1161	Handling

Machine Work

082	1174	Operating-Controlling
084	2209	Tending

Merchandising

097	186	Demonstration & Sales

Personal Service

101	9	Beautician & Barbering Service
102	21	Customer Service Work, N.E.C.
103	22	Miscellaneous Customer Service
105	66	Miscellaneous Personal Service (Food Serving, Portering, Valeting & Related Activities)
107	10	Animal Care

APPENDIX A

Explanation of Worker Functions: Data, People, and Things

EXPLANATION OF WORKER FUNCTIONS: DATA, PEOPLE, AND THINGS [FOURTH EDITION OF THE *DICTIONARY OF OCCUPATIONAL TITLES* (1977)]

Much of the information is based on the premise that every job requires a worker to function in some degree to Data, People, and Things. These relationships are identified and explained below. They appear in the form of three listings arranged in each instance from the relatively simple to the complex in such a manner that each successive relationship includes those that are simpler and excludes the more complex. (As each of the relationships to People represents a wide range of complexity, resulting in considerable overlap among occupations, their arrangement is somewhat arbitrary and can be considered a hierarchy only in the most general sense.) The identifications attached to these relationships are referred to as *worker functions*, and provide standard terminology for use in summarizing exactly what a worker does on the job.

A job's relationship to Data, People, and Things can be expressed in terms of the lowest numbered function (most complex) in each sequence. These functions taken together indicate the total level of complexity at which the worker performs. The fourth, fifth, and sixth digits of the occupational code numbers reflect relationships to Data, People, and Things, respectively. (Only those relationships which are occupationally significant in terms of the requirements of the job are reflected in the code numbers. The incidental relationships that every worker has to Data, People, and Things, but which do not seriously affect successful performance of the essential duties of the job, are not reflected.) These digits express a job's relationship to Data, People, and Things by identifying the highest appropriate function in each listing as reflected by the following table:

DATA (4th digit)	PEOPLE (5th digit)	THINGS (6th digit)
0 Synthesizing	0 Mentoring	0 Setting-Up
1 Coordinating	1 Negotiating	1 Precision Working
2 Analyzing	2 Instructing	2 Operating-Controlling
3 Compiling	3 Supervising	3 Driving-Operating
4 Computing	4 Diverting	4 Manipulating
5 Copying	5 Persuading	5 Tending
6 Comparing	6 Speaking-Signaling	6 Feeding-Offbearing
	7 Serving	7 Handling
	8 Taking Instructions- Helping	

DEFINITIONS OF WORKER FUNCTIONS

DATA: Information, knowledge, and conceptions, related to data, people, or things, obtained by observation, investigation, interpretation, visualization, and mental creation. Data are intangible and include numbers, words, symbols, ideas, concepts, and oral verbalization.

0 *Synthesizing:* Integrating analyses of data to discover facts and/or develop knowledge concepts or interpretations.
1 *Coordinating:* Determining time, place, and sequence of operations or action to be taken on the basis of analysis of data; executing determination and/or reporting on events.
2 *Analyzing:* Examining and evaluating data. Presenting alternative actions in relation to the evaluation is frequently involved.
3 *Compiling:* Gathering, collating, or classifying information about data, people, or things. Reporting and/or carrying out a prescribed action in relation to the information is frequently involved.
4 *Computing:* Performing arithmetic operations and reporting on and/or carrying out a prescribed action in relation to them. Does not include counting.
5 *Copying:* Transcribing, entering, or posting data.
6 *Comparing:* Judging the readily observable functional, structural, or compositional characteristics (whether similar to or divergent from obvious standards) of data, people or things.

PEOPLE: Human beings; also animals dealt with on an individual basis as if they were human.

0 *Mentoring:* Dealing with individuals in terms of their total personality in order to advise, counsel, and/or guide them with regard to problems that may be resolved by legal, scientific, clinical, spiritual, and/or other professional principles.

1 *Negotiating:* Exchanging ideas, information, and opinions with others to formulate policies and programs and/or arrive jointly at decisions, conclusions, or solutions.

2 *Instructing:* Teaching subject matter to others, or training others (including animals) through explanation, demonstration, and supervised practice; or making recommendations on the basis of technical disciplines.

3 *Supervising:* Determining or interpreting work procedures for a group of workers, assigning specific duties to them, maintaining harmonious relations among them, and promoting efficiency. A variety of responsibilities is involved in this function.

4 *Diverting:* Amusing others (usually accomplished through the medium of stage, screen, television, or radio).

5 *Persuading:* Influencing others in favor of a product, service, or point of view.

6 *Speaking-Signaling:* Talking with and/or signaling people to convey or exchange information. Includes giving assignments and/or directions to helpers or assistants.

7 *Serving:* Attending to the needs or requests of people or animals or the expressed or implicit wishes of people. Immediate response is involved.

8 *Taking Instructions-Helping:* Helping applies to "nonlearning" helpers. No variety of responsibility is involved in this function.

THINGS: Inanimate objects as distinguised from human beings, substances, or materials; machines, tools, equipment, and products. A thing is tangible and has shape, form, and other physical characteristics.

0 *Setting-up:* Adjusting machines or equipment by replacing or altering tools, jigs, fixtures, and attachments to prepare them to perform their functions, change their performance, or restore their proper functioning if they break down. Workers who set up one or a number of machines for other workers or who set up and personally operate a variety of machines are included here.

1 *Precision Working:* Using body members and/or tools or work aids to work, move, guide, or place objects or materials in situations where ultimate responsibility for the attainment of standards occurs and selection of appropriate tools, objects, or materials, and the adjustment of the tool to the task require exercise of considerable judgment.

2 *Operating-Controlling:* Starting, stopping, controlling, and adjusting the progress of machines or equipment. Operating machines involves setting up and adjusting the machine or material(s) as the work progresses. Controlling involves observing gauges, dials, etc., and turning valves and other devices to regulate factors such

as temperature, pressure, flow of liquids, speed of pumps, and reactions of materials.

3 *Driving-Operating:* Starting, stopping, and controlling the actions of machines or equipment for which a course must be steered, or which must be guided, in order to fabricate, process, and/or move things or people. Involves such activities as observing gauges and dials; estimating distances and determining speed and direction of other objects; turning cranks and wheels; pushing or pulling gear lifts or levers. Includes such machines as cranes, conveyor systems, tractors, furnace charging machines, paving machines, and hoisting machines. Excludes manually powered machines, such as handtrucks and dollies, and power-assisted machines, such as electric wheelbarrows and handtrucks.

4 *Manipulating:* Using body members, tools, or special devices to work, move, guide, or place objects or materials. Involves some latitude for judgment with regard to precision attained and selecting appropriate tool, object, or material, although this is readily manifest.

5 *Tending:* Starting, stopping, and observing the functioning of machines and equipment. Involves adjusting materials or controls of the machine, such as changing guides, adjusting timers and temperature gauges, turning valves to allow flow of materials, and flipping switches in response to lights. Little judgment is involved in making these adjustments.

6 *Feeding-Offbearing:* Inserting, throwing, dumping, or placing materials in or removing them from machines or equipment which are automatic or tended or operated by other workers.

7 *Handling:* Using body members, handtools, and/or special devices to work, move or carry objects or materials. Involves little or no latitude for judgment with regard to attainment of standards or in selecting appropriate tool, object, or material.

Selected Worker Function Numbers (WFN, DPT)
Within Representative Worker Trait Groups (WTG)

WTG Code	Number of Jobs	WTG Titles	WTG Jobs
Clerical Work			
021	14	Cashiering (Drug Stores, Theaters, Restaurants & Related)	.462-8; .467-6
022	211	Inspecting & Stock Checking	.364-18; .367-58; .382-12; .384-32; .387-77

WTG Code	Number of Jobs	WTG Titles	WTG Jobs
024	88	Classifying, Filing & Related	.362-10; .367-34; .387-35
027	531	Sorting, Inspecting, Measuring & Related	.487-15; .567-10; .587-47; .667-28; .684-60; .685-20; .687-305
028	16	Typing & Related Recording	.562-4; .582-9; .587-2
029	53	Routine Checking & Recording	.567-10; .587-31; .687-3
030	7	Switchboard Service	.462-1; .562-1; .662-5

Crafts

037	21	Cooking & Related	.361-9; .381-10
038	865	Craftsmanship & Related	.261-123; .281-243; .361-96; .381-393
040	1351	Manipulating	.364-24; .384-57; .484-43; .584-29; .664-78; .684-1066

Elemental Work

051	396	Feeding-Offbearing	.666-17; .686-366
052	1161	Handling	.587-38; .667-51; .687-1063

Machine Work

082	1174	Operating-Controlling	.362-111; .382-254; .462-34; .482-79; .562-16; .582-38; .662-76; .682-560
084	2209	Tending	.385-17; .485-50; .565-28; .585-103; .665-126; .685-1871

Merchandising

097	186	Demonstration & Sales	.257-19; .354-6; .357-148

Personal Service

101	9	Beautician & Barbering Services	.071-1; .271-4; .371-4
102	21	Customer Service Work, N.E.C.	.467-7; .477-6; .677-2
103	22	Miscellaneous Customer Service Work	.464-2; .467-2; .477-2; .665-2; .667-2; .677-5
105	66	Miscellaneous Personal Service Work (Food Serving, Portering, Valeting & Related)	.367-2; .374-2; .474-3; .477-13; .674-8; .677-30
107	10	Animal Care	.674-8; .677-1

APPENDIX B

Physical Demands

Physical demands are those physical activities required of a worker in a job.

The physical demands referred to serve as a means of expressing both the physical requirements of the job and the physical capacities (specific physical traits) that a worker must have to meet the requirements. For example, "seeing" is the name of a physical demand required by many jobs (perceiving by the sense of vision), and also the name of a specific capacity possessed by many people (having the power of sight). The worker must possess physical capacities at least in an amount equal to the physical demands made by the job.

THE FACTORS

1 LIFTING, CARRYING, PUSHING, AND/OR PULLING (STRENGTH)

These are the primary "strength" physical requirements, and, generally speaking, a person who engages in one of these activities can engage in all. Specifically, each of these activities can be described as:

- Lifting: Raising or lowering an object from one level to another (includes upward pulling).
- Carrying: Transporting an object, usually holding it in the hands or arms or on the shoulders.
- Pushing: Exerting force upon an object, so that the object moves away from the force (includes slapping, striking, kicking, and treadle actions).
- Pulling: Exerting force upon an object so that the object moves toward the force (includes jerking).

The five degrees of Physical Demands for factor No. 1 (Lifting, Carrying, Pushing, and/or Pulling) are as follows:

S *Sedentary Work:* Lifting 10 lb. (4.5 kg) maximum and occasionally lifting and/or carrying such articles as dockets, ledgers, and small tools.

Although a sedentary job is defined as one that involves sitting, a certain amount of walking and standing often is necessary in carrying out job duties. Jobs are sedentary if walking and standing are required only occasionally and other sedentary criteria are met.

L *Light Work:* Lifting 20 lb. (9 kg) maximum with frequent lifting and/or carrying of objects weighing up to 10 lb. (4.5 kg). Even though the weight lifted may be only a negligible amount, a job is in this category when it requires walking or standing to a significant degree, or when it involves sitting most of the time with a degree of pushing and pulling of arm and/or leg controls.

M *Medium Work:* Lifting 50 lb. (22.5 kg) maximum with frequent lifting and/or carrying of objects weighing up to 25 lb. (11.4 kg).

H *Heavy Work:* Lifting 100 lb. (45 kg) maximum with frequent lifting and/or carrying of objects weighing up to 50 lb. (22.5 kg).

V *Very Heavy Work:* Lifting objects in excess of 100 lb. (45 kg) with frequent lifting and/or carrying of objects weighing 50 lb. (22.5 kg) or more.

2 CLIMBING AND/OR BALANCING

- Climbing: Ascending or descending ladders, stairs, scaffolding, ramps, poles, ropes, and the like, using the feet and legs and/or hands and arms.
- Balancing: Maintaining body equilibrium to prevent falling when walking, standing, crouching, or running on narrow, slippery, or erratically moving surfaces; or maintaining body equilibrium when performing gymnastic feats.

3 STOOPING, KNEELING, CROUCHING, AND/OR CRAWLING

- Stooping: Bending the body downward and forward by bending at the waist.
- Kneeling: Bending the legs at the knees to come to rest on the knee or knees.
- Crouching: Bending the body downward and forward by bending the legs and spine.
- Crawling: Moving about on the hands and knees or hands and feet.

4 REACHING, HANDLING, FINGERING, AND/OR FEELING

- Reaching: Extending the hands and arms in any direction.
- Handling: Seizing, holding, grasping, turning, or otherwise working with the hand or hands (fingering not involved).

■ Fingering: Picking, pinching, or otherwise working with the fingers primarily (rather than with the whole hand or arm as in handling).

■ Feeling: Perceiving such attributes of objects and materials as size, shape, temperature, or texture, by means of receptors in the skin, particularly those of the finger tips.

5 TALKING AND/OR HEARING

■ Talking: Expressing or exchanging ideas by means of the spoken word.

■ Hearing: Perceiving the nature of sounds by the ear.

6 SEEING

Obtaining impressions through the eyes of the shape, size, distance, motion, color, or other characteristics of objects. The major visual functions are: (1) acuity, far and near, (2) depth perception, (3) field of vision, (4) accommodation, (5) color vision. The functions are defined as follows:

■ Acuity, far: Clarity of vision at 20 feet or more. Acuity, near: Clarity of vision at 20 inches or less.

■ Depth perception: Three-dimensional vision. The ability to judge distance and space relationships so as to see objects where and as they actually are. Ascertaining the thickness, length, and width of objects.

■ Field of vision: The peripheral area that can be seen up and down or to the right or left while the eyes are fixed on a given point.

■ Accommodation: Adjustment of the lens of the eye to bring an object into sharp focus. This item is especially important when doing close work at varying distances from the eye.

■ Color vision: The ability to identify and distinguish various shades and hues of colors.

Physical Demands

WTG Code	Number of Jobs	WTG Titles (S)	(L)	(M)	(H)	Levels/Jobs (V)	(2)	(3)	(4)	(5)	(6)
Clerical Work											
021	14	Cashiering (Drug Stores, Theaters, Restaurants & Related)									
		(4)	(10)						(14)	(12)	(9)
022	211	Inspecting & Stockchecking									
		(7)	(155)	(45)	(4)		(20)	(40)	(207)	(34)	(176)

WTG Code	Number of Jobs	WTG Titles				Levels/Jobs					
		(S)	(L)	(M)	(H)	(V)	(2)	(3)	(4)	(5)	(6)

Clerical Work (continued)

WTG Code	Number of Jobs	Title	(S)	(L)	(M)	(H)	(V)	(2)	(3)	(4)	(5)	(6)
024	88	Classifying, Filing & Related	(49)	(36)	(2)	(1)		(1)	(6)	(73)	(19)	(61)
027	531	Sorting, Inspecting, Measuring & Related	(55)	(405)	(57)	(13)	(1)	(15)	(57)	(523)	(24)	(445)
028	16	Typing & Related Recording	(16)							(16)	(5)	(11)
029	53	Routine Checking & Recording	(21)	(31)	(1)			(2)	(2)	(49)	(6)	(26)
030	7	Switchboard Service	(5)	(2)						(7)	(7)	(3)

Crafts

WTG Code	Number of Jobs	Title	(S)	(L)	(M)	(H)	(V)	(2)	(3)	(4)	(5)	(6)
037	21	Cooking & Related		(3)	(16)	(2)		(2)	(4)	(21)	(3)	(16)
038	865	Craftsmanship & Related	(47)	(325)	(387)	(101)	(5)	(188)	(359)	(863)	(175)	(758)
040	1315	Manipulating	(82)	(539)	(478)	(198)	(18)	(155)	(387)	(1314)	(29)	(866)

Elemental Work

WTG Code	Number of Jobs	Title	(S)	(L)	(M)	(H)	(V)	(2)	(3)	(4)	(5)	(6)
051	396	Feeding-Offbearing	(3)	(133)	(151)	(107)	(2)	(24)	(125)	(395)	(4)	(75)
052	1161	Handling	(72)	(512)	(372)	(187)	(18)	(114)	(350)	(1159)	(14)	(266)

Machine Work

WTG Code	Number of Jobs	Title	(S)	(L)	(M)	(H)	(V)	(2)	(3)	(4)	(5)	(6)
082	1174	Operating-Controlling	(9)	(523)	(515)	(123)	(4)	(122)	(213)	(1173)	(83)	(842)
084	2209	Tending	(35)	(1081)	(816)	(272)	(5)	(144)	(405)	(2201)	(43)	(909)

Merchandising

WTG Code	Number of Jobs	Title	(S)	(L)	(M)	(H)	(V)	(2)	(3)	(4)	(5)	(6)
097	186	Demonstration & Sales Work	(6)	(174)	(6)				(6)	(67)	(186)	(47)

Personal Service

WTG Code	Number of Jobs	Title	(S)	(L)	(M)	(H)	(V)	(2)	(3)	(4)	(5)	(6)
101	9	Beautician & Barbering Services		(9)						(9)	(8)	(9)
102	21	Customer Service Work, N.E.C.	(1)	(15)	(3)	(2)			(3)	(19)	(20)	(8)
103	22	Miscellaneous Customer Service Work		(11)	(9)	(2)			(3)	(10)	(22)	(17)	(6)
105	66	Miscellaneous Personal Service Work (Food Serving, Portering, Valeting & Related Activities)	(3)	(50)	(13)			(5)	(19)	(64)	(51)	(17)
107	10	Animal Care		(3)	(6)	(1)		(2)	(3)	(10)	(2)	(7)

A P P E N D I X C

Environmental Conditions

Environmental conditions are the physical surroundings of a worker in a specific job.

1 INSIDE, OUTSIDE, OR BOTH

I—Inside: Protection from weather conditions but not necessarily from temperature changes.
O—Outside: No effective protection from weather.
B—Both: Inside and outside.

A job is considered "inside" if the worker spends approximately 75 percent or more of the time inside, and "outside" if he or she spends approximately 75 percent or more of the time outside. A job is considered "both" if the activities occur inside or outside in approximately equal amounts.

2 EXTREMES OF COLD PLUS TEMPERATURE CHANGES

■ Extremes of Cold: Temperature sufficiently low to cause marked bodily discomfort unless the worker is provided with exceptional protection.
■ Temperature Changes: Variations in temperature which are sufficiently marked and abrupt to cause noticeable bodily reactions.

3 EXTREMES OF HEAT PLUS TEMPERATURE CHANGES

■ Extremes of Heat: Temperature sufficiently high to cause marked bodily discomfort unless the worker is provided with exceptional protection.
■ Temperature Changes: Variations in temperature changes which are sufficiently marked and abrupt to cause noticeable bodily reactions.

222

4 WET AND HUMID

■ Wet: Contact with water or other liquids.
■ Humid: Atmospheric condition with moisture content sufficiently high to cause marked bodily discomfort.

5 NOISE AND VIBRATION

Sufficient noise, either constant or intermittent, to cause marked distraction or possible injury to the sense of hearing and/or sufficient vibration (production of an oscillating movement to strain on the body or its extremities from repeated motion or shock) to cause bodily harm if endured day after day.

6 HAZARDS

Situations in which the individual is exposed to the definite risk of bodily injury.

7 FUMES, ODORS, TOXIC CONDITIONS, DUST, AND POOR VENTILATION

■ Fumes: Smoky or vaporous exhalations, usually odorous, thrown off as the result of combustion or chemical reaction.
■ Odors: Noxious smells, either toxic or nontoxic.
■ Toxic Conditions: Exposure to toxic dust, fumes, gases, vapors, mists, or liquids which cause general or localized disabling conditions as a result of inhalation or action on the skin.
■ Dust: Air filled with small particles of any kind, such as textile dust, flour, wood, leather, feathers, etc., and inorganic dust, including silica and asbestos, which make the workplace unpleasant or are the source of occupational diseases.
■ Poor Ventilation: Insufficient movement of air causing a feeling of suffocation; or exposure to drafts.

Environmental Conditions

WTG Code	Number of Jobs	WTG Titles (I)	(O)	(B)	(2)	(3)	(4)	(5)	(6)	(7)
Clerical										
021	14	Cashiering (Drug Stores, Theaters, Restaurants & Related)								
		(13)		(1)						
022	211	Inspecting & Stockchecking								
		(173)	(14)	(24)	(1)	(4)	(7)	(36)	(19)	(11)
024	88	Classifying, Filing & Related								
		(81)	(1)	(6)				(3)		

WTG Code	Number of Jobs	WTG Titles (I)	(O)	(B)	(2)	(3)	(4)	(5)	(6)	(7)
Clerical (continued)										
027	531	Sorting, Inspecting, Measuring & Related								
		(495)	(14)	(22)	(4)	(9)	(20)	(95)	(27)	(24)
028	16	Typing & Related Recording								
		(16)								
029	53	Routine Checking & Recording								
		(50)	(2)	(1)				(3)		
030	7	Switchboard Service								
		(7)						(1)		
Crafts										
037	21	Cooking & Related								
		(21)			(1)	(12)	(5)	(3)	(6)	(1)
038	865	Craftsmanship & Related								
		(683)	(47)	(135)	(2)	(23)	(32)	(235)	(227)	(84)
040	1315	Manipulating								
		(1108)	(106)	(101)	(8)	(59)	(116)	(298)	(252)	(169)
Elemental Work										
051	396	Feeding-Offbearing								
		(375)	(8)	(13)	(2)	(29)	(46)	(156)	(62)	(70)
052	1161	Handling								
		(963)	(112)	(86)	(16)	(54)	(142)	(238)	(153)	(144)
Machine Work										
082	1174	Operating-Controlling								
		(1090)	(43)	(41)	(4)	(129)	(98)	(627)	(312)	(220)
084	2209	Tending								
		(2122)	(41)	(46)	(12)	(150)	(239)	(923)	(291)	(333)
Merchandising										
097	186	Demonstration & Sales Work								
		(173)		(13)			(1)	(1)	(1)	(1)
Personal Service										
101	9	Beautician & Barbering Services								
		(9)								
102	21	Customer Service Work, N.E.C.								
		(16)	(1)	(4)			(1)			
103	22	Miscellaneous Customer Service Work								
		(7)	(7)	(8)	(1)	(1)	(3)	(3)	(1)	
105	66	Miscellaneous Personal Service Work (Food Serving, Portering, Valeting & Related Activities)								
		(59)	(3)	(4)		(2)	(3)	(7)	(1)	
107	10	Animal Care								
		(6)	(2)	(2)			(1)		(6)	(1)

APPENDIX D

General Educational Development

This embraces those aspects of education (formal and informal) which contribute to the worker's (1) reasoning development and ability to follow instructions, and (2) acquisition of "tool" knowledges, such as language and mathematical skills. It is education of a general nature which does not have a recognized, fairly specific, occupational objective. Ordinarily, such education is obtained in elementary school, high school, or college. It derives also from experience and individual study. This is meant to be a very general guide for each qualifications profile. Requirements for specific jobs particularly in certain industries and geographical areas may deviate above or below the specified GED levels.

REASONING DEVELOPMENT

6 Apply principles of logical or scientific thinking to a wide range of intellectual and practical problems. Deal with nonverbal symbolism (formulas, scientific equations, graphs, musical notes, etc.) in its most difficult phases. Deal with a variety of abstract and concrete variables. Comprehend the most abstruse classes of concepts.

5 Apply principles of logical or scientific thinking to define problems, collect data, establish facts, and draw valid conclusions. Interpret an extensive variety of technical instructions, in books, manuals, and mathematical or diagrammatic form. Deal with several abstract and concrete variables.

4 Apply principles of rational systems (e.g., bookkeeping, internal combustion engines, electric wiring systems, house building, nursing, farm management, ship sailing) to solve practical problems and deal with a variety of concrete variables in situations where only limited standardization exists. Interpret a variety of instructions furnished in written, oral, diagrammatic, or schedule form.

3 Apply common sense understanding to carry out instructions furnished in written, oral, or diagrammatic form. Deal with problems involving several concrete variables in or from standardized situations.

2 Apply common sense understanding to carry out detailed but uninvolved written or oral instructions. Deal with problems involving a few concrete variables in or from standardized situations.

1 Apply common sense understanding to carry out simple one- or two-step instructions. Deal with standardized situations with occasional or no variables in or from these situations encountered on the job.

MATHEMATICAL DEVELOPMENT

6 Apply knowledge of advanced mathematical and statistical techniques such as differential and integral calculus, factor analysis, and probability determination, or work with a wide variety.

5 Apply knowledge of theoretical mathematical concepts and make original applications of mathematical procedures, as in empirical and differential equations.

4 Perform ordinary arithmetic, algebraic, and geometric procedures in standard, practical applications.

3 Make arithmetic calculations involving fractions, decimals and percentages.

2 Use arithmetic to add, subtract, multiply, and divide whole numbers.

1 Perform simple addition and subtraction, reading and copying of figures, or counting and recording.

LANGUAGE DEVELOPMENT

6 Comprehension and expression of a level to—

- Report, write, or edit articles for such publications as newspapers, magazines, and technical or scientific journals. Prepare and draw up deeds, leases, wills, mortgages, and contracts.
- Prepare and deliver lectures on politics, economics, education, or science.

5 Comprehension and expression of a level to—

- Interview, counsel, or advise such people as students, clients, or patients, in such matters as welfare eligibility, vocational rehabilitation, mental hygiene, or marital relations.
- Evaluate engineering technical data to design buildings and bridges.

4 Comprehension and expression of a level to—

- Transcribe dictation, make appointments for executives and handle their personal mail, interview and screen people wishing to speak to them, and write routine correspondence on own initiative.

■ Interview job applicants to determine work best suited for their abilities and experience, and contact employers to interest them in services of agency.

■ Interpret technical manuals as well as drawings and specifications, such as layouts, blueprints, and schematics.

3 Comprehension and expression of a level to—

■ File, post, and mail such material as forms, checks, receipts, and bills.

■ Copy data from one record to another, fill in report forms, and type all work from rough draft or corrected copy.

2 Comprehension and expression of a level to—

■ Interview members of household to obtain such information as age, occupation, and number of children, to be used as data for surveys, or economic studies.

■ Guide people on tours through historical or public buildings, describing such features as size, value, and points of interest.

1 Comprehension and expression of a level to—

■ Learn job duties from oral instructions or demonstration.

■ Write identifying information, such as name and address of customer, weight, number, or type of product, on tags, or slips.

■ Request orally, or in writing, such supplies as lye, soap, or work materials.

General Educational Development (GED)

WTG Code	Number of Jobs	WTG Titles		Levels/Jobs					
				(1)	(2)	(3)	(4)	(5)	(6)
Clerical Work									
021	14	Cashiering (Drug Stores, Theaters, Restaurants &	R			(14)			
			M		(10)	(4)			
			L	(2)	(10)	(2)			
022	211	Inspecting & Stock Checking	R		(4)	(181)	(26)		
			M	(11)	(119)	(79)	(2)		
			L	(9)	(103)	(96)	(3)		
024	88	Classifying, Filing & Related	R			(58)	(30)		
			M	(12)	(38)	(36)	(2)		
			L		(12)	(65)	(11)		

(continued)

WTG Code	Number of Jobs	WTG Titles		Levels/Jobs					
				(1)	(2)	(3)	(4)	(5)	(6)

Clerical Work (continued)

WTG Code	Number of Jobs	WTG Titles		(1)	(2)	(3)	(4)	(5)	(6)
027	531	Sorting, Inspecting, Measuring & Related	R	(26)	(291)	(212)	(2)		
			M	(284)	(226)	(20)	(1)		
			L	(148)	(343)	(39)	(1)		
028	16	Typing & Related Recording	R		(1)	(11)	(4)		
			M	(6)	(7)	(3)			
			L	(1)	(3)	(12)			
029	53	Routine Checking & Recording	R		(18)	(32)	(3)		
			M	(201)	(30)	(3)			
			L	(2)	(30)	(19)	(2)		
030	7	Switchboard Service	R			(7)			
			M	(2)	(4)	(1)			
			L		(1)	(6)			

Crafts

WTG Code	Number of Jobs	WTG Titles		(1)	(2)	(3)	(4)	(5)	(6)
037	21	Cooking & Related	R			(13)	(8)		
			M	(1)	(14)	(6)			
			L	(1)	(12)	(8)			
038	865	Craftsmanship & Related	R			(222)	(64)		
			M	(7)	(241)	(486)	(129)		
			L	(5)	(201)	(562)	(96)		
040	1351	Manipulating	R	(14)	(753)	(535)	(13)		
			M	(788)	(491)	(33)			
			L	(583)	(660)	(72)			

Elemental Work

WTG Code	Number of Jobs	WTG Titles		(1)	(2)	(3)	(4)	(5)	(6)
051	396	Feeding-Offbearing	R	(191)	(203)	(2)			
			M	(384)	(12)				
			L	(374)	(22)				
052	1161	Handling	R	(430)	(718)	(13)			
			M	(1090)	(71)				
			L	(1014)	(147)				

Machine Work

WTG Code	Number of Jobs	WTG Titles		(1)	(2)	(3)	(4)	(5)	(6)
082	1174	Operating-Controlling	R		(107)	(951)	(116)		
			M	(259)	(689)	(214)	(12)		
			L	(254)	(653)	(260)	(7)		
084	2209	Tending	R	(155)	(1701)	(353)			
			M	(1699)	(502)	(8)			
			L	(1373)	(810)	(26)			

WTG Code	Number of Jobs	WTG Titles		Levels/Jobs					
				(1)	(2)	(3)	(4)	(5)	(6)
Merchandising									
097	186	Demonstration & Sales	R			(25)	(146)	(15)	
			M		(17)	(161)	(8)		
			L		(1)	(31)	(150)	(4)	
Personal Service									
101	9	Beautician & Barbering Services	R			(5)	(4)		
			M		(5)	(4)			
			L		(1)	(8)			
102	21	Customer Service Work, N.E.C.	R		(7)	(13)	(1)		
			M	(2)	(12)	(7)			
			L	(1)	(14)	(5)	(1)		
103	22	Miscellaneous Customer Service	R		(10)	(12)			
			M	(7)	(15)				
			L	(2)	(16)	(4)			
105	66	Miscellaneous Personal Service Work (Food Serving, Portering, Valeting & Related Activities	R	(1)	(38)	(26)	(1)		
			M	(26)	(39)	(1)			
			L	(10)	(43)	(13)			
107	10	Animal Care	R		(4)	(5)	(1)		
			M	(4)	(5)	(1)			
			L	(4)	(3)	(2)	(1)		

Guide to approximate grade levels: 1(1–3); 2(4–5); 3(6–8); 4(9–12); 5(13–14); 6(15–16).

APPENDIX E

Specific Vocational Preparation and Training

Specific Vocational Preparation is the amount of time required to learn the techniques, acquire information, and develop the facility needed for average performance in a specific job-worker situation. This training may be acquired in a school, work, military, institutional, or avocational environment. It does not include orientation training required of even fully qualified workers to become accustomed to the special conditions of any new job. Specific vocational training includes training given in any of the following circumstances:

- Vocational education (such as high school business or shop training, technical school, art school, and that part of college training which is organized around a specific vocational objective);
- Apprentice training (for apprenticeable jobs only);
- In-plant training (given by an employer in the form of organized classroom study);
- On-the-job training (serving as learner or trainee on the job under the instruction of a qualified worker);
- Essential experience in other jobs (serving in less responsible jobs that lead to the higher grade job or serving in other jobs that qualify).

The following is the key to the chart entitled "Vocational Preparation and Training" pertaining to general requirements for jobs within each of the 66 work groups:

G *Graduate:* Graduate level college studies required. May require a master's or doctor's degree entailing 1 to 4 or more years of study beyond the baccalaureate degree.

C *College:* Requires undergraduate studies toward a 4 year baccalaureate degree.

T *Technical:* Requires 2 years of vocational-technical school, junior college, community college, or 4 year college and university leading to an associate of arts or science degree; or 6 months to 2 years study resulting in a certificate of completion.

V *Vocational:* Requires high school level vocational program, or equivalent, offered during sophomore to senior years. Such programs may be offered in the vocational department of the high school, or at a comprehensive high school.

N *No formal training:* Designates that no formal training or education required beyond a general education.

The following is an explanation of the various levels of specific vocational preparation.

Level	*Time* (Short)	*Level*	*Time* (Medium)
1	Short demonstration only.	5	Over 6 months up to and including 1 year
2	Anything beyond short demonstration up to and including 30 days	6	Over 1 year up to and including 2 years.
3	Over 30 days up to and including 3 months.	7	Over 2 years up to and including 4 years.
4	Over 3 months up to and including 6 months.	8	Over 4 years up to and including 10 years.
		9	Over 10 years.

Specific Vocational Preparation

WTG Code	Number of Jobs	WTG Titles			Levels/Jobs					
		(1)	(2)	(3)	(4)	(5)	(6)	(7)	(8)	(9)
Clerical Work										
021	14	Cashiering (Drug Stores, Theaters, Restaurants & Related)								
		(6)	(5)	(2)	(1)					
022	211	Inspecting & Stockchecking								
		(1)	(28)	(67)	(79)	(22)	(10)	(4)		
024	88	Classifying, Filing & Related								
		(2)	(19)	(32)	(21)	(13)				
027	531	Sorting, Inspecting, Measuring & Related								
		(3)	(163)	(211)	(136)	(11)	(7)			
028	16	Typing & Related Recording								
		(2)	(2)	(7)	(5)					
029	53	Routine Checking & Recording								
		(18)	(19)	(14)	(2)					
030	7	Switchboard Service								
		(4)	(1)ʾ	(2)						

(continued)

WTG Code	Number of Jobs	WTG Titles	Levels/Jobs								
			(1)	(2)	(3)	(4)	(5)	(6)	(7)	(8)	(9)
Crafts											
037	21	Cooking & Related				(1)	(3)	(8)	(9)		
038	865	Craftsmanship & Related				(13)	(28)	(27)	(434)	(115)	
040	1351	Manipulating	(253)	(477)	(324)	(196)	(62)				
Elemental Work											
051	396	Feeding-Offbearing	(40)	(346)	(9)	(1)					
052	1161	Handling	(137)	(827)	(179)	(14)					
Machine Work											
082	1174	Operating-Controlling		(29)	(101)	(442)	(358)	(140)	(99)	(5)	
084	2209	Tending		(1038)	(797)	(294)	(27)				
Merchandising											
097	186	Demonstration & Sales		(4)	(19)	(33)	(66)	(59)	(5)		
Personal Service											
101	9	Beautician & Barbering Services				(1)	(2)	(5)	(1)		
102	21	Customer Service Work, N.E.C.		(10)	(8)	(2)		(1)			
103	22	Miscellaneous Customer Service Work	(1)	(7)	(14)						
105	66	Miscellaneous Personal Service Work (Food Serving, Portering, Valeting & Related Activities)	(1)	(28)	(33)	(3)	(1)				
107	10	Animal Care		(3)	(1)	(5)	(1)				

Training Time: Short (1),(2),(3),(4); Medium (5),(6); Long (7),(8),(9)

APPENDIX F

Aptitudes

Aptitudes are the specific capacities and abilities required of an individual in order to learn or perform adequately a task or job duty.

G INTELLIGENCE: General learning ability. The ability to "catch on" or understand instructions and underlying principles; ability to reason and make judgments; closely related to doing well in school.

V VERBAL: Ability to understand meanings of words and ideas associated with them, and to use them effectively. Ability to comprehend language, to understand relationships between words, and to understand meanings of whole sentences and paragraphs; ability to present information or ideas clearly.

N NUMERICAL: Ability to perform arithmetic operations quickly and accurately.

S SPATIAL: Ability to comprehend forms in space and understand relationships of plane and solid objects. May be used in such tasks as blueprint reading and in solving geometry problems; frequently described as the ability to "visualize" objects of two or three dimensions, or to think visually of geometric forms.

P FORM PERCEPTION: Ability to perceive pertinent detail in objects or in pictorial or graphic material; to make visual comparisons and discriminations and see slight differences in shapes and shadings of figures and widths and lengths of lines.

Q CLERICAL PERCEPTION: Ability to perceive pertinent detail in verbal or tabular material. Ability to observe differences in copy, to proofread words and numbers, and to avoid perceptual errors in arithmetic computation.

K MOTOR COORDINATION: Ability to coordinate eyes and hands or fingers rapidly and accurately in making precise movements with speed. Ability to make a movement response accurately and quickly.

F FINGER DEXTERITY: Ability to move the fingers and manipulate small objects with the fingers rapidly or accurately.

M MANUAL DEXTERITY: Ability to move the hands easily and skillfully. To work with the hands in placing and turning motions.

E EYE-HAND-FOOT COORDINATION: Ability to move the hand and foot coordinately with each other in accordance with visual stimuli.

C COLOR DISCRIMINATION: Ability to perceive or recognize similarities or differences in colors, or in shades or other values of the same color; to identify a particular color, or to recognize harmonious or contrasting color combinations, or to match colors accurately.

EXPLANATION OF LEVELS

The digits indicate how much of each aptitude the job requires for satisfactory (average) performance. The average requirements, rather than maximum or minimum, are cited. The amount required is expressed in terms of equivalent amounts possessed by segments of the general working population. The following scale is used:

1 The top 10 percent of the population. This segment of the population possesses an extremely high degree of the aptitude.
2 The highest third exclusive of the top 10 percent of the population. This segment of the population possesses an above average or high degree of the aptitude.
3 The middle third of the population. This segment of the population possesses a medium degree of the aptitude, ranging from slightly below to slightly above average.
4 The lowest third exclusive of the bottom 10 percent of the population. This segment of the population possesses a below average or low degree of the aptitude.
5 The lowest 10 percent of the population. This segment of the population possesses a negligible degree of the aptitude.

SIGNIFICANT APTITUDES

Certain aptitudes appear in the qualifications profiles for the worker trait groups. These aptitudes are considered to be occupationally significant for the specific group; that is, essential for average successful job performance. All of these aptitudes are not necessarily required of a worker for each individual job within a worker trait group, but some combination of them is essential in every case.

Aptitudes*

WGT Code	Number of Jobs	WTG Titles	APT	Levels/Jobs				
				(5)	(4)	(3)	(2)	(1)

Clerical Work

WGT Code	Number of Jobs	WTG Titles	APT	(5)	(4)	(3)	(2)	(1)
021	14	Cashiering (Drug Stores, Theaters, Restaurants & Related	G			(14)		
			V			(14)		
			N			(14)		
			S	(3)	(11)			
			P		(11)	(3)		
			Q			(12)	(2)	
			K		(6)	(7)	(1)	
			F		(3)	(10)	(1)	
			M		(10)	(4)		
			E	(14)				
			C	(6)	(4)	(4)		
022	211	Inspecting & Stockchecking	G		(3)	(205)	(3)	
			V		(69)	(140)	(2)	
			N		(93)	(116)	(2)	
			S	(2)	(93)	(109)	(7)	
			P	(2)	(37)	(140)	(32)	
			Q	(6)	(97)	(101)	(7)	
			K		(131)	(78)		
			F		(121)	(83)	(6)	
			M	(2)	(71)	(137)		
			E	(164)	(39)	(7)		
			C	(86)	(85)	(34)	(6)	
024	88	Classifying, Filing & Related	G		(3)	(82)	(3)	
			V		(5)	(82)	(1)	
			N		(35)	(48)	(5)	
			S	(8)	(72)	(7)	(1)	
			P	(1)	(47)	(34)	(6)	
			Q		(2)	(52)	(34)	
			K	(2)	(57)	(26)	(3)	
			F	(1)	(50)	(35)	(2)	
			M	(2)	(66)	(20)		
			E	(83)	(5)			
			C	(62)	(20)	(5)	(1)	

(continued)

WGT Code	Number of Jobs	WTG Titles	APT	Levels/Jobs (5)	(4)	(3)	(2)	(1)
Clerical Work (continued)								
027	531	Sorting, Inspecting, Measuring & Related	G		(286)	(245)		
			V	(3)	(477)	(50)		
			N	(45)	(429)	(57)		
			S	(14)	(393)	(122)		
			P	(4)	(170)	(331)	(26)	
			Q	(75)	(370)	(83)	(3)	
			K	(2)	(331)	(193)	(5)	
			F	(3)	(346)	(170)	(12)	
			M	(2)	(173)	(354)	(2)	
			E	(476)	(51)	(3)	(1)	
			C	(247)	(178)	(95)	(11)	
028	16	Typing & Related Recording	G		(1)	(15)		
			V		(2)	(13)	(1)	
			N		(10)	(6)		
			S	(1)	(12)	(3)		
			P	(1)	(7)	(7)	(1)	
			Q			(6)	(10)	
			K		(3)	(8)	(5)	
			F		(3)	(8)	(5)	
			M		(6)	(10)		
			E	(15)	(1)			
			C	(14)	(2)			
029	53	Routine Checking & Recording	G		(13)	(38)	(2)	
			V		(25)	(26)	(2)	
			N		(36)	(17)		
			S	(10)	(38)	(5)		
			P	(2)	(39)	(11)	(1)	
			Q		(1)	(45)	(6)	(1)
			K	(1)	(42)	(10)		
			F	(2)	(36)	(15)		
			M	(3)	(39)	(11)		
			E	(52)	(1)			
			C	(36)	(16)	(1)		

WGT Code	Number of Jobs	WTG Titles	APT	Levels/Jobs (5)	(4)	(3)	(2)	(1)

Clerical Work (continued)

WGT Code	Number of Jobs	WTG Titles	APT	(5)	(4)	(3)	(2)	(1)
030	7	Switchboard Service	G			(7)		
			V			(7)		
			N		(7)			
			S		(7)			
			P	(2)	(1)	(4)		
			Q		(2)	(5)		
			K			(7)		
			F			(7)		
			M		(7)			
			E	(7)				
			C	(5)	(2)			

Crafts

WGT Code	Number of Jobs	WTG Titles	APT	(5)	(4)	(3)	(2)	(1)
037	21	Cooking & Related	G			(21)		
			V		(7)	(14)		
			N		(14)	(7)		
			S		(18)	(3)		
			P		(1)	(20)		
			Q	(1)	(12)	(8)		
			K		(11)	(10)		
			F		(16)	(5)		
			M			(19)	(2)	
			E	(19)	(1)	(1)		
			C		(20)	(1)		
038	865	Craftsmanship & Related	G		(4)	(777)	(84)	
			V		(159)	(691)	(15)	
			N	(3)	(177)	(645)	(39)	(1)
			S		(47)	(515)	(301)	(2)
			P		(45)	(491)	(329)	
			Q	(34)	(683)	(140)	(8)	
			K		(127)	(671)	(67)	
			F		(95)	(614)	(155)	(1)
			M		(22)	(604)	(239)	
			E	(535)	(238)	(75)	(17)	
			C	(352)	(330)	(152)	(30)	(1)

(*continued*)

WGT Code	Number of Jobs	WTG Titles	APT	Levels/Jobs (5)	(4)	(3)	(2)	(1)

Crafts (continued)

WGT Code	Number of Jobs	WTG Titles	APT	(5)	(4)	(3)	(2)	(1)
040	1315	Manipulating	G		(642)	(673)		
			V	(4)	(1252)	(58)	(1)	
			N	(166)	(1051)	(97)	(1)	
			S	(6)	(701)	(597)	(11)	
			P	(5)	(469)	(808)	(33)	
			Q	(468)	(821)	(26)		
			K		(371)	(933)	(11)	
			F	(3)	(576)	(694)	(42)	
			M		(69)	(1224)	(22)	
			E	(972)	(288)	(47)	(8)	
			C	(840)	(371)	(95)	(9)	

Elemental Work

WGT Code	Number of Jobs	WTG Titles	APT	(5)	(4)	(3)	(2)	(1)
051	396	Feeding-Offbearing	G		(392)	(4)		
			V	(12)	(384)			
			N	(170)	(226)			
			S	(21)	(361)	(14)		
			P	(12)	(364)	(20)		
			Q	(243)	(152)	(1)		
			K		(277)	(118)	(1)	
			F	(4)	(340)	(51)	(1)	
			M	(1)	(117)	(277)	(1)	
			E	(329)	(62)	(5)		
			C	(322)	(61)	(3)		
052	1161	Handling	G		(1135)	(26)		
			V	(49)	(1108)	(4)		
			N	(550)	(606)	(5)		
			S	(70)	(1015)	(76)		
			P	(33)	(955)	(172)	(1)	
			Q	(783)	(372)	(6)		
			K	(6)	(779)	(374)	(2)	
			F	(10)	(855)	(285)	(11)	
			M		(316)	(843)	(2)	
			E	(930)	(204)	(26)	(1)	
			C	(918)	(224)	(19)		

WGT Code	Number of Jobs	WTG Titles	APT	(5)	(4)	(3)	(2)	(1)
Machine Work								
082	1174	Operating-Controlling	G		(166)	(1005)	(3)	
			V		(854)	(318)	(2)	
			N	(7)	(796)	(369)	(2)	
			S		(436)	(707)	(31)	
			P		(304)	(825)	(45)	
			Q	(174)	(869)	(130)	(1)	
			K		(347)	(817)	(10)	
			F	(1)	(690)	(408)	(75)	
			M		(92)	(1066)	(16)	
			E	(795)	(267)	(110)	(2)	
			C	(653)	(422)	(93)	(6)	
084	2209	Tending	G		(1806)	(403)		
			V	(8)	(2170)	(31)		
			N	(303)	(1829)	(77)		
			S	(38)	(1917)	(253)	(1)	
			P	(19)	(1484)	(701)	(5)	
			Q	(630)	(1540)	(39)		
			K	(5)	(1317)	(884)	(3)	
			F	(9)	(1747)	(446)	(7)	
			M		(405)	(1796)	(8)	
			E	(1618)	(562)	(27)	(2)	
			C	(1675)	(478)	(56)		
Merchandising								
097	186	Demonstration & Sales	G		(1)	(136)	(49)	
			V			(123)	(63)	
			N		(13)	(161)	(12)	
			S	(5)	(89)	(82)	(10)	
			P	(2)	(71)	(110)	(3)	
			Q	(1)	(25)	(157)	(3)	
			K	(1)	(141)	(44)		
			F	(1)	(134)	(51)		
			M	(2)	(136)	(48)		
			E	(175)	(7)	(4)		
			C	(79)	(78)	(26)	(2)	

(continued)

Aptitudes (*continued*)

WGT Code	Number of Jobs	WTG Titles	APT	(5)	(4)	(3)	(2)	(1)
						Levels/Jobs		

Personal Service

WGT Code	Number of Jobs	WTG Titles	APT	(5)	(4)	(3)	(2)	(1)
101	9	Beautician & Barbering Services	G		(1)	(7)	(1)	
			V			(8)	(1)	
			N		(8)	(1)		
			S		(1)	(8)		
			P			(4)	(5)	
			Q		(9)			
			K			(4)	(5)	
			F			(7)	(2)	
			M			(9)		
			E	(8)	(1)			
			C	(1)	(3)	(3)	(2)	
102	21	Customer Service Work, N.E.C.	G		(6)	(15)		
			V		(7)	(14)		
			N		(8)	(13)		
			S	(2)	(16)	(3)		
			P		(18)	(2)	(1)	
			Q		(8)	(13)		
			K		(17)	(4)		
			F		(18)	(3)		
			M		(14)	(7)		
			E	(15)	(4)	(2)		
			C	(13)	(7)	(1)		
103	22	Miscellaneous Customer Service	G		(10)	(12)		
			V		(17)	(5)		
			N		(18)	(4)		
			S		(19)	(3)		
			P	(1)	(17)	(4)		
			Q	(1)	(19)	(2)		
			K		(11)	(11)		
			F		(21)	(1)		
			M		(6)	(16)		
			E	(10)	(6)	(6)		
			C	(16)	(6)			

WGT Code	Number of Jobs	WTG Titles	APT	(5)	(4)	(3)	(2)	(1)
					Levels/Jobs			

Personal Service (continued)

WGT Code	Number of Jobs	WTG Titles	APT	(5)	(4)	(3)	(2)	(1)
105	66	Miscellaneous Personal Service (Food Serving, Portering, Valeting & Related)	G		(41)	(25)		
			V		(44)	(22)		
			N	(4)	(57)	(5)		
			S	(7)	(54)	(5)		
			P	(1)	(56)	(8)		(1)
			Q	(8)	(46)	(12)		
			K	(1)	(42)	(22)	(1)	
			F	(1)	(54)	(9)	(2)	
			M	(1)	(19)	(44)	(2)	
			E	(33)	(27)	(6)		
			C	(41)	(20)	(4)		(1)
107	10	Animal Care	G		(3)	(7)		
			V		(6)	(4)		
			N	(1)	(8)	(1)		
			S		(6)	(4)		
			P	(1)	(4)	(5)		
			Q	(3)	(5)	(1)		(1)
			K		(1)	(7)	(2)	
			F		(2)	(8)		
			M			(10)		
			E	(3)	(6)	(1)		
			C	(3)	(6)	(1)		

*Aptitudes: Low = (5),(4); Medium = (3); High = (2),(1)

APPENDIX G

Interests

Preferences for certain types of work activities or experiences, with accompanying rejection of contrary types of activities or experiences. Five pairs of interest factors are provided below. A positive preference for one factor of a pair implies rejection of the other factor of that pair. However, these opposites are only general, and an interest in the one does not always preclude an interest in the other type situation.

1a Situations involving a preference for activities dealing with things and objects.

1b Situations involving a preference for activities concerned with people and communication of ideas and information.

2a Situations involving a preference for activities involving business contact with people.

2b Situations involving a preference for activities of a scientific and technical nature.

3a Situations involving a preference for activities of a routine concrete, organized nature.

3b Situations involving a preference for activities of an abstract and creative nature.

4a Situations involving a preference for working with people for their presumed good, as in the social welfare sense, or for dealing with people and language in social situations.

4b Situations involving a preference for activities that are nonsocial in nature, and are carried on in relation to processes, machines, and techniques.

5a Situations involving a preference for activities resulting in prestige or the esteem of others and entailing a high level of data and people worker functions.

5b Situations involving a preference for activities resulting in tangible, productive satisfaction, involving building, producing, repairing, or restoring things.

WTG Code	Number of Jobs	WTG Titles				Levels/Jobs					
		(1a)	(1b)	(2a)	(2b)	(3a)	(3b)	(4a)	(4b)	(5a)	(5b)

Clerical Work

WTG Code	Number of Jobs	(1a)	(1b)	(2a)	(2b)	(3a)	(3b)	(4a)	(4b)	(5a)	(5b)
021	14	Cashiering (Drug Stores, Theaters, Restaurants & Related)									
		(4)	(2)	(14)		(13)			(2)		
022	211	Inspecting & Stockchecking									
		(191)	(1)	(10)	(6)	(124)		(2)	(175)		(4)
024	88	Classifying, Filing & Related									
		(35)	(29)	(24)	(1)	(81)			(19)		
027	531	Sorting, Inspecting, Measuring & Related									
		(489)	(2)		(3)	(434)		(1)	(318)		(5)
028	16	Typing & Related Recording									
		(1)	(2)	(4)		(13)			(9)		
029	53	Routine Checking & Recording									
		(31)	(8)	(8)		(51)			(3)		
030	7	Switchboard Service									
				(7)		(7)			(2)		

Crafts

WTG Code	Number of Jobs	(1a)	(1b)	(2a)	(2b)	(3a)	(3b)	(4a)	(4b)	(5a)	(5b)
037	21	Cooking & Related									
		(10)						(2)	(19)		(20)
038	865	Craftsmanship & Related									
		(703)	(3)	(11)	(39)	(60)	(27)	(1)	(815)	(8)	(534)
040	1315	Manipulating									
		(1183)		(1)	(1)	(985)	(2)	(1)	(1013)	(1)	(67)

Elemental Work

WTG Code	Number of Jobs	(1a)	(1b)	(2a)	(2b)	(3a)	(3b)	(4a)	(4b)	(5a)	(5b)
051	396	Feeding-Offbearing									
		(387)				(384)			(106)		
052	1161	Handling									
		(1138)	(2)	(2)	(2)	(1128)			(228)	(1)	(4)

Machine Work

WTG Code	Number of Jobs	(1a)	(1b)	(2a)	(2b)	(3a)	(3b)	(4a)	(4b)	(5a)	(5b)
082	1174	Operating-Controlling									
		(1088)		(1)	(3)	(538)	(1)	(2)	(1159)	(1)	(63)
084	2209	Tending									
		(2098)	(1)			(1991)	(2)		(1993)		(2)

(continued)

WTG Code	Number of Jobs	WTG Titles	Levels/Jobs									
			(1a)	(1b)	(2a)	(2b)	(3a)	(3b)	(4a)	(4b)	(5a)	(5b)
Merchandising												
097	186	Demonstration & Sales	(4)	(179)	(180)	(5)	(1)	(3)		(4)	(2)	
Personal Service												
101	9	Beautician & Barbering Services		(7)				(7)		(6)		(5)
102	21	Customer Service Work, N.E.C.	(8)	(1)	(17)	(16)		(1)	(1)	(1)		
103	22	Miscellaneous Customer Service	(8)	(1)	(18)	(15)		(2)	(5)			
105	66	Miscellaneous Personal Service (Food Serving, Portering, Valeting & Related)	(14)	(2)	(51)	(52)		(5)	(4)		(1)	
107	10	Animal Care	(1)				(5)	(1)	(4)	(2)		(2)

APPENDIX H

Job Worker Situations

Different types of occupational situations to which workers must adjust:

V Situations involving a variety of duties often characterized by frequent change.

R Situations involving repetitive or short cycle operations carried out according to set procedures or sequences.

D Situations involving the direction, control, and planning of an entire activity or the activities of others.

P Situations involving the necessity of dealing with people in actual job duties beyond giving and receiving instructions.

I Situations involving influencing people in their opinions, attitudes, or judgments about ideas or things.

S Situations involving performing adequately under stress when confronted with the critical or unexpected or when taking risks.

J Situations involving the evaluation (arriving at generalizations, judgments, or decisions) of information against sensory or judgmental criteria.

M Situations involving the evaluation (arriving at generalizations, judgments, or decisions) of information against measurable or verifiable criteria.

F Situations involving the interpretation of feelings, ideas, or facts in terms of personal viewpoint.

T Situations involving the precise attainment of set limits, tolerances, or standards.

Job Worker Situations

WTG Code	Number of Jobs	WTG Titles (V)	(R)	Levels/Jobs (D)	(P)	(I)	(S)	(J)	(M)	(F)	(T)
Clerical Work											
021	14	Cashiering (Drug Stores, Theaters, Restaurants & Related)									
		(1)	(8)		(13)		(1)		(1)		(13)
022	211	Inspecting & Stockchecking									
		(25)	(32)	(2)	(9)	(1)	(2)	(57)	(167)		(182)

(continued)

WTG Code	Number of Jobs	WTG Titles	Levels/Jobs									
			(V)	(R)	(D)	(P)	(I)	(S)	(J)	(M)	(F)	(T)
Clerical Work (continued)												
024	88	Classifying, Filing & Related	(7)	(31)		(10)	(1)	(1)	(16)	(37)		(62)
027	531	Sorting, Inspecting, Measuring & Related	(9)	(358)	(2)	(1)		(1)	(63)	(191)		(410)
028	16	Typing & Related Recording	(2)	(9)		(2)				(1)		(12)
029	53	Routine Checking & Recording	(2)	(39)		(3)				(8)		(27)
030	7	Switchboard Service		(6)		(7)		(1)				
Crafts												
037	21	Cooking & Related	(10)		(1)	(3)			(19)	(3)	(3)	(17)
038	865	Craftsmanship & Related	(295)	(25)	(6)	(17)		(24)	(164)	(790)	(9)	(844)
040	1315	Manipulating	(72)	(986)	(2)	(3)		(24)	(84)	(254)		(1066)
Elemental Work												
051	396	Feeding-Offbearing	(1)	(393)				(1)		(4)		(50)
052	1161	Handling	(29)	(1117)	(1)	(1)		(8)	(14)	(21)		(183)
Machine Work												
082	1174	Operating-Controlling	(73)	(434)	(6)	(2)		(8)	(92)	(728)		(1136)
084	2209	Tending	(8)	(1970)				(4)	(67)	(216)		(1426)
Merchandising												
097	186	Demonstration & Sales Work	(5)	(1)	(1)	(184)	(182)		(160)	(27)	(6)	(6)

WTG Code	Number of Jobs	WTG Titles / Levels/Jobs									
		(V)	(R)	(D)	(P)	(I)	(S)	(J)	(M)	(F)	(T)

Personal Service

WTG Code	Number of Jobs	(V)	(R)	(D)	(P)	(I)	(S)	(J)	(M)	(F)	(T)
101	9	Beautician & Barbering Services									
		(6)			(9)			(8)	(1)	(1)	(3)
102	21	Customer Service Work, N.E.C.									
		(1)	(4)	(1)	(20)			(2)	(5)		(4)
103	22	Miscellaneous Customer Service Work									
		(6)	(9)	(1)	(21)			(3)			(1)
105	66	Miscellaneous Personal Service Work (Food Serving, Portering, Valeting, & Related)									
		(21)	(26)		(60)		(2)	(4)	(4)	(1)	(6)
107	10	Animal Care									
		(5)	(1)		(3)	(1)		(3)	(5)	(1)	(3)

A P P E N D I X I

Vocational Evaluation Tests in Special Education

Aptitude and Achievement Tests

Test	Description	Student Population*	Publisher
Differential Aptitude Test (DAT)	Individual or group paper and pencil test that measure eight aptitudes: verbal reasoning, numerical ability, abstract reasoning, clerical speed and accuracy, mechanical comprehension, spatial relations, language usage, spelling.	Requires 6th grade reading level. All disability groups but VI	Psychological Corporation
Career Ability Placement Survey (CAPS)	Paper and pencil test measuring mechanical reasoning, verbal reasoning, numerical, language, perceptual speed, manual speed and accuracy, word knowledge.	All disability groups but VI	EDITS Publishers
General Clerical Test	An individual or group paper and pencil test measuring alphabetizing, checking, arithmetic computation, error location, arithmetic reasoning, spelling, reading comprehension, vocabulary, grammar.	PH, ED, LD, HI, Requires 6th grade reading level	Psychological Corporation
Woodcock Reading Mastery	Individual administration. Separate subtests measure letter identification, word identification, word attack, word comprehension. Both norm- and criterion-referenced results, useful for developing an IEP.	All disability groups but VI	American Guidance Service

*VI = Visually Impaired; ED = Emotionally Disturbed; MR = Mentally Retarded; PH = Physically Handicapped; LD = Learning Disabled; HI = Hearing Impaired.

Test	Description	Student Population*	Publisher
Key Math Diagnostic Arithmetic Test	Individually administered math achievement test measuring math content, operations, and application. No reading is required. Takes between 30 to 40 minutes to administer.	All disability groups but VI	American Guidance Service

Performance Tests

Test	Description	Student Population*	Publisher
Minnesota Rate of Manipulation Test	Individually or group administered test, taking between 25 to 35 minutes. Student performs five separate manipulation tasks including placing, turning, displacing, and one-hand and two-hand turning.	All disability groups; limited with PH	American Guidance Service
O'Connor Finger and Tweezer Dexterity Test	Individual administration to measure motor coordination and manual dexterity. Fingers are used to insert pins into small holes; tweezers used to pick up and place pins in hole. Relatively short test, taking from 10 to 20 minutes.	All disability groups but VI	Stoelting Company
Minnesota Spatial Relations Test	Individually administered test to measure student's speed and accuracy in discriminating size and shape, spatial visualization, and eye-hand coordination. Task consists of manipulating blocks into 58 cutouts on four separate boards.	All disability groups but VI	American Guidance Service

*VI = Visually Impaired; ED = Emotionally Disturbed; MR = Mentally Retarded; PH = Physically Handicapped; LD = Learning Disabled; HI = Hearing Impaired.

Test	Description	Student Population*	Publisher
Career Assessment Inventory (CAI)	Measures vocational interest as they relate to John Holland's occupational themes. Student responds to various activities, school subjects, and occupations. Paper and pencil test in which student indicates preference for written statement.	LD, ED, PH, HI; requires 6th grade reading level	National Computer Systems
Kuder Occupational Interest Survey (Form DD)	Student responds to 100 triad items of different activities to indicate preference. Best liked and least liked are indicated. The test is intended for higher functioning individuals who may seek training after high school.	LD, ED, PH	Science Research Associates
Ohio Vocational Interest Survey (OVIS)	A computer scored paper and pencil interest test. Students respond to test items on a scale from "like very much" to "dislike very much." Either individual or group administration and takes approximately 90 minutes.	HI, ED, LD, PH; 6th grade reading level	Psychological Corporation
Interest Checklist	Students indicate "like," "uncertain," or "dislike" for 210 work activities. Items are grouped in sets of threes reflecting a close relationship to the GOE. No formal scoring is used; the list is reviewed with the student to discuss and explore vocational interest.	All disability groups	U.S. Dept. of Labor
Geist Picture Interest Inventory, Revised	Separate male and female booklets are used to measure general interest areas, including outdoors, artistic, mechanical, personal service. Of interest, the text attempts to measure motivation behind vocational choice.	All disability groups but VI. Some reading involved	Western Psychological Services

*VI = Visually Impaired; ED = Emotionally Disturbed; MR = Mentally Retarded; PH = Physically Handicapped; LD = Learning Disabled; HI = Hearing Impaired.

TEST PUBLISHERS

AMERICAN GUIDANCE
  SERVICE
Publisher's Building
Circle Pines, MN 55014
1-800-328-2560

AMERICAN ASSOCIATION
  ON MENTAL DEFICIENCY
5101 Wisconsin Ave., N.W.
Washington, DC 20016
(202) 857-5400

CONSULTING
  PSYCHOLOGICAL PRESS,
  INC.
577 College Avenue
Palo Alto, CA 94306
(415) 857-1444

EDITS CAREER GUIDANCE
  CATALOG
P.O. Box 7234
San Diego, CA 92107
(619) 222-1666

JASTAK ASSOCIATES, INC.
1526 Gilpin Ave.
Wilmington, DE 19806
1-800-221-9718

NATIONAL COMPUTER
  SYSTEMS
P.O. Box 1416
Minneapolis, MN 55440
1-800-328-6759

THE PSYCHOLOGICAL
  CORPORATION
555 Academic Court
San Antonio, TX 78204
(512) 299-1061

SCIENCE RESEARCH
  ASSOC., INC.
155 N. Wacker Dr.
Chicago, IL 60606
1-800-621-0476

VOCATIONAL
  PSYCHOLOGY RESEARCH
N620 Elliott Hall
University of Minnesota
75 East River Rd.
Minneapolis, MN 55455
(612) 376-7377

WESTERN PSYCHOLOGICAL
  SERVICES
12031 Wilshire Blvd.
Los Angeles, CA 90025
(213) 478-2061

APPENDIX J

Work Sample Systems

Title: Comprehensive Occupational Assessment and Training System (COATS)

Description: The COATS System represents a comprehensive process to assess and predict the vocational capability of students prior to placement into a training program or simulated work situation. COATS consists of the following four components:

(1) Job Matching System–This component matches a student's abilities, preferences, and experiences to training or employment opportunities. The student responds to 15 audiovisual cartridges about different skill categories which are based on the Data-People-Things hierarchy of the *Dictionary of Occupational Titles*. A computer print-out provides a match to training or job areas.

(2) Employability Attitudes System–Six audiovisual cartridges present "real life" scenarios to assist the student in comparing his or her attitudes and behavior with the attitude that employers view as being important in an employment situation. The scenarios cover job seeking, job maintenance, and job advancement situations.

(3) Work Sample System–COATS uses 28 simulated work samples which are independent of each other, including; Drafting, Clerical, Sales, Metal Construction, Food Preparation, Medical Services, Cosmetology, Small Engine, Police Science, Masonry, Electronics, Automotive, Commercial Art, Nutrition, Bookkeeping, Fire Science, Communication Services, Refrigeration, Solar Technology, and Computer Technology.

(4) Living Skills System–Six individual cartridges present scenarios to evaluate the student's skill to function in the

community. The system evaluates reading, writing, computational problem solving, speaking-listening, consumer resources, health, and government law.

All four system components are independent of each other and the Job Matching System may be used to select the most appropriate Work Sample components. The work samples replicate actual work tasks and provide opportunity for significant vocational exploration.

All components are computer scored and provide a detailed printout for the student. An eighth grade reading level is required, but much of the material can be read to the student.

Comments: As one of the most comprehensive and versatile systems available, the system is able to involve the student in the evaluation process to assess interest, capabilities, work behavior, and transition skills.

Student
Population: The audiovisual presentation may create difficulties for students with hearing and visual impairments. The evaluator may read the material for students at below eighth grade reading level. Appropriate for all other disabilities.

Publisher: Prep, Inc.
                1575 Parkway Avenue
                Trenton, N.J. 08628

Title: Hester Evaluation System

Description: Rather than being a traditional work sample evaluation system, the Hester is a series of 26 separate performance and paper and pencil tests that relate the student's abilities to the Data-People-Things hierarchy of the *Dictionary of Occupational Titles.* The 26 tests are used to measure 28 ability areas that are then grouped into 7 primary categories as follows:

                (1) Unilateral Motor Ability
                (2) Bilateral Motor Activity
                (3) Perceptual
                (4) Perceptual Motor Coordination
                (5) Intelligence
                (6) Achievement
                (7) Physical Strength

As the tests are administered in a traditional testing situation, there is little opportunity for interaction between the student and evaluator. Similarly, as the tests are of a more abstract nature and do not closely replicate work situations, there is little opportunity for vocational exploration. The entire battery may be administered in 5 to 7 hours.

The test is scored by computer and the evaluator may either mail the results to the publisher or use a terminal for direct input. Results are provided to show the student's level of functioning in relation to the Data-People-Things hierarchy, the test scores, and specific test scores.

Comments: The Hester system uses a trait and factor approach to assessment that has long been accepted in psychological testing. Although the traditional testing format may not promote the desired student involvement in vocational evaluation, the testing results are closely related to the worker function structure of the DOT. As such, the system may have greatest utility as a screening process to acquire a quick picture of the student's ability.

Student
Population: Appropriate for all disability groups.

Publisher: Evaluation Systems, Inc.
640 N. LaSalle Street
Suite 698
Chicago, IL 60610

Title: Micro-TOWER

Description: The Micro-TOWER uses a group aptitude battery approach to vocational evaluation, using work samples and group discussion to promote assessment of vocational potential. The evaluation process measures 7 aptitudes through 13 work samples as follows:

(1) Motor: Electronic connector assembly (finger dexterity-F), bottle capping and packing (manual dexterity-M), lamp assembly (motor coordination-K).
(2) Spatial: Blueprint reading (spatial reasoning-S), graphics illustration (spatial reasoning-S); motor coordination-K).
(3) Clerical Perception: Filing (clerical perception-Q; motor coordination-K), mail sorting (clerical perception-Q; manual dexterity-M), zip coding (clerical perception-Q), record checking (clerical perception-Q).

(4)   Numerical: Making change (numerical reasoning-N), payroll computation (numerical reasoning-N).
(5)   Verbal-want ads (verbal comprehensive-V), message taking (verbal comprehension-V).

Of particular use to many special education students is the evaluation sequence employed. All instructions are provided to the student on an audio cassette tape which stops at preselected points for additional instruction. There are also visual illustrations, demonstrations of task expectation, and opportunity for practice. No written instructions are used. After completion of a task the student completes a self rating form. The student also participates in a group discussion to discuss interests, perceived abilities, work values, supervisor concerns, and other suggested topics.

Comments: The Micro-TOWER is closely related to the DOT and uses a desired work sample approach to assessment. Two unique features of the system that are of significance for special education students are the structured administration process that separates instruction, demonstration, and practice from timed evaluation and the structured group format that promotes discussion on Career Exploration and Career Awareness themes.

Student
Populations: The Micro-TOWER is useful for all disability groups, except moderately mentally retarded.

Publisher: Micro-TOWER
2CD Rehabilitation and Research Center
340 East 24th Street
New York, NY 10010

Title: Valpar #17–Pre-Vocational Readiness Battery

Description: Valpar #17 was designed to evaluate the functional characteristics of mentally retarded individuals that are important to vocational potential. Evaluation activity focuses on five areas, each with separate components as follows:

(1)   Development Assessment: measuring pattern/color discrimination and manipulation, manual coordination, work range/dynamic strength/walking, and matching/vocational knowledge/measurement.

(2)   Workshop Evaluation: simulated assembly process with multiple steps.

(3)   Vocational Interest Screening: six basic areas are explored, including social service, sales, machine operation, office work, physical science, and outdoor. Students make choices in response to a sound and slide presentation.

(4)   Social-Interpersonal Skills: a rating form format evaluates the student on (a) personal skill, (b) socialization, (c) aggravating behaviors, (d) work-related skills.

(5)   Independent Living Skills: simulations and games are used to assess transportation, money handling, grooming, and living environments.

The evaluation process promotes high student/evaluator involvement. Instructions are provided based on the student's ability, either through verbal, verbal plus demonstration, or verbal plus demonstration and a sample.

Comments: Because of the level of evaluation activity, the system is best used with more severely mentally retarded students. As adjustment behaviors are critical for job success with severely mentally retarded students, the emphasis on work behaviors is informative and useful. Technical elements of the system are not clear and in some cases not available.

Publisher: Valpar Corporation
3801 East 34th Street
Tucson, AZ 85713

Title: Project Discovery Training System

Description: Although Project Discovery was originally developed as a series of independent and separate vocational modules to promote vocational and career exploration, modifications have been made to provide more systematic application needed in evaluation. Project Discovery consists of 27 modules to provide hands-on exposure to different occupations to promote exploration of the typical duties, responsibilities, and work tasks of the job. The following career clusters have been developed: communications and media, public service, construction transportation, business and office, marketing and distribution, agri-business and natural resources, consumer and home making, health occupations, and manufacturing. Each module contains an analysis of the skills and abilities in terms of work characteristics related to the *Dictionary of Occupational Titles.*

Rather than a norm-referenced approach to assessment, Project Discovery uses observation and experience to establish criterion reference results of performance.

Comments: Project Discovery represents a useful approach to career exploration for special needs students. There is ample opportunity for student/evaluator interaction and comparison of student's performance on a "Qualifications Profile" to jobs listed in the DOT.

Student
Population: All student disability groups

Publisher: Experience Education
401 Reed Street
Red Oak, IA 51566

Distributor: Prentice-Hall Media
ServCode CM
150 White Plains Road
Tarrytown, NY 10591

A P P E N D I X K

Job Site Analysis Form

Name of Company: _____

Address: _____

Job Title: _____ D.O.T. Code Number _____

Name of Supervisor:_____ Title: _____

Brief Job Description:

Previous Training Required:
(including math, reading, writing, speaking levels)

Major Job Duties
    What the Worker Does:

    Tools, Equipment, Machinery Used:

Required Knowledge (Machines, Work Procedures, Techniques):

Work Hours: _____ Shifts: _____
Hourly Pay/Salary: _____ Pay Schedule: _____
Describe Supervision Received:

Describe Supervision Given:

Work Demands
Dexterity: (Describe speed, precision needed to perform tasks)

Production Demands: (items, activities to be completed/hour)

Rate of Errors Permitted/Tolerated:

Physical Demands
Walking:
Lifting:
Carrying:
Pushing:
Pulling:
Communications:
Hearing:
Seeing:
Coordinating:
Fingering/Feeling:
Manipulating:
Working Conditions
Work Room Size: Small _____ Many Rooms _____
                 Large _____ Outside   _____
Noise Level:
Temperature Ranges & Changes:
Hazards:
Moving Machinery:

Dangerous Equipment:
Working Alone/With Others:
Auditory/Visual Stimuli:
Accessibility:
Social Environment: Describe relationships with others:
Coworkers _____
Supervisor _____
Public _____
Transportation available:

Decision Making
Responsibility for Equipment, Supplies, Material, Safety:

Independent Judgement Required:

Planning Activities:

Employment Outlook:

Career Mobility & Advancement Opportunities:

Union Memberships Required:

Previous Experience Required:

Other Relevant Information

SUBJECT INDEX

Achievement tests, 105–109,
248–249
Peabody Individual Achievement
Test (PIAT), 106, *106, 116*
publishers, 251
Wide Range Achievement Test—
Revised (WRAT), 105, *116*
Apticom work sample system, *135,*
146–147
Aptitude tests, 105–109, 248–249
Bennett Mechanical
Comprehension Test,
106–107, *107, 116*
General Aptitude Test Battery,
108, *116*
Minnesota Clerical Test, 107, *108,
116*
Non-Reading Aptitude Test
Battery, 109
publishers, 251
Revised Minnesota Paper Form
Board, 107, *108, 116*

Bennett Hand-Tool Dexterity
Test, 114, *116*
Bennett Mechanical
Comprehension Test,
106–107, *107*

Career education, 9
current programs, 13–14
history, 9–11
legislation, 12–13
state implementation, 11–13, *12*
Carl D. Perkins Act, 8–9, 43
Commercial work samples. *See*
Work samples.

Comprehensive Occupational
Assessment and Training
System (COATS), 252–253
Crawford Small Parts Dexterity
Test, 113–114, *116*
Criterion-referenced testing, 91–92
Critical function analysis, 161, 162,
164–165, *166–167*
Curriculum-Based Vocational
Assessment, 59, 61, 62, 63
with learning-disabled students,
185–186

Dictionary of Occupational Titles, 41,
42, 43, 71–77, 120
in commercial work samples,
Apticom system, 147
JEVS, 138–140
Valpar Component Work
Samples, 141–142
Vocational Information and
Evaluation Work
Samples, 142–144
DOT definition parts, 72, *73*
occupational code number,
72–73
fourth edition development, 71–72
occupational titles arrangement,
75
alphabetical index, 76
occupational group
arrangement, 75–76
industry designations, 77, *78*
test validity, 94
worker functions, 213–214
data, 214
people, 214–215

Italic page numbers refer to figures and tables

261